**ARCHITECTURAL ENCOUNTERS WITH
ESSENCE AND FORM IN MODERN CHINA**

ARCHITECTURAL ENCOUNTERS WITH ESSENCE AND FORM IN MODERN CHINA

PETER G. ROWE AND SENG KUAN

WITHDRAWN

THE MIT PRESS

CAMBRIDGE, MASSACHUSETTS

LONDON, ENGLAND

This book was set in Kievit by Graphic Composition, Inc., and was printed and bound in the United States of America.

Library of Congress Cataloging-in-Publication Data

Rowe, Peter G.
   Architectural encounters with essence and form in modern China / Peter G. Rowe and Seng Kuan.
      p.   cm.
   Includes bibliographical references and index.
   ISBN 0-262-18219-X (hc. : alk. paper)
   1. Architecture—China—20th century. 2. Architecture—Europe—Influence. I. Kuan, Seng. II. Title.

NA1545 .R68 2002
720′.951′0904—dc21   2001054624

For Anthony and his youthful curiosity

P. G. R.

For my grandfather, for his pancakes and inspiration

S. K.

Contents

List of Illustrations

Acknowledgments

This book came about from a long-standing curiosity toward the roles of tradition and modernism in shaping the architecture and architectural environment of modern China, developed during numerous trips both to and within the mainland over the years. We owe a special debt to Wu Liangyong, Zhang Jie, Wu Jiang, Zheng Shiling, Zhang Jinqiu, Lü Junhua, Sun Fengqi, and Hu Shaoxue for sharing their prodigious knowledge with us and for their patient guidance in helping us understand what was going on around us. Any mistakes or misinterpretations are solely ours. In a similar vein, we would like to express our thanks to Qin Youguo, Zhao Bingshi, Bo Xilai, Liu Hui, Qi Kang, Michael Hwa, Liu Bomin, Wu Qingzhou, and He Jingtang for their insights as well as local knowledge and to C. F. and Paul Tao, Frank Tsao, and David Lie for their generous support over the years and for sharing their experiences in China.

In testing out ideas and concepts, we received timely assistance from several faculty members at Harvard. In particular, we would like to thank Leo Lee, Michael Hays, Cherie Wendelken, Christine Smith, Eduard Sekler, and Toshiko Mori for both their observations and encouragement. We would also like to thank Lai Delin for his review of the text before it went to press. In addition, several remarkable graduate students gave generously of their time. To Wu Yue, Wang Bing, Cheng Yan, Shen Yahong, Huang Lei, Yan Jiahui, and Hiroshi Koike we owe a special debt of gratitude, and in many ways it is to them and their kindred spirits that this book is addressed.

Many thanks also go to Maggie Zong and Celia Slattery, for their patient assistance throughout, and especially to Maria Moran, who tirelessly converted our scribbles into a polished manuscript. Also, without the general support and understanding from Neil Rudenstine of the necessity to engage in such ventures, this book never would have materialized. Finally, we wish to express our enduring gratitude to Lauretta Vinciarelli, Toi Choi, and Mario Kuan, for their selfless support and constant encouragement.

ARCHITECTURAL ENCOUNTERS WITH
ESSENCE AND FORM IN MODERN CHINA

THE FAN OF THE AIR-CONDITIONING UNIT droned on in the corner, drowning out the noises from the courtyard below that doubled as a makeshift foundry for the work unit. The ubiquitous fluorescent light flickered, bathing the shiny gray painted walls in an odd greenish light to the point that you could not tell what time of day or night it was without opening the window. Soon the design institute was moving—or so they were told—into better, more modern quarters. In the meantime, even in their preliminary design discussions, they were continuing to tread familiar ground. All three of them—Zhang Shaoshu, Lu Hui, and Wu Feng—had graduated from Beijing's top school, though some years apart, and all, remarkably, now found themselves in a position of relative design responsibility. Unlike earlier times, when invariably they would have joined an established studio within the design institute and worked their way up, they were now given a comparatively free hand, at least before their boss started issuing them explicit instructions from on high. These days, there was so much design work to be done and very little in the way of a specific doctrine or style to be followed. So much freedom made some of their older colleagues think it was a moment of crisis in Chinese architecture; and even if this sentiment was exaggerated, it was certainly a time for experimentation and, hence, a chance for them to show what they could do.

"It is a civic building, after all," interjected Lu Hui, somewhat taken aback by the slightly younger Wu Feng's flight of fancy in the direction of colliding volumes and planes, as he sketched out a basic concept for the project. "Surely it must reflect some sort of Chineseness!" she continued forcefully.

"And tell me—if you can—what exactly is that?" responded Feng sarcastically. "We are, after all, finally living in the modern world," he continued, mimicking Hui's cadence.

"Yes, that's undoubtedly true," said Zhang Shaoshu, the oldest of the three, also in an ironic tone, as he was also becoming somewhat exasperated with Wu Feng's constant striving for fashionable design novelty as an architect. "But Hui has a point. Otherwise we might as well be doing this for—I don't know—Hong Kong!"

"I wish!" Feng shot back, who since his return from the design institute's branch office in the south was sporting a punk hairdo and spending his money on the hippest clothes he could find, frequenting foreign bars, and even sprinkling his Mandarin speech with a Cantonese twang.

"Your trouble is, you have no sense of tradition!" Hui blurted out, again becoming frustrated with Wu Feng's persistent avant-gardism. "Just look at yourself," she added more for rhetorical effect than to be nasty, as she liked Feng and thought that he was probably the most talented designer in their group.

"Like I've said before, what good is it?" Feng replied emphatically. "It hasn't got us anywhere in the past, why should it now?"

"That's not true!" interjected Shaoshu indignantly; "besides, surely what has happened before should not invalidate our continuing efforts to try to find a way of being both modern and Chinese at the same time."

TRADITIONALISM VERSUS MODERNISM IN CHINA emerged strongly as an issue of cultural development, though not for the first time, in the aftermath of the Opium War of 1840 to 1842. The ceding of the treaty ports to foreign powers, which accompanied the Treaty of Nanjing in 1842, forcefully opened China to the West in an unprecedented manner. This Anglo-Chinese conflict followed on the heels of failed diplomatic efforts to open China to the West during the late eighteenth and early nineteenth centuries; although opium was a factor, the deeper and more central issue was trade. Laws banning opium then in force in China led to the destruction of supplies from foreign warehouses and resulted in a blockade of Chinese ports by the British. After the siege of Guangzhou and the occupation of Shanghai in 1842, which also prevented supplies from traveling along the Grand Canal to the Chinese capital, the Qing government, under duress, finally acceded to British demands. Following the Treaty of Nanjing, five treaty ports were opened for foreign trade—Shanghai, Ningbo, Fuzhou, Xiamen, and Guangzhou—together with land use rights; in those areas foreign powers began to establish their own communities, under their own extraterritorial rule and modeled on life in their home countries.[1] Eventually, these "Concessions" or "Settlements," as they were called, in places like Shanghai, became the centers of modern cities from which contemporary Western ideas and technologies were propagated.

There was, however, little overt cultural response by the Chinese at the time, largely in the hope that the treaty could be annulled and the foreign influence dismissed. More fundamentally, this inaction can also be attributed to the traditional cosmological Chinese view of harmonious balance and to the classical Confucian and Neo-Confucian legacy that flowed from it and remained entrenched in Chinese family life, education, and state institutions. These gave the Chinese a sense that they were superior in civilized behavior, ethical conduct, and minding their own business, a response that sprang up immediately in the face of unvarnished Western expansionism. In brief, harmony was achieved by striking a balance by conceptualizing an oppositional binary—the *yang* (expansion) and the *yin* (concentration) of a given set of relations—as exemplified in the central values of Chinese civilization, passed on down through the ages via the *Analects,* the *Mencius,* and other works. These writings stressed concepts of noble virtue, the need for rites and rituals and propriety in their performance, and filial respect and reverence.[2]

Noble virtue, for its part, promoted a depth of practical wisdom, enabling the past to be appreciated and the present understood through active learning and scholarship: the result was personal autonomy, responsibility, and a capacity both to deal with specific situations and to transcend a particular walk of life. Indeed, the scholarly class ultimately created was largely meritocratic and was entered into solely through rigorous examination. Rites and rituals were understood as necessary to nourish the much-appreciated appetites of life in a manner that would avoid conflict and disorder, rather than to transcend such appetites altogether—as, for instance, Buddhists and Taoists would have it. More specifically, the Confucian notion of *li* (adhering to what is correct) applied to that which was used to influence social outcomes and to bring forth good fortune; from it the *li* of propriety, etiquette, protocol, and courtesy were formed, defining a model social order and an effective system of interpersonal relations.[3] Furthermore, filial respect and reverence were seen as a cornerstone of life's renewal, family perpetuation, and, by extension, dynastic precedents—and ultimately claims to sovereignty.

As teaching and as code of conduct, Confucianism, in its various incarnations, often proved well-suited to the governance and cultural cultivation of a vast expanse of an otherwise disparate people, where a more personalized form of administration and adjudication was preferable to impersonal top-down bureaucratic procedures. It was, as William Theodore de Bary described it, a "decentralized enfeoffment system," unlike the more centralized feudalism encountered earlier in the West and in Japan.[4] Moreover, its orientation toward matters immediately at hand, within personal grasp and therefore within the internal affairs of China, was essentially civil rather than militaristic, nationalistic, and expansionist. This is not to say that the institutional conduct and mind-set of the Qing dynasty measured up fully to the Confucian mandate—it did not, and the regime ultimately fell because of that failure. Certainly, many transactions were marred by favoritism and corruption, often including the sense that admission into the scholarly or "nobly virtuous" class was a prize in itself, rather than a stepping-stone toward doing well by others and the country at large. Those who ruled could and often did become despotic. Also, a certain sense of xenophobia and a fear of radicalism, especially with regard to the future, undermined the prescribed harmonious balancing of the power of positive thinking (*yang*) against the power of negative thinking and arbitrary sanctions (*yin*).[5] Nevertheless, the Chinese elite undoubtedly felt, at the time of the Opium War, that they came closer to meeting the standards of their own complex mandate, developed over the centuries, than did the Western powers who were invading them. Small wonder, then, that they thought they were right and would prevail.

Yet mounting pressure from the West only exacerbated the situation, culminating in the Second Opium (or *Arrow*) War of 1856 through 1860, which pitted Britain and France against China over matters of trade and diplomatic representation. The conflict started on October 8, 1856, when Chinese troops boarded the *Arrow*, a ship sailing under a British flag on the Pearl River in the vicinity of Guangzhou; the British and French retaliated by shelling the city. Under the Treaty of Tianjin in 1858, the Chinese officially conceded to demands for opening further treaty ports and for providing foreign diplomats the right to reside in Beijing, as well as offering free access by foreign missionaries and traders to China's vast interior. In spite of an attempt by the Chinese to renege on the agreement, it was again forcibly imposed on Prince Gong through the Convention of Beijing in 1860—though not before Lord Elgin's troops had burned down the Summer Palace (*Yuanmingyuan*).[6] In all, ten treaty ports were opened. Among them were Tianjin, Zhenjiang on the Yangtze River (*Changjiang*) near Nanjing, Jiujiang and Hankou farther upriver, and Shantou on the southern coast near Guangzhou.

The impact of the West's military prowess had a lasting effect on at least certain prominent segments of the Qing dynasty court. One result was a program of military modernization and advancement, broadly referred to as the Self-Strengthening Movement (*Ziqiang yundong*) or sometimes as the Westernization Movement, which was to last through the 1860s and 1870s, and even, in its later phases, well into the 1890s. During the Tongzhi Restoration of 1861 (*Tongzhi zhongxing*), which symbolized a revival of the flagging Qing dynasty, officials, deeply aware of how far behind the West China had fallen, made strenuous efforts to acquire Western military technology and scientific knowledge. Later, under what was referred to as the Foreign Matters Movement (*Yangwu yundong*) within the idea of self-strengthening, applications from a wider range of Western technology and industry were copied, such as techniques of shipbuilding and mining, the telegraph, and railways.[7] The slogan "Self-Strengthening" itself had a classical and therefore nonforeign ring to it. It eventually became identified with the doctrine of "Chinese learning for essential principles, Western learning for practical functions" (*Zhongxue weiti, xixue weiyong*), and particularly with the binary concepts of *ti* (referring to body, essence, or foundation) and *yong* (standing for use, function, application, or form).[8] More specifically, the phrase "self-strengthening" came from a sentence in the Book of Changes (*Yijing*): "Heaven moves on strongly; the gentlemen, therefore, incessantly strengthen themselves."[9] The statement coincides with a primary tenet of Confucian thinking and conduct, whereby learning and self-reflection, guided again by the aim of reaching harmonious balance in changed circumstances, through virtuous nobility, institutional respect, filiality, and so on, were to be both admired and put into action.

This was not the first time that China had confronted an influx of new ideas or of foreign pressures. After the relative decline of Buddhism in the ninth century C.E., the Neo-Confucians, who became well-established during the Song Dynasty, called for a new kind of learning in which the "solid," "real," and "practical" would replace the "emptiness" of Buddhism and Taoism, which they regarded as having no useful principles for dealing effectively with human problems.[10] Indeed, the terms *ti* and *yong* were drawn from Song metaphysics, where they stood for the ontological and functional aspects of the same reality.[11] Identified within a longer view of Chinese history as the "early modern period," the Song dynasty saw intensive internal development and the need for numerous teachers, scholars, and administrative officials. It was also a period during which new agricultural methods flourished, technology was deployed, paper money was used, and industry, commerce, and urbanization expanded rapidly—all ostensible hallmarks of modernization.

Furthermore, this mass of new knowledge and technique required a new model of education: the School of Hu Yuan (993–1059) combined classical study with practical learning and specialization in such areas as civil administration, engineering, and mathematics. There, the "substance," "function," and "literary expression" of Confucian teaching were emphasized, where "substance" referred to ethical principles, "function" to practical application, and "literary expression" to explicit communication.[12] Rather than being inflexible, or resistant to modernization, the Confucian classics provided values and principles for structuring and giving priority to new technical knowledge and applications. Indeed, their study proved so flexible that during the late thirteenth and early fourteenth centuries, the invading Mongols quickly adopted and institutionalized this approach as a basis for their educational system and as a way of reaffirming universal, as distinct from Chinese, values. Therefore, the application of the concepts of *ti* and *yong* during the Self-Strengthening Movement should be viewed not as some novel way of seeing the world but as a continuation of Neo-Confucian thought: the interaction of the two terms could be broadened, contracted, and balanced depending on the situation at hand—namely, the introduction of foreign technology. It also provided the basis for something of an intellectual tug-of-war, supplying the rationale for conservatives and progressives alike to pursue and promote their own scholarly views of this changing world, with the result that a dominant and consistent sense of direction was often hard to come by.

In other ways the Self-Strengthening Movement took place largely within the cordial atmosphere between China and the Western powers that followed closely on the heels of the Taiping Rebellion (1851–1864). The successful defense of Shanghai against the Taiping was a joint effort between loyalist troops—*Huaiyong*—under the command of Li Hongzhang (1823–1901) and foreign detachments, all armed with Western weapons.[13] A number of sources have attributed the first use of the phrase "self-strengthening" to Feng Guifen (1809–1874), an official, scholar, and proponent of Western reforms who authored a series of essays that he presented to Zeng Guofan (1811–1872), a loyal statesman of the late Qing. In one, Feng wrote, in connection with foreign humiliation, that "our inferiority is not something allotted us by heaven, but is rather due to ourselves. . . . And, if we feel ashamed, there is nothing better than Self-Strengthening."[14] Zeng, in turn, immortalized the term.[15] Essentially, Feng argued for selectively adopting Western learning. "If we let Chinese ethics and famous [Confucian] teachings serve as an original foundation," he said, "and let them be supplemented by the methods used by various nations for the attainment of prosperity and strength, would it not be the best of procedures?"[16] More subtly, such writings as his 1860 "Protests of the Jiaobin Studio" (*Jiaobinlu kanyi*) formed a substantial part of the theoretical underpinnings of the Self-Strengthening Movement.[17] Feng, who taught for about twenty years in Shanghai, Nanjing, and Suzhou, also argued for limited institutional reforms to advance his program of Western learning; if that learning were recognized by being incorporated into the civil services examinations, students would be encouraged to study it.

Over time the Self-Strengthening Movement broadened from a focus on strictly military matters to a general sentiment embracing outside influences. That sentiment was expressed by the *Yangwu* faction of the Qing court under the leadership of Prince Gong, the founder of the *Zongli yamen* or Office of Foreign Affairs, in a further illustration of *yong* being expanded though still guided by *ti*. It also saw practical application by Zeng Guofan and Li Hongzhang, who collaborated to successfully create a number of arsenals, shipyards, and steel mills in southern and coastal China. In addition to being a statesman, Zeng Guofan was also a scholar and a general, as well as the inspiration for Li Hongzhang's Huai army. Not coincidentally, Li's father was a fellow student with Zeng, who, in turn, extended patronage to the son. Li Hongzhang, for his part, provided distinguished service to the Qing court in a number of important positions; he eventually fell into disfavor because he was seen as partly responsible for the abject Chinese defeat during the Sino-Japanese War of 1894 to 1895.[18]

In the final analysis, however, the Self-Strengthening Movement was essentially an effort to compartmentalize Western influences and Western expertise in the collective Chinese mind, to prevent interference with local laws and institutions; it was to fail precisely because of this unreasonable selectivity and its inability to bring both frameworks together.[19] Western arms and industries, after all, are not just products but artifacts of ways of life and of ideologies. As John King Fairbank puts it, "in retrospect we can see that gunboats and steel mills bring their own philosophy with them."[20] One cannot halfway Westernize. There were also strategic failures: Vietnam was lost by China to the French by force of arms in 1885, and the humiliating defeats suffered at the hands of the Japanese during the Sino-Japanese conflict of 1894 to 1895 only highlighted the lopsided comparison between the modern advances made during the Meiji Restoration in Japan, beginning in 1868, and those accomplished in China under its own far more shaky Tongzhi Restoration. Under the 1895 Treaty of Shimonoseki, China was forced to cede Taiwan, the Pescadores, and the Liaodong Peninsula to Japan; to recognize the independence of

Korea, which in 1910 was annexed to Japan; and to allow Japanese citizens into China to trade. Soon after, the Liaodong Peninsula became the beachhead for the development of Japanese mining and railway interests in Manchuria; this influx, together with competition from the Russians that eventually led to the Russo-Japanese War of 1904 to 1905, was to have a strong influence (as described later) on the urban character of such emerging cities as Harbin, Changchun, and Mukden (now Shenyang). Finally, the Self-Strengthening Movement lacked the full support of the Qing administration. Certainly it was resisted by members of the entrenched scholarly class, whose fortunes were directly connected to traditional forms of Chinese learning.[21] But probably more important, the diffusion of ideas among intellectuals about appropriate courses of action led to factionalism at court and also prevented the emergence of a sharper or more distinct national focus. In contrast to Japan, which in the Meiji Restoration immediately shifted to a vigorous outward-oriented policy reflecting a new mode of thinking—albeit partly Confucian in origin—China remained mired in its assumptions about dynastic rule and lacked the alternative form of leadership needed to effectively halt and reverse the damage to its prestige.

At about the same time that Li Hongzhang was negotiating the Treaty of Shimonoseki, two erstwhile reformers—Kang Youwei (1858–1927) and Liang Qichao (1873–1929)—were in Beijing to take the Metropolitan Examinations that, once passed, would grant them the highest degree and award them lofty positions in the officialdom of scholars. Together they organized a protest among some twelve hundred other candidates, asking for the rejection of the peace terms with Japan and portraying Li as a traitor. After receiving his *jinshi* degree, Kang Youwei returned to Guangdong province to complete a book titled *The Study of Confucius as a Reformer* (*Kongzi gaizhi kao,* 1897), in which he suggested that Confucius was not just a self-admitted transmitter of ancient knowledge but an innovator who used the cloak of antiquity to advance more radical ideas about life and moral experience. This proved to be yet another provocative work by Kang; the first, *Study of the Forged Xin Classics* (*Xinxue weijingkao*), had rocked the scholarly Chinese world when it was published in 1891.

Kang's theory of progress and the idea of a "grand commonality," for which he is well known, was set out in *The Book of Great Harmony* (*Datongshu,* 1898) in terms of three ages: the Age of Disorder, into which Confucius was born; the Age of Order; and, finally, the Age of Great Peace, which was yet to come. As he put it, "the course of humanity progresses according to a fixed sequence. From the clans come tribes, which in turn are transformed into nations. And from nations the Grand Unity comes about." Idealistically, he then went on to say that at the final juncture, "there will be no longer any nations, no more racial distinctions, and customs will be everywhere the same." For him, the present was the Age of Order, although he admonished those around him "to propagate the doctrines of self-rule and independence, and to discuss publicly the matter of constitutional government. If the laws are not reformed, greater disorder will result."[22] Kang then went on to write about the Meiji Reform Movement in Japan. In 1898, amid the Western powers' scrabbling for still further concessions in China—including Qingdao, sought by the Germans; Lüshun, by the Russians; and the Kowloon New Territories, by the British—he returned to Beijing to once again petition the emperor to start a reform movement modeled after those in Russia and Japan. After two more attempts, including meetings with high officials like Li Hongzhang, Kang Youwei finally gained an audience with the Guangxu emperor; the result was the Hundred Days' Reform (*Wuxu bianfa*).[23]

During the summer months that followed—spanning 103 days, from June 11 until September 21, 1898—more than two hundred rescripts, decrees, and edicts were handed down from the throne: they called for modernization of practically all aspects of the Chinese government and institutional structure. The reformers' aim was to drag China forward to meet world standards, using the time-honored albeit here dangerous tactic of "truth from the top."[24] Liang Qichao, a younger compatriot and former pupil of Kang Youwei in Guangzhou, was also a part of the reform group from the outset. In 1898 he wrote an influential paper, "Proposals for Reform" (*Bianfa tongyi*), urging radical institutional reform and the introduction of a constitutional monarchy modeled loosely on Western precedents.[25] Unfortunately for those involved, the empress dowager, at the instigation of the conservative faction at court, effectively brought the reform movement to an end. Zaitian (Guangxu) was placed under house arrest; Kang and Liang fled, warned in advance by the emperor. Kang, traveling via Shanghai and Hong Kong to Japan and then on to Canada and Britain, remained throughout much of the rest of his life in loyal opposition, opposing Republicanism after 1911 and, instead, attempting to restore the monarchy. Liang also escaped to Japan with Kang; he remained there and established the *Xinmin congbao,* an intellectual review through which he carried on the reformist cause. In 1912, after the downfall of the Qing regime, he returned with his family to China, taking up an appointment as minister of justice in 1913.[26] Six others, however, were summarily executed for their role in the movement.[27]

Again the reforms threatened vested interests, especially among the large conservative faction of the scholarly class who wished to perpetuate their version of traditional Chinese culture and its way of life. The reformers were supported by the emperor, but his power base, especially in comparison to the empress dowager Cixi's grasp on the throne and the Qing court, was weak.[28] Indeed, real reform would at last come only with the downfall of the Qing dynasty—the Boxer Rebellion and foreign retaliations by the Eight Power invasion force of 1900 and then outright revolution in 1911—and not, as their Confucian backgrounds might have led Kang and Liang to imagine it, through the emperor.

Taken together, proponents of both the Hundred Days' Reform and the Self-Strengthening Movement shared certain philosophical concepts. All were more or less strongly committed to some essential set of Chinese values, embodied in traditional thought and scholarship. Similarly, they all identified the threat of modernization with Westernization and attempted to avoid this conflation by somehow putting Chinese principles and Western know-how into distinct and compatible realms. A striking example is provided by Zhang Zhidong, a moderate scholar during the Hundred Days' Reform who coupled gradual reform with adherence to Neo-Confucianism. While he borrowed the terms *ti* and *yong* from Neo-Confucian doctrine, his essay of 1898, titled "Exhortations to Learn" (*Quanxuepian*), made it clear that the survival of Chinese culture required active engagement with Western knowledge. As he put it (rather prophetically, as events turned out), "If we wish to make China strong and preserve Chinese knowledge, we must study Western knowledge. Furthermore, if we do not use Chinese knowledge to consolidate the foundation first and, therefore, get straight in our minds what our interests and purposes are, then the strong will become rebellious leaders and the weak will become slaves of others."[29]

In China, unlike in other modernizing countries, the underlying sense of nationalism was not necessarily attached to some specific political program; it was more often part of the scholarly tradition of *youhuanyishi*—the general anxiety with which intellectuals regarded their civilization.[30] In effect, this was an independent scholarly habit of mind; not only did it produce an intellectually uncoordinated and often factionalized attitude at court that was quite unlike the sharper focus seemingly required for nationalism, but it also tended to lose contact, in its idealism, with local realities and interests.

But there were also significant differences between the programs of the Self-Strengthening Movement and the Hundred Days' Reform and between their attitudes toward *ti* and *yong*. First, they were dissimilar in orientation and degree. By taking a narrowly technological view, naively unencumbered by much of a conscious ideological perspective, those in the Self-Strengthening Movement could with relative ease detach questions of essence from those of form. Some thirty years later, after much more contact with the West and a rapidly modernizing Japan, supporters of the Hundred Days' Reform no longer had such naïveté; their emphasis shifted much further toward their institutional setting and they called for reform—albeit often gradual—largely by way of adopting and emulating available Westernized models, while maintaining a core of Chinese values and essential principles. Their view of the interaction between *ti* and *yong* was, therefore, often dynamic and expansive, at least among the more radical group. Kang Youwei, as noted above, went so far as to cast Confucius in the role of a reformer, with the clear implication that his writings should be interpreted from this perspective and that at another time he might have had different things to say.

Second, the groups differed in how they regarded Western and Chinese knowledge. For those in the Self-Strengthening Movement, the two forms of thought were like separate mental compartments with relatively clear boundaries and uses. By contrast, the later reformers, while clearly putting Chinese knowledge first, argued for active engagement with Western knowledge to sharpen and update the sense of Chinese essence. This attitude of self-reflection, so strong in the Confucian tradition, is of course not uncommon when different knowledge and value systems substantially engage. Such encounters can lead, for example, in the direction of intermingling and broader pluralistic attitudes, as seen recently in the West—and, for that matter, at times during the Roman Empire. They can also lead in the opposite direction, encouraging a further congealing or muddled combining of more closely held traditional beliefs, as is frequent in beleaguered authoritarian regimes. China and the Qing generally tended more toward the latter than the former.

Undoubtedly the collective mission of both movements was heightened and given direction by the defeats suffered in the Opium and Sino-Japanese Wars; the need for new strength and direction, in turn, strongly influenced the dualistic logic inherent in the defensive stand taken by many toward Chinese culture, deemed necessary for the *ti,* or essence, of China to survive. Their stand was also influenced by the mounting presence of modern foreign powers on Chinese soil, resulting in a state of affairs that not only was semifeudal but was also verging on semicolonial. Since 1842, the foreign foothold in China had grown to numerous treaty ports in addition to the earlier fifteen; by 1911 more than thirty Aihun ports were opened along most of China's navigable waterways and there were at least six extensive leasehold areas along the coastal regions, including the French-controlled Guangzhou Bay, almost opposite Hainan Island.

Following the failure of the Hundred Days' Reform, the suppression of the Boxer Rebellion, and the return of the Qing court from largely self-imposed exile in Xi'an in 1901, steps were taken to institute constitutional and administrative reforms, amid broadening anti-Qing sentiment and revolutionary activities abroad. But again, the "Constitutional Movement," as it generally became known, was led by scholars and wealthy landowners whose opposition to the imperial court reflected more a desire for power sharing and the ascendancy of local interests than a hope for the radical overturn of Chinese society. Modern-thinking though many of the reformers were, they also enjoyed relatively entrenched positions and were mindful of the continuing imperial presence. Indeed, the conservatives among them continued to insist on ancestral institutions and believed, in a Confucian manner, that good government depended on men and not on laws. Consequently, too much institutional change too quickly not only threatened them but also was antithetical to their fundamental position—an attitude that was certainly revealed in the diffidence of many of their actions over the next ten years.

The first real change occurred in 1905 and 1906, when the imperial examination system was abolished, Ministries of Education, Police, and War were established, and the idea that China should move to a constitutional form of government—based on the Japanese model—was publicly discussed. An outline of the new constitution was published in 1908, and the death of the empress dowager and the Guangxu emperor that year seemed to clear the way for more rapid reform. The following year, provincial assemblies met to discuss the constitutional provisions; in 1910 they called for a parliament to be convened, with a cabinet of high officials and Manchu nobles to be appointed in April 1911 and a parliament promised for 1913. As events turned out, this was too little reform and too late, as anti-Qing feelings and revolutionary activities strengthened.[31] Sun Yat-sen (or Sun Zhongshan, 1866–1925), for example, then in exile in Japan, in 1905 became the head of the United League (*Tongmenghui*), an alliance of radicals from about seventeen different provinces in China; in 1912, it became the Guomindang.[32]

Exercising its assumed authority, the Qing government decided to nationalize all railroads in 1911 and borrowed heavily from foreign banks to do so; local officials in Sichuan province, who were trying to establish their own system, were especially outraged by what they saw as a local affront and an unpatriotic sellout. Shortly thereafter, events snowballed out of Qing control, with local takeovers, strikes, attacks on government offices, and declarations of independence in several areas sympathetic to the United League.[33] On October 10, 1911, units of the new regular army stationed in Wuchang, a suburb of Wuhan, mutinied and, a day later, torched the city. Other units in Hanyang and Hankou also broke away, and a new independent military government was declared. From then on, the hopes for Qing imperial rule—constitutional or otherwise—deteriorated quickly; the Republic of China was declared at the end of 1911, with Sun Yat-sen as its president. Matters did not end there, however, as threats to split the country led Sun to resign in 1912 in favor of Yuan Shikai (1859–1916).[34] In 1913 Yuan, who had a military background, suppressed the "Second Revolution" of the southern republics; in 1915 he had himself declared emperor, but he died in 1916 before he could be truly enthroned. China then slid into an often tumultuous period of factionalism and partial rule by warlords.[35]

Although not very effectively and certainly well behind the rising popular tide of anti-Qing sentiment and events, those in the Constitutional Movement had tried to put into effect sweeping institutional changes similar in orientation to those attempted by proponents of the Hundred Days' Reform. In fact, many were involved in both movements. Certainly, the new Chinese society was commingling essence and form to a higher degree, with external models of governance and recently arrived modern and foreign technologies, as it confronted and tried to shape a more modern world. In this regard, application, use, and outward form (*yong*) were uppermost in the reformers' minds and were beginning to take precedence over the essence, body, or inner structure (*ti*) of Chinese culture.

For one thing, geographical differences in development and in decentralized power sharing were beginning to surface. The semicolonial and outright colonial foreign influence in the coastal concessions and, to the north, in Manchuria created a very real disparity in modes of economic production and wealth between these areas and regions of central and western China, as well as areas outside the larger modernizing cities near the coast and to the north. For another, those living in many of the same developing areas were undoubtedly beginning to question the necessity of the established imperial and Confucian cultural mold of life. Quite apart from having an ideological source, as indisputably was true at certain points along the sociopolitical spectrum, such questioning also reflected the decreasing utility and applicability of older ways of conducting daily life; other, modern systems of valuation and social intercourse seemed to be needed. Like many other modernizing societies at the time, although much more gradually, China was beginning to banish essential, traditional cultural rites and rituals to less public realms of life, where they were performed more selectively. Nevertheless, most of those in the Constitutional Movement ultimately opted for privilege over suffrage, choosing in spite of modern appearances to preserve their conservative intellectual positions, entrenched interests, and essentially traditional way of life.

Yet the Constitutional Movement did provide a transition to the revolutionary movements of Sun Yat-sen and, later, of Mao Zedong. Sun, like Kang, projected the idea of a "grand commonwealth"—or, as classical scholars would have it, "all under heaven shared in common"; but under greater Western influence, he moved further outside the Confucian orbit in rejecting the evolutionary aspect of Chinese culture in favor of revolution. Indeed, he saw China as resistant to modern nation building precisely because of such Neo-Confucian traits as individualism, which he considered to have become excessive, and loyalty to family and clan. On both points he went so far as to say that "even though we have four hundred million people gathered together in one China, in reality they are just a heap of loose sand."[36] His remedy was a three-stage revolutionary process: it began with military government, went on to a provisional constitution granting local self-government, and ended in a full constitutional government under a republican system. Key to this process was what he called "the necessity of political tutelage"; he explained, "as a school boy must have good teachers and helpful friends, so the Chinese people, being for the first time under republican rule, must have a far-sighted revolutionary government for their training."[37] Again like Kang Youwei, he saw the alternative to his three-stage process as "unavoidable disorder." Seen in hindsight, Sun's doctrine of political and hence party tutelage, first enunciated in 1905, represents perhaps the first conscious advocacy among the leaders of Asian nationalism of "guided democracy."

Sun Yat-sen differed from the other reformers discussed in that he was taught almost entirely in Western schools and lived for a long time outside of China. He was not classically trained and initially saw the task of bridging the gap between China's past and his Western-oriented future as being relatively straightforward. This opinion was to change quickly, however, as he was forced to reevaluate his position and to turn toward Chinese tradition as the source of national solidarity. Not only was this tradition already in place, and therefore readily at hand, but Sun was also growing critical of Western materialism; like others before him, he sought a more steadfast Chinese essence on which to base his movement. In other ways as well, Sun Yat-sen's doctrine seems to have been formed within a Confucian framework, albeit in opposition to it. As noted earlier, he largely blamed two bedrock tenets of Confucian conduct for the presumed Chinese malaise: excessive individualism, stemming from the habits of mind of the autonomous scholar, and fealty to family or clan. He thus aimed his critique more directly at the essence (*ti*) of Chinese culture than his predecessors had done.

Many long-held convictions about the integrity and enduring capacity of Chinese culture were to change dramatically during these upheavals, precipitating the May Fourth Movement (*Wusi yundong*) of 1919 and its immediate predecessor, the New Culture Movement (*Xinwenhua yundong*) of 1917.[38] Ostensibly, the May Fourth Movement began on a Sunday afternoon when some 3,000 students assembled in Tiananmen Square in Beijing, in front of the Gates of Heavenly Peace, specifically to demonstrate against the decision of the Paris peace conference to award Japan the treaty rights previously held by the Germans in Qingdao and parts of Shandong Province, and more generally to awaken the masses to the impending threat of further dismemberment at the hands of foreign powers.[39] A subsequent march toward the foreign legation quarters was deflected by police, with the assistance of foreign guards; the students then headed toward the home of the Chinese minister of communications, which they ransacked in protest of his direct negotiations with the Japanese and his role in the Versailles agreement. During the ensuing violence, one student was killed and thirty-two others were arrested.

In the days that followed, broad-based student unions spread from Beijing to Shanghai, Tianjin, Wuhan, and beyond, and in June 1919 the Student Union of the Republic of China was formed. Shop owners, industrial workers, and others supported the students, and the resulting sympathy strike in Shanghai involved some 60,000 workers from forty-three enterprises. The press also became involved: numerous May Fourth journals sprang up, such as *The Dawn, Young China,* and *New Society,* all proclaiming the arrival of a new and better era.[40] As the historian Jonathan Spence observes, "it was as if far off events at [Paris and] Versailles and the mounting evidence of the spinelessness of corrupt local politicians coalesced in people's minds and impelled them to search for a way to return meaning to the Chinese culture."[41]

Like participants in other broad-based movements of this kind, the reformers followed different avenues and predilections, although they were all in some way attempting to redefine Chinese culture as a valid part of the modern world; in particular, they strove to bring new ideas of science and democracy, as well as their newfound patriotism, into a stronger common focus. Indeed, they were unified around the idea of a rejuvenated China capable of coping successfully with such chronic ills as warlordism, a feudal landlord system, and foreign imperialism.[42] As it turned out, the institutional setting most important to the movement was Peking University (Beida), which, with its first modern chancellor, Yan Fu (1854–1921), who took office in 1912, had earlier played a vital role in the New Culture Movement. Yan Fu was also a renowned translator, who with Lin Shu and others was responsible for providing wide access to numerous important foreign texts. In 1916–1917 Yan Fu was succeeded as chancellor at Beida by Cai Yuanpei, who, together with Chen Duxiu, the dean of the university, and Hu Shi (Hu Shih), a professor of philosophy, was to rise to special prominence in the May Fourth Movement.[43]

Cai Yuanpei (1868–1940) was something of a prodigy, passing his *jinshi* exam in classical studies in 1890, at age twenty-two, and then going on to study philosophy in Germany. Conspicuously anti-Qing, Cai served as minister of education under Sun Yat-sen during the early Republican era; he was chancellor of Beida from 1916 until 1926. Throughout his academic life, Cai was a staunch advocate of intellectual freedom and helped position Peking University as the leading center in China for the propagation of new social, literary, and political ideas emanating from the May Fourth Movement.[44]

Chen Duxiu (1879–1942) was more intuitive and less classically skilled than Cai, passing his more lowly civil service exam in 1896. Under the influence of the 1898 reformers he then began to engage with Western ideas, and between 1900 and 1910 he periodically studied overseas in

France and Japan. In 1915 he founded *New Youth* or *La Jeunesse* (*Xinqingnian*), a magazine that arguably became the most influential intellectual journal of its time in China, actively pressing for "scientific content" and the use of everyday language; it ceased publication in 1921.[45] An opponent of Confucianism, Chen urged that liberal concepts of science and democracy were essential for China's future progress.[46] For him, notes Spence, "the basic task [of reform] is to import the foundation of Western society, that is the new belief in equality and human rights. [In so doing] we must [also] be thoroughly aware of the incompatibility between Confucianism and the new belief, the new society and the new state."[47] By 1920, Chen Duxiu was gravitating toward Marxism; he became one of the first members of the Chinese Communist Party in Shanghai and served as its general secretary until 1927.

Much younger than the other two men, Hu Shi (1891–1962) attended a new-style school in Shanghai in 1904; he traveled to Cornell University in the United States on a scholarship in 1910, graduating with a bachelor of arts in philosophy in 1914. He then completed a doctorate at Columbia University under the supervision of the philosopher John Dewey, whom he greatly admired; he remained a lifelong advocate of pragmatism. Relatively early in his career Hu made a pioneering social interpretation of Cao Xueqin's classic novel *The Dream of the Red Chamber* (*Hongloumeng*, ca. 1760). Hu consistently believed in Western interpretive and analytical methodology; unlike Chen the Marxist, he was a political conservative, continuing his association with the Guomindang during the 1920s.[48]

Others, such as Li Dazhao (1888–1927) and Lu Xun (1881–1936), also rose to prominence and helped shape the May Fourth Movement. Li Dazhao was the librarian at Peking University and another member of the philosophy department. Like Hu, he studied abroad, at Waseda University in Japan; he wrote on Marxism for *New Youth*—Chen's journal—in 1918, arguing for a synthesis of Eastern and Western values, as well as rather disconcertingly advocating violent overthrows of ruling regimes when necessary. During this period he hired Mao Zedong as a temporary office assistant, Mao apparently having been attracted by Li's leftist rhetoric and ideas about reform.[49] Lu Xun, who also taught at Peking University and Peking Normal University, was unquestionably the most brilliant author to emerge from the May Fourth Movement, publishing numerous stories between 1917 and 1921. One of these, "The True Story of Ah Q," parodied the 1911 revolution, to paraphrase Jonathan Spence, as both a muddled and inconclusive event.[50] Serialized in the *Beijing Morning Post* in 1920, "Ah Q" told the story of a self-deluding and cowardly bully, humiliated by people more powerful than himself though simultaneously thinking himself the victor, who in his greed for status attempts to intimidate and harass those who are weaker. It eventually ends in his execution. In the "Diary of a Madman," an earlier work published in *New Youth* in 1918, Lu Xun launched a similar attack on the cruelty, backwardness, and hypocrisy of Chinese society, as the "madman" sees his fellow countrymen as cannibals.[51] In fact, Lu Xun was the pen name of Zhou Shuren, who went to Japan in 1902 to study medicine at Sendai University, returning to China in 1909. In 1930, shortly before his death of tuberculosis in Shanghai, he founded the League of Left-Wing Writers.[52] Like many of his colleagues, Lu Xun advocated something equivalent to a Chinese "enlightenment."

At this juncture, it seemed that nothing short of the replacement of traditional Chinese learning by modern Western knowledge and intellectual practices would suffice. Prior attempts to mediate and circumscribe some sense of a Chinese "essence," by applying modern institutional and technological principles, were being abandoned. To put it another way, the focus of the May Fourth Movement's cultural program shifted away from trying to do things in a modern way (*yong*), while leaving intact more closely held beliefs, to seeking an apparently fundamental reform of the structure of Chinese thinking per se (*ti*). Moreover, the particular liberal scientific, or positivist, brand of knowledge and social practice being proposed was almost completely at odds with the battered but still reigning paradigm of traditional moral discourse combined with classical learning, tied in practice at least to an exclusive system of acquisition and dissemination.

Despite the rhetoric, however, the May Fourth Movement's proposals were not all-encompassing. The emphasis was still largely on matters of application and methodology and the replacement of one form of reasoning with another. Presumably, over time, such replacement could have resulted in a sweeping change of essential values, since how one thinks and what one thinks are thoroughly intertwined—although that outcome is not inevitable, because as thinking takes place the "what" and "how" influence one another. Nevertheless, while the intellectuals involved probably entertained thoughts of this kind, their writings demonstrate that they were rather more interested in undertaking broad-based social reform by mounting a critique relying on a certain form of Western intellectual apparatus—moving also, in short, in the direction of *yong*. Yet the May Fourth Movement did result in a substantial change of intellectual consciousness in China; it created greater openness to modernism in the Western sense, principally, as stated, through science and practical reasoning. It also resulted in a critique of entrenched traditional hypocrisy; for instance, its arguments for women's emancipation led to the first female students being admitted to Peking University in 1920. Politically, the Shandong problem that started it all was finally settled at the Washington Conference of 1922, and the twenty-one punitive demands that had previously been placed on China were effectively eradicated with the signing of the Nine Powers Act at the close of the conference.[53]

As was perhaps predictable, given the historical vacillation that had taken place between advocacy of traditional and modern forms of cultural enterprise, as well as the more pressing issue of the need for national solidarity and identity, during the later 1920 and 1930s a reaction set in to the Western tide of thought, inspired once again by Neo-Confucianism. Those leading it hoped to find a spiritual basis that would enable them to meet the evident challenges of modernization, joining a radical questioning of the inner truth of humankind and a philosophy of the mind and heart (*Xinxue*) together with a call for collective action.[54] Proponents like Liang Shuming, a professor of philosophy at Peking University who later became director of the Shandong Rural Research Institute, tried, as Jonathan Spence describes, "to obviate the need for class struggle" and called for "a synthesis of Chinese and Western cultures which, nevertheless, would be distinctively Chinese."[55] More directly, the New Life Movement, also referred to as the National Rejuvenation Movement, was officially launched in 1934 by Chiang Kai-shek (or Jiang Jieshi, 1887–1975), the leader of the Guomindang and the Nationalist Government. Chiang called for greater adherence to traditional Confucian values of politeness, righteousness, integrity, and self-respect; reflecting the sense of national crisis, he emphasized sacrifice, a capacity to endure hardship, a love of country, and a loyalty to national ideals.[56] He declared that "a new national consciousness and mass psychology have to be created and developed": "It is to this end that peoples' thoughts are now being directed to the ancient high virtues of the nation for guidance namely propriety, justice, integrity and conscientiousness, expressed in *li*, *i*, *lien* and *ch'ih*. These four virtues were highly respected by the Chinese people in the past, and they are vitally necessary now if the rejuvenation of the nation is to be effected."[57]

As played out in everyday life, this ideology in many ways mirrored contemporary fascist movements in Europe and Japan, which often placed considerable and violent emphasis on social decorum and meddled incessantly in citizens' private lives.[58] Thus the first two campaigns concerned "good manners" and "cleanliness"; and all instruction related to the regular life of citizens flowed from the New Life Movement Headquarters through local associations, which were responsible for inspections. A militarist, Chiang had joined Sun Yat-sen's army in 1924, and after Sun's death in 1925 he gained political power; in 1926 he won leadership of the Guomindang. He went on to lead the military expedition that reunified China in 1927, bringing to an end more than a decade of unruly factionalism, and he established the capital of the Nationalist Government in Nanjing. He deployed this Neo-Confucian line of thought, wrapped in a sense of nationalism (or vice versa), as a response to "the unpreparedness of the [Chinese] people for the responsibilities of public life," hampered as they were "by the age-long influences of apparently sanctified customs" of the late Qing dynasty;[59] he used it as a tool in the nation-building process.

Despite its fascist tendencies, however, this reaction proved to be relatively short-lived in the culture. It displayed no real theoretical engagement with the essential problems of Chinese modernity at the time—unlike the May Fourth Movement, with its emphasis on sweeping institutional reform and a radical change in the collective mind-set. Instead, Chiang's program returned to a belief that earlier, venerable aspects of Chinese culture could be called on as a defense in current circumstances and, by implication, that China's long, relatively uniform history produced a strength that could be marshaled to resist an encroaching Eurocentric view. Thus the essentialism of Chinese culture was again emphasized for protective and nationalistic purposes, even as the proverbial modern genie was already coming out of the bottle.

Finally, in the period before the end of the War of Resistance against Japan in 1945 and the civil war in 1949, Mao Zedong (1893–1976), the leader of the Chinese Communist Party, formulated a syncretic framework for dealing with tradition and modernism that also turned in the direction of *ti* and *yong*. Mao, who became actively involved in politics during the May Fourth Movement and rose in the Communist Party during the 1930s, had also enjoyed a classical education, sometimes writing poetry. In his 1940 treatise on cultural theory, *On New Democracy* (*Xinminzhuzhuyilun*), he introduced two terms: *jinghua*, loosely translated as "quintessence," or that which can be boiled down, and *zaopo,* loosely interpreted as "sediment."[60] While advocating an idea of a socialist nation and an objective and materialist culture for China, free from the fetters of religion and social class, Mao was mindful that China could also benefit by drawing on ideas and achievements from the West and from China's own feudal past. As he put it, "anything foreign is like food to us; we must digest it, to separate the *jinghua* from the *zaopo,* release the *zaopo* and absorb the *jinghua.*"[61] More specifically, Mao's distinction turned on the repression in feudalistic practices and the liberation in democratic practices, as he stressed that one must discard the feudalistic *zaopo* and absorb the democratic *jinghua* when confronting culture from a different time or place. But this was not to say that *jinghua* could not be found in a place like feudal China. On the contrary, Mao reasoned that many of the creations of the people were non-exploitative and were therefore worthy of potential cultural emulation. Mao approached the concept of a socialist-materialist culture for China in a dialectical manner by initially placing Chinese and foreign cultural practices on a more or less equal footing and then pitting one against the other, with the intent of formulating a new set of liberating social and political practices. He could also be seen as implicitly conflating *ti* and *yong,* though more likely he disregarded the earlier distinction altogether in favor of a process aimed directly at addressing essential social action and cultural features together.

Thus intellectual circles in China between about 1860 and 1940 underwent an episodic process of change, usually pushed and mandated by both internal and external agents; through that process, the traditional edifice of Chinese knowledge, together with practices stemming from it, was incrementally and then more thoroughly (although still selectively) modified to accommodate China to the exigencies of modernization and China's ambitions to a changing world. As described, change did not move uniformly forward. For instance, the Republicans and Nationalists reinstated a traditionally inclined Confucian scheme through the New Life Movement, though clearly their aim was control and the essentially modern purpose of nationalism. Nor were the episodes focused entirely at a core of essential values and beliefs; they were concerned instead with how such values, from a profoundly unitary initial starting position, would or could play out in modernizing Chinese life and in philosophically reframing modernization in Chinese terms. This episodic process can therefore also be regarded as an important part of an evolving "master narrative" that helped orchestrate responses to outside challenges as well as to internal needs for change, preparing the nation to face further modern incursions without abandoning its (admittedly dwindling) essential Chinese characteristics.

Altogether there were five shifts that occurred. First came the initial detachment of form and application (*yong*) from essence, body, and structure (*ti*) during the Self-Strengthening Movement, as a way of reorganizing and actively taking up foreign modern technology by casting it as essentially nonideological. Second, this distinction was further enlarged to encompass social and political institutions during the Hundred Days' Reform and the Constitutional Movement, when it became much more ideologically charged. Third, this expansion culminated in the May Fourth Movement, which advocated a thoroughgoing embrace of largely positivist Western thinking and modern practical reasoning. Fourth, the Republican and Nationalist period of the 1920s and '30s brought a reaction back in the direction of the primacy of traditional culture and a belief in its enduring robustness and appropriateness, while still viewing modernization as necessary. Finally, Mao's reformulation in a new direction—once again unitary—obliterated many of the earlier distinctions almost entirely, or blurred the once-sharp lines between tradition and modernism and between *ti* and *yong* as they were drawn into the same process.

By the early years of the twentieth century, the binary concepts of *ti* and *yong,* which surfaced during the Self-Strengthening Movement, had well and truly moved in the direction of a strong practical emphasis on modern and, thus, Western application, use, and form, especially when it came to modern technology and institutions, despite rearguard actions in favor of Chinese essence and structure. Yet even with the later radicalism, the role of traditionalism in China's project of modernization still remained in contention in many walks of life.

*"**WHAT'S THE CONNECTION WITH ARCHITECTURE?** I don't see it," said Wu Feng rather emphatically, having listened impatiently to another one of Zhang Shaoshu's diatribes about the past. "Those old guys were all philosophers or writers. They didn't design things, like we do," he went on.*

"In fact, they probably wouldn't have been caught dead getting their hands dirty, or making something," Lu Hui interjected, for once agreeing with Feng. "You have to remember the Confucian scheme of things was pretty much hierarchical. Master builders and craftsmen might not have been as low-grade as merchants, but they weren't exactly at the top of the tree either!" she added emphatically.

"Why does she keep doing that?" hissed Feng.

"Who? Doing what?" inquired Shaoshu, somewhat confused by Feng's sudden digression.

"Her, the tea lady!" replied Feng, gesturing in the direction of an old woman, with a kerchief around her hair, who had shuffled into the conference room and was quietly filling a new set of cheap porcelain cups from a thermos and carefully replacing their domed lids.

"Doesn't she know by now that we don't drink the stuff?" Feng continued indignantly.

"The pause that refreshes—ahh!" intoned Hui, sardonically.

"I hadn't noticed," Shaoshu said. "Besides, I like tea from time to time. It helps keep your throat from getting too dehydrated from the dry air."

"The pollution, you mean," interjected Hui.

"Yes, I suppose so," Shaoshu responded quickly, eager to get back to the topic at hand. He had certainly learned, during his recent graduate studies abroad, that architecture could be regarded as an autonomous discipline in which the design of successive projects drew on prior works as precedents, allowing it to remain relatively self-contained. "But that doesn't explain very well the big changes that have occurred here at various times along the way," he thought to himself. "Like all forms of cultural production, architecture reflects what's in the air. It is part of what is going around at the time," Shaoshu proffered out loud, perhaps a little too authoritatively, as Feng began to make a face.

"Oh, here we go again!" said Feng, disparagingly.

"We must remember that as time went on, China became more and more open to the rest of the world and especially to the West," Shaoshu continued, ignoring Feng's comment. "Also, architecture couldn't help but be a part of the general discussion," he went on emphatically, "especially with all the modernization that was taking place in the big cities and the need there for new types of buildings. . . . Not to mention the stamp the Guomindang wanted to put on things," he added, almost as an afterthought.

"And let's not forget all those guys like you who came back from America," interjected Hui once again, making a momentary sideways reference to Shaoshu, but also thinking of a much earlier time and her architect father's teacher at Central.

FOREIGN INFLUENCES AND THE FIRST GENERATION OF CHINESE ARCHITECTS were, in fact, to have a lasting effect on the evolution of modern architecture in China and the degree to which tradition was combined with contemporary, internationally available practices. Before the Qing dynasty finally began to unravel, most building was carried out by Chinese master builders and craftsmen in a time-honored manner; the exceptions were structures in the foreign concessions and other foreign missions, designed primarily by foreign architects, and Chinese facilities incorporating new modern programs, in line with the Self-Strengthening Movement. Until the second decade of the twentieth century, China had no professional architects to speak of in the Western sense, as there were in nineteenth-century Europe or America. Building, and indeed architecture, was the responsibility of craftsmen and master builders following tradition, sometimes guided by old illustrated treatises on bracketed timber systems and other earlier forms of construction. In most cases, knowledge about how to build was passed down, from generation to generation, by word of mouth and by practice as the young worked alongside the old. In fact, as those seeking a clearer, well-documented account of traditional Chinese architecture and building later discovered, the earlier treatises, usually ignored over the years, were difficult to comprehend in detail, despite explanations by craftsmen working in the field.

This declining state of affairs during the later years of Qing rule did not entirely prevent the straightforward approximation of past practices from having an architectural impact, as demonstrated during the reconstruction of what became the Summer Palace in Beijing. The empress dowager Cixi had the palace and its superb gardens secretly rebuilt, after their destruction at the hands of Lord Elgin's foreign forces in 1860, under the pretext that the building would house a naval academy. The secrecy was necessary in order to avoid the strong opposition of others in the ruling class who regarded such a project, first broached in the mid-1860s, as a prolifigate use of imperial resources. Completed in 1888, the palace was again destroyed in 1900 by members of the Eight Powers Forces in the Boxer War; it was restored again by Cixi in 1902, after her return from self-imposed exile when she was more firmly, if fleetingly, in control.¹ At least until the beginning of the twentieth century, when cultural separation widened and debate grew over matters of "essence" and "form," differences in *ti* and *yong* went largely unregistered in the making and remaking of Chinese architecture.

According to the Confucian virtues, ancient town planning and building formed a part of the *li,* or ritualistic aspect, of Chinese social and moral character. One of its earliest expressions is found in the *Zhouli kaogongji* (*Record of Trades*) section of the *Zhouli,* written around the twelfth century B.C.E.[2] Within its ambit, the *wangcheng* (ruler's city) plan emerged as an idealization of city form; the palace, or official *yamen,* was located at its center, facing south. The overall square, walled enclosure of the city, oriented north to the polestar, was then punctuated with gates, corresponding to an evenly spaced grid of three streets each, running north-south and east-west.[3] Another set of principles was *guanxi* (relations), which guided a more flexible layout of cities according to natural advantages of landforms. It drew heavily on the spatial harmony that begins with the oppositional conceptualization of *yin* and *yang,* expressed in such *feng shui* practices as always situating urban centers either at the foot of a mountain or above the bank of a broad river. Throughout, a southern orientation was important, for, as it was said, "the sage faces south when he listens to reports and exposes himself to the light when he deals with administrative affairs."[4] Under certain circumstances, these two sets of city-building principles might seem contradictory. However, they should be regarded as being complementary. Flat land in the correct orientation tended to yield regular plans, whereas other topography tended to produce irregular plans. Topologically speaking, though, the proscriptions of the *Zhouli kaogongji* remained intact.[5]

In practice, and over time, bell towers and drum towers were located near city centers, ritually providing an aural parenthesis to the morning and evening, respectively. *Pailou* gates also bracketed the ends of streets and neighborhoods, acting both as memorials and as means of controlling the movement of residents. Extensive city markets, under the *fangli* (ward) system of the Han and Tang dynasties, were walled and located away from the center; during the Song and Ming dynasties, they were largely replaced by shopping streets, after the *fangli* system was abandoned in favor of aggregations of shophouses in which each aggregation corresponded, again largely for reasons of control, to a particular kind of merchandise.[6]

Connected, low-rise courtyard housing, in either the expansive northern style or the more compact southern style, lined relatively narrow and secluded residential lanes, usually running east-west, like the *hutongs* of Beijing; they made up the bulk of urban areas. Three-sided (*sanheyuan*) or, more usually, four-sided (*siheyuan*) in overall arrangement, these courtyard houses

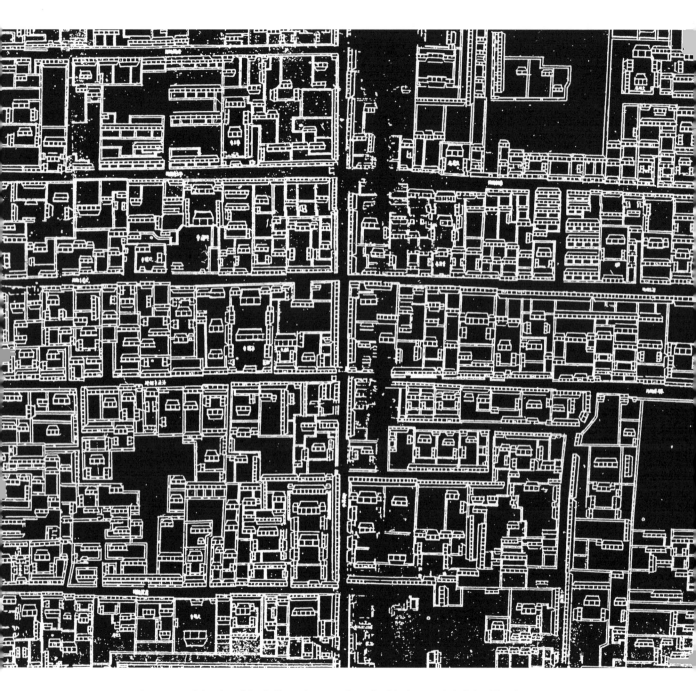

1   A segment of the plan of the Beijing urban area, from the Qianlong period of the Qing dynasty, ca. 1735.

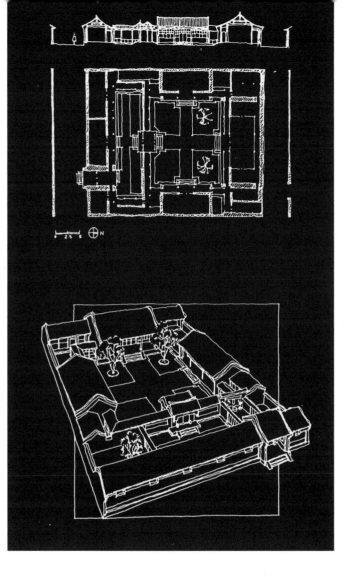

2   A northern-style *siheyuan* courtyard house.

were effectively walled compounds for extended families, sometimes with several courtyards, surrounded by pavilions and arcades and stretching back from the street; their extent depended on a family's wealth or status. Internally, the arrangement of rooms and pavilions also reflected Confucian doctrine. The main hall, facing south, was considered the sacred family space; it was flanked symmetrically on both sides by other rooms, reserved for family progeny in descending order of importance (with the first son located to the east, nearest the main hall). So-called reverse rooms were located along the street, integral with the outside wall facing north, to accommodate servants and lower-status functions such as cooking and storage. In the typical northern-style *siheyuan,* formal entry to the compound was gained through an elaborate entry and gate—a hanging lotus gate—located on the propitious southeast corner of the outside street wall. From there, the entry proceeded ritually in a zigzag through an outer court, before the main courtyard—"heaven's well"—could be broached. Building construction rules, embodying the numerology of "auspicious numbers" and elements of the trigrams, which draw from *yin* and *yang,* were also employed in developing the overall harmonious proportions of buildings and elements of their detailing; their orientation, in doubtful cases, was given by a geomancer.[7] Indeed, on at least two occasions these rules became codified as construction laws, or formal shape grammars: first during the Song dynasty in 1103 and then during the Qing dynasty in Beijing, around 1734.[8] In addition these laws extended to the often elaborate system of timber bracketing, *dougong,* which supported the heavy gabled roofs, as well as the color scheme, mandating yellow for imperial buildings and red for those of higher rank.[9]

In sum, traditional Chinese towns and buildings formed a unified, organic ritual landscape, in conformance with the *li* of proper behavior and outward form, discussed earlier.[10] Not surprisingly, they often embodied spatial principles of "self-similarity" implicit in the *li,* linking household member to family to society and, therefore, room to house to city. Significant urban spaces, like pre-Communist Tiananmen in Beijing, were also interesting in this respect, conforming to the long parallel structure of streets rather than acting as wide-open plazas, or open spaces, as they might have done in the West. As alluded to earlier, building also embodied the harmonious balance (*yin* and *yang*) necessary for appropriate comportment, again implicit in the *li,* through the use of volumetric spatial components, structural and decorative symmetry, and a balanced hierarchy of spaces and functions. There, an ability to reassemble a disaggrega-

3　An ocular system of proportions in the Qing Tombs.

tion of rooms, spaces, and pavilions, each often a microcosm of the others in descending scale and order, into larger ensembles was also used to advantage, lending a sense of completeness and organic wholeness—essence and form—to the entire composition. Finally, again under the *li* of Confucian conduct, spatial sequences usually unfolded in a gradual and visually semioccluded fashion, thus helping to safeguard against the impropriety of unwanted contact and contention, as well as promoting protocol, etiquette, and courtesy. Ocular systems of composition, based on a normal cone of vision, were also often deployed brilliantly to help orchestrate a well-framed and well-connected, unfolding vision for "correct" passage through high-ritual spaces, such as the Qing Tombs, west of Beijing, and the Imperial Academy within the city.[11] The placement of buildings and pavilions, within a complex, on masonry plinths—*xumizuo*—with steps at varying heights also strengthened the intended senses of protocol and guided reception in such a spatial sequence; the technique found similar uses in much more mundane circumstances.

The relatively few exceptions to this continuation of tradition by the Chinese were in the munitions factories and other military and quasi-military industrial establishments called for by those in the Self-Strengthening Movement. In these cases, the new uses of the buildings themselves outstripped the capacity for traditional building practices to respond adequately, though often many older stylistic architectural aspects remained. For instance, the Jiangnan (*Kiangnan*) Arsenal in Shanghai of 1865, sponsored by Li Hongzhang among others, combined a thoroughly Western-style layout of production facilities and building forms with tiled roofs, wooden decorative lattice work, and other traditional construction details.[12] Moreover, this architectural convergence of Western and Chinese elements was understandable, for at the time it was widely believed, as mentioned earlier, that foreign technology could be borrowed and then absorbed into a Chinese scheme of things without too much fuss.

Within the treaty ports and other foreign concessions and missions, foreign architects designed mostly in an eclectic variety of the revivalist styles fashionable in the West and elsewhere during the last half of the nineteenth and early twentieth centuries, strongly reflecting the architectural ambitions of their colonial patrons and providing architectural familiarity. After all, these ports and concessions were effectively foreign "states" or administrative units within the broader, although often disputed, sovereignty of China; consequently, in places like Shanghai and later in Qingdao, they were sites of Western city building and architecture.

4   Gothic-revival Xujiahui Catholic church, Shanghai.

5   The New Science Building at St. John's University, Shanghai, 1923.

Moreover, this denotation of European occupancy also followed what was becoming a well-established formula for public building, particularly in British colonial possessions. Close stylistic parallels can be drawn easily, for instance, between the early railway station in Shanghai and its counterpart in Bombay, India, and between nineteenth-century Victorian public buildings in, say, Melbourne, Australia, and those in Hong Kong and Shanghai.

One of the earliest foreign architects to arrive on the scene during this period was a Briton named Strachan, who practiced between 1849 and 1866 largely in a neoclassical style.[13] Conspicuous among the early churches were St. Francis Xavier in Shanghai, a neobaroque structure of 1853, and the Holy Trinity, the first Episcopal church in the same city rebuilt in 1893 and designed in a neo-Gothic manner by William Kidner.[14] Later revivalist buildings included the 1906 Palace Hotel in Shanghai, by the British architect Walter Gilbert Scott; the seven-story neoclassical structure with a mansard roof also incorporated the first use of elevators in China.[15] Subsequently, this revivalist stylistic profusion increased; for instance, the monumental neoclassical facade of the Shanghai Club by R. B. Morehead of 1906 incorporated a two-story-high Ionic columnar order defining its *piano nobile,* or main floor area.[16] One exception to this persistence of imported styles was St. John's University, again in Shanghai, where the Sherachevsky Building of 1884, the Graves Building of 1898, and both Yen and Mann Halls of 1904 and 1909, respectively, incorporated traditional Chinese upturned tiled roofs and other details on otherwise relatively restrained Western neoclassical buildings.[17] One probable reason for this architectural nod in the Chinese direction, discussed later in more detail, was a self-conscious realization by church-affiliated educationalists that they should be mindful of and respect, at least in part, host traditions. Unlike the many mercantile and early industrial interests bent on exploiting the Chinese, they had a somewhat different role, inclined in the direction of conversion and modern education.

Apart from its foreign architecture, Shanghai was also a multinational jurisdiction in which various forms of Western municipal administration, planning, public improvement, and modernization took place alongside the much earlier walled Chinese settlement, near the banks of the Huangpu River. Prior to becoming a treaty port, Shanghai, which acquired its name (literally, "above the sea") in 1200, had had little significance. In fact, for centuries it was relatively isolated from the trade that took place along China's extensive internal network of roads and the

Grand Canal, which stretched from Hangzhou in the south eventually to Beijing in the north. Nevertheless, as the "silk road" to the west became more dangerous to negotiate and the need for trade further south—beyond the reach of the Grand Canal—increased, along with the need for coastal defenses, Shanghai did become slightly more prominent. A circular wall was erected around the town in 1554, enclosing a traditional settlement (*Nanshi* area) made up of an irregular community block structure and markets in the neighborhood of temples. Retail trade spilled out beyond the gates of the wall along a few major roads, making their way through low-lying poorly drained territory.[18] Unlike Hangzhou and Suzhou immediately to the south and west, which were designated as subprefectures, Shanghai remained merely a stop along the Huangpu River and was not an administrative center of any importance.

Between the 1840s and the 1930s, with the arrival of foreign powers, Shanghai was to lose its obscurity and be transformed into a place like no other in China, at first gradually and then with accelerating speed. First, with the enactment of Land Regulations in 1854, administration of the earlier British, American, and French Settlements conceded under the Treaty of Nanjing was combined into a single elected municipal council, superseding the prior British claim to complete jurisdiction. The purpose of this council was to administer the making of roads; the building of public jetties; the cleaning, lighting, and draining of the settlements; and the establishment of a police force. To accomplish these ends, the municipal council was also given the power to raise ad valorem taxes on the use of the land, even though it continued to acknowledge underlying sovereign Chinese rights. Also, unlike in some other concessions, nothing was said about the legality of selling property or letting homes to Chinese, a large number of whom were already living in the settlements. If anything, opposition came from the adjacent Chinese town administration, fearing that taxes would be lost if Chinese claimed exemption.[19] But the French withdrew from this arrangement in 1862, setting up their own municipal council in what became known as the French Concession; the British and Americans concluded a formal amalgamation of their municipal interests in 1863, with the founding of the International Settlement.[20] As time went on, commercial trade boomed as it never had before; significant improvements were made to the growing city, which, after the influx of refugees from the Taiping Rebellion, had reached close to half a million inhabitants, overwhelmingly Chinese. The Shanghai Gas Company was formed in 1864, providing gas lighting; a modern volunteer fire brigade was also formed; a new

6   A view of the Bund, Shanghai, ca. 1936.

race course and other recreational and cultural institutions were constructed; and in the 1880s, running water, electricity, and sewers were introduced, under the auspices of the municipal council, which extended these services also into the Chinese areas to stop the potential spread of waterborne diseases.

A second change occurred shortly after the signing of the Treaty of Shimonoseki in 1895, as Shanghai, a thriving commercial center, became dominated by manufacturing (although strong commercial trade also continued). Cotton manufacturing by modern methods, for instance, arrived in China relatively late, in spite of the high demand—China at this time was sometimes referred to as "the land of the (cotton) blue gown" even though the well-to-do continued to dress in silk.[21] Having been allowed to engage in manufacturing within the treaty ports, the Japanese soon surpassed even the British in the large number of spinning and weaving mills that they erected. Along with cotton manufacture also came flour mills and chemical plants—the most notable being the new facility for the long-standing Jiangsu Chemical Works—as well as greatly expanded shipbuilding facilities. Apart from foreign technology and know-how, Shanghai's comparative advantages, in what amounted to an industrial revolution, were its proximity to raw materials (including prosperous cotton-growing areas), a cheap supply of electricity, good financial institutions for handling increasingly sophisticated transactions, and an extensive and already-skilled labor force.[22] After the Boxer Rebellion in 1901, massive harbor development along the Huangpu River added to these advantages a capacity for significant international transportation, as Shanghai also became a major world port.

Finally, before its heyday during the 1930s—when Shanghai became, to many in China, the "model of modernity" for its cosmopolitanism, its high-rise commercial buildings, and its popular cultural enterprises[23]—the city became entangled in the civil war simmering between the Nationalists and the Communists. Though a policy of continuous neutrality was adopted in the International Settlement and the French Concession, there was considerable social and industrial upheaval, as to the exigencies of other rapidly modernizing societies were added strong local and national overtones. In 1925, strikes at Japanese-owned mills quickly led to clashes between police and students—no doubt strongly influenced by the earlier May Fourth Movement—leading to a general strike. Demands within the foreign concessions for Chinese representation on the municipal councils also strengthened appreciably, as an antiforeign mood prevailed; particular targets of resentment were Great Britain, the United States, and Japan, all now seen as at least paternalistic, if not exploitative capitalist powers. Sheer numbers and, therefore, arguably legitimate Chinese interests also probably had something to do with the mood; the 1925 census showed more than a million Chinese residents and only 38,000 foreign residents in foreign-administered areas, a disparity that led at least the French to grant representation. Then, as the Nationalist forces moved to take Shanghai in 1927, foreign powers dispatched troops, including a territorial force of some 20,000 British soldiers; they erected barbed wire fences and roadblocks around the International Settlement and the French Concession, as well as declaring a curfew.

During the subsequent uneasy standoff, these areas became more or less safe havens for Chinese protagonists from both sides; continual political intrigue flourished until Chiang Kai-shek managed to smash the Communist presence and foreign–Chinese relations gradually got back to normal. In spite of this upheaval, however, during the late 1920s Shanghai posted its largest volumes of trade, accounting for something like 42 percent of the national total. Socially, what followed was a matter of business as usual, only more of it. Members of the middle class, never very numerous, were unable to play a significant political role as they did in other parts of the world after similar convulsions; they were caught on the horns of a dilemma, aspiring toward modernization in all its varied manifestations and yet simultaneously feeling constrained by resentment of foreign paternalism and by rising nationalism with, ironically, its own anti-materialist stance.[24]

A colonial presence of a similar stamp was also rife in other treaty ports, such as German Qingdao, acquired militarily under a ninety-nine-year lease from the Chinese government through the Jiaozhou (Kiaochow) Treaty of 1897; here, any conspicuous Chinese settlement was swept away, and Qingdao did not reach the same modern stature as Shanghai. By 1899, a development plan had been prepared, laying stress on adequate light and ventilation and on the hilly topography of what was to become a German colony and seaside resort.[25] Unlike other treaty ports, the town proper was located three kilometers south of the port facility, making possible a well-appointed waterfront promenade. The town itself was constructed in five districts: the European section, a villa quarter, a Chinese trade and commercial center, and two districts for (Chinese) workers. By 1913, the total population of Qingdao numbered almost 60,000 inhabitants; all but about 2,500 were Chinese.[26] In fact, after the fall of the Qing dynasty in 1911, Qingdao, like other foreign possessions, became a refuge for disenfranchised citizens and families—including Prince Gong, the elder brother of the emperor, who was mentioned earlier in connection with the Self-Strengthening Movement.

Nevertheless, the architectural presence of what was described in 1913 as being "a little piece of Germany"[27] was unmistakable, fitting into at least two stylistic camps. First, there were those building in the neoclassical style of late-nineteenth- and early-twentieth-century German officialdom, such as the headquarters of the German Administration (1904–1906) by the government architect Mahlke, and the later Imperial Court Building (1914) by Fritz Fitkau. Second, there were the so-called neo-Nürnberg buildings with steep roofs, towers, and facsimiles of half-timbered wall decoration, such as the Police Headquarters and District Town Hall (1904–1905) by the government architect Wentrup, as well as the abattoir building of 1906.[28] The administrative headquarters, for instance, was built with an imposing masonry formal facade, featuring two stories of open-arched arcades formed of plastered barrel vaults and centered symmetrically on the central mass of the entry pavilion with public rooms above. The entire composition also formed a backdrop to the formal layout of the Gouvernement Platz and adjacent streets leading down the southern slope of the complex's hillside location. One exception to this colonial stylistic hegemony was the Weimarer Mission (1899–1900) by Franz Xaver Mauerer, which, like other foreign religious missions noted earlier, was composed of an arrangement of buildings around courtyards, in what was presumed to be a Chinese manner; it also incorporated a decorative program of traditional upturned roofs with terra-cotta figures along the ridge lines, as well as a distinctly Chinese-style entry gateway.[29]

Over time, again particularly in some of the treaty ports like Shanghai, what became known as the "compradoric style" emerged, sometimes as an outlandish amalgam of Western and Chinese motifs and other forms of expression, as in some of the concessions Chinese and foreign economic interests commingled. In fact, the style's name itself derives from the go-betweens necessary to effectuate trade between China and the West—the so-called compradors, who became wealthy as a consequence of this burgeoning business and sought to express their newfound economic status in their establishments. Housing also began to be produced under the same joint interests; in Shanghai, this gave rise to the hybrid form of *lilong* houses, which com-

7　The headquarters of the German Administration, Qingdao, by Mahlke, 1904–1906.

8 Government building in the Taisho neoclassical style, Zhongshan Plaza, Dalian, 1919.

bined a Western terrace house tradition with the Chinese courtyard house in a manner that perpetuated the narrow lanes of earlier Chinese settlements mentioned earlier. Furthermore, as real estate and related market conditions stabilized in the 1870s, after the Taiping Rebellion, foreign architectural practices slowly began to thrive, such as that of Thomas Kingsmill, a Briton who worked successfully from Shanghai between 1875 and 1910.[30] In 1880, there were very few foreign practices in Shanghai, and the numbers rose to seven by 1893 and fourteen by 1910; the first meeting of the Shanghai Society of Engineers and Architects was held in 1901.[31]

Consistent foreign architectural and planning influence also occurred in northeast China late in the Qing dynasty under the aegis of Russia and Japan, with activities concentrated in Manchuria and around parts of Bohai Bay. The Russians, in building the Trans-Siberian Railroad, which they began in Vladivostok in 1891, encountered difficulties in running the rail line north and realized they would save about 340 miles by going directly through Manchuria. One of the outcomes of the Treaty of Shimonoseki and of Russia's role in the retroceding of the Liaodong Peninsula by Japan was the concession to build this line—under a thinly veiled state subsidiary, the Chinese Eastern Railway Company—with an eighty-year lease dating from 1896. In 1898, again by flexing its military muscle, Russia acquired another concession to build a line south, linking Harbin—the headquarters of the Chinese Eastern Railway—through Changchun and Shenyang, with year-round ice-free port facilities on the Liaodong Peninsula at Port Arthur (Lüshun) and the adjacent town of Dairen (Dalian).[32] After its victorious conclusion of the Russo-Japanese War of 1904 and 1905, Japan immediately seized the southern rail link from Changchun down to the coast, which then became known as the Southern Manchurian Railway. The political seesawing did not end there, however; the Japanese Kwantung Army in 1931 and 1932 gained control of the Manchurian cities, including Harbin, and in 1934 established the puppet state of Manchukuo (Manzhouguo), formally headed by Pu Yi—the last emperor of the Qing—who became the emperor of Manchukuo, with Changchun as its capital.[33] Harbin and other settlements had sprung up along the railroad lines and developed into largely well-planned cities with adjacent Chinese settlements, structured much as the earlier treaty port concessions had been, principally to accommodate railway and some mining company activities, the companies' employees, and civic as well as religious institutions.

In Harbin itself, three parts of the city had emerged by 1904. Pristan, later to be called Daoli, and Fujiadian or Daowai—the Chinese settlement—were on the southern side of the Songhuajiang (Sungari River); Nangang was a new-town development to the south of the railway properties that divided the three districts.[34] Over time, Daoli became the recreational and bourgeois center, while Nangang became the center of officialdom and the site of the villas of Russian railway company executives and other leaders. Outside of the Chinese settlement, the Russian architectural influence was dominant and continued well into the early 1930s, even though Russia had lost direct control of the city by 1907. Orthodox churches sprang up in parishes; dominating all was the cathedral of St. Sophia, with its large onion-shaped cupola over the transept of the main body of the church. It was surrounded on all sides by smaller octagonal cupolas covering side chapels and had an immense, well-decorated semicircular front portal. By contrast, the Moderne Hotel (Madier) of 1913 was an opulent, multistory, French-style fin-de-siècle establishment, with a strong cornice line and a small tower above a well-decorated Western-style chamfered corner entry.[35] As in the other foreign concessions, there was a profusion of architectural styles, reflecting the taste of the day. For instance, the later Bank of Communication (1930) was a neoclassical four-story building, with a prominent peristylar entrance of four freestanding, fluted columns and two side pilasters.[36] On the residential side, palatial and not-so-palatial villas dotted an often curvilinear and well-landscaped roadway network, strongly adhering, in layout, to European garden city principles.[37]

In this foreign context, the Japanese plans for Changchun—renamed Xinjing in 1931—were even more ambitious; they were directed in part by Gotō Shimpei, who had been the civilian governor of Taiwan in 1895 and president of the Southern Manchurian Railway between 1906 and 1915.[38] Gotō, who was educated in Germany and enamored of European town-planning principles, had and was to continue to have a profound impact on Japanese planning (notably in Tokyo before the Kanto Earthquake of 1923), and he seemed to find fuller expression of these ideas in Japan's colonial holdings, away from the thorny problems of property acquisition and budgets that plagued him at home. In any event, the plan of Xinjing featured large ceremonial axes, in the manner of Sir Edwin Lutyens's and Herbert Baker's plan for New Delhi in India (1912–1913); it also had radial links to circumferentially inscribed multiple centers, like Walter Burley Griffin's layout (1907–1921) for Canberra, the Australian capital. A separation of function was also prescribed in the plan, with the Construction Bureau, Central Bank, and other related institutions concentrated around Mizoe Satsuki's Unity Plaza (Datong), the major nucleus of the plan, and a nearby ministerial district along one of the city's major avenues.[39] In general, the prominent form of architectural expression was a Western-based, post–Meiji Restoration style of building. The Ministry of Justice (1937), for instance, one of seven such buildings completed, had two three-story wings of offices, well-proportioned and relatively plain, flanking a substantial tower of more public accommodations that was crowned by a multilayered gabled roof structure and a peristylar neoclassical entryway.

Meanwhile, during the waning days of the Qing dynasty, official attitudes toward foreign and primarily Western architecture were to change appreciably from the limited and sinified inclusivity of the Self-Strengthening Movement. As described earlier, the One Hundred Days' Reform of 1898 and the Constitutional Movement of the early 1900s had led to considerable broadening in the use, application, and form component of the binary concepts of *ti* and *yong,* as reformers attempted to philosophically reconcile China, on its own terms, with challenging political realities outside the nation as well as with the need for more thoroughgoing institutional reform and modernization within it. The immense High Victorian Qing Army Barracks in Beijing designed by Shen Qi (1909), for instance, and the even more immense Chinese Parliament Building in the same city that was to be built—symbolically, one imagines—on the site of the old examination hall were both almost entirely foreign in their architectural conception. The German architect Curt Rothkegel's proposal for the Parliament Building was almost twice the size of Berlin's Reichstag (completed in 1894) and similar in architectural character.[40] Instead of just one massive dome at the center, fronted by a neoclassical portico, there were two additional smaller domes, placed over the side flanks of the building, that were to house the assembly halls of the upper and lower branches of government. Although construction of this monumental edifice was begun in the autumn of 1910, work was discontinued after the revolution of 1911. Rothkegel went on to design and construct in 1912 the much more modest Provisional Parliament Building, where the Republican Chinese parliament met in 1924.[41]

This architectural turn of events, in the last days of Qing imperial rule, might be facilely ascribed to a large-scale conversion of those at the seat of power to reform and the general project of modernization. After all, a program of constitutional reform had been announced in 1908,

9   The Qing Army Barracks in Beijing, by Shen Qi, 1909.

and provincial elections took place in 1909. Alternatively, it might be seen as a reinforcement of the cultural separation of modern use from Chinese essence, undertaken as a matter of expediency or perhaps even resistance. Although the young emperor died on November 14, 1908, followed by the empress dowager one day later, those remaining in power hardly made a sudden about-face from their beleaguered and still conservative stance or appreciably accelerated the rate of reform. Both buildings, quite apart from representing the taste for foreign architecture of some in a relatively well-traveled imperial elite, were distinctly foreign expressions for what seemed to be inevitable (though not fully assimilated) imported modern uses. No doubt, they were also intended to impress foreigners with the late Qing's capacity both for modern institutional building and for holding on to power and, therefore, to the past. Furthermore, it may be useful to keep in mind Edward Said's observation that "orientalism" is essentially a Western construct;[42] thus it did not stand in the way of expedient borrowing from the West. Nevertheless, both China's architectural seclusion and its selective architectural celebration of the outside world were soon to change irrevocably, even though the seeds of Western architecture had already been well and truly sown on Chinese soil.

From early on in the Republican period, modern city planning and administration began to be applied in a number of Chinese cities, relying on procedures modeled directly on those used in the West, those imported from the West via Japan, or those found close at hand in the foreign concessions. In fact, the earlier reformer Kang Youwei was most impressed by the planning and administration of the British colony of Hong Kong, during his visit there in 1879.[43] As in both Europe and the United States, a powerful impetus for these undertakings was the need to improve public health, safety, and welfare. The political crises that China had endured during the previous decades left the old state structure defunct and many, if not most, urban areas inadequately served, grossly run-down, and in disrepair. As freedom and an emphasis on modern economic development increased, interest in mobility and other new concerns replaced earlier needs for population control. Consequently, city walls were torn down to make way for wide paved roads, often used by mass transit, and thoroughfares within the cities were widened, straightened, and paved to make possible modern forms of movement. Similarly, public hygiene was addressed: public utilities and services, such as the provision of sewers and drinking water and the removal of storm water and garbage, were gradually implemented in many urban areas. Relaxation of old forms of population control and surveillance, not to mention old manners governing public decorum and comportment under the *li* of Confucian conduct, gave rise to a modern uniformed police force, again as in the West; not only were they tasked with controlling crime but they also doubled as tax collectors, health inspectors, and general arbiters of public behavior. So drastic were these changes that some cities, like Tianjin, published guides for public behavior with more than one hundred stipulations, much like similar published prescriptions that were widely promulgated during the late nineteenth century in the United States when urbanization was booming.[44]

Street lighting and electrical power service also became prevalent, improving public safety after dark and also providing new opportunities for nighttime entertainment. Public spaces within cities were opened up, generally for the first time—often around new railway stations that, because of their accessibility, frequently became the focal points for new institutions, as well as in confiscated imperial precincts, such as those that gave rise to Beijing'spublic park program of the 1920s.[45] These and other public improvements must certainly have encouraged the formation of anonymous groups—the street crowd—as never before in China, promoting the enticing possibility of greater self-expression and the formation of new social connections quite unlike those condoned by older Confucian norms and rites. In contrast to imperial cities, commercial centers and downtowns replete with banking institutions and a range of other public and private enterprises began to form; new kinds of public buildings began to emerge, including libraries, museums, sports stadiums, and concert halls, mirroring the rise of a new form of urban administration.

Until the national regulation of 1919 that authorized the formation of municipal governments (*shizheng*) in the modern sense, cities were not constituted as separate administrative units, serving rather as imperial outposts overseeing their rural hinterlands. Their rational and progressive changes were no doubt spurred by sentiments similar to those expressed by reformers in 1917 and during the May Fourth Movement of 1919, as well as by the enviable contrast presented by the relatively up-to-date and well-functioning urban environments of the foreign concessions. But that progress was often thwarted by undercapitalization and an overall weakness of China's public finances, together with inadequate coordination and lack of trained personnel for the tasks at hand. Many public improvement projects, for instance, were privately contracted—often to foreign firms, immediately raising questions about private profit gained from public enterprises and, in some instances, about national interest and control.

The early Republican period also saw foreign architectural influences become more firmly established and extended with the return of the first generation of overseas-trained Chinese architects. Zhuang Jun (1888–1970) was the first, having graduated from the University of Illinois in 1914; he proceeded to open his own firm shortly thereafter, and established the Society of Chinese Architects in 1926.[46] In 1928, a professional architectural infrastructure began to take shape with the creation of a department of architecture at the Northeastern University (Dongbei) in Mukden, headed by Liang Sicheng (1901–1972), son of the reformer and scholar Liang Qichao. The younger Liang had studied with Paul Cret at the University of Pennsylvania; after graduating in 1927, he remained briefly in the United States to work for Cret with his wife Lin Huiyin (Phyllis Lin), also a Penn graduate in fine arts, and to pursue studies at Harvard on the history of oriental architecture.[47] In fact, Yang Tingbao (1901–1982), a 1924 architecture graduate from the University of Pennsylvania, had originally been asked to lead the new school at Northeastern University but declined because of his position as a partner in the firm of Kwan, Chu, and Yang, headquartered in Tianjin; he recommended in his stead his friend and fellow schoolmate from both Penn and Tsinghua College. Liang the elder, in the absence of his son, also helped organize the new department at Northeastern. Liang Sicheng was joined on the faculty by Lin Huiyin and the next year, in 1929, by Chen Zhi (or Benjamin Chen, b. 1902), Tong Jun (1900–1983), and Cai Fangyin—all three University of Pennsylvania graduates in architecture familiar with a Cret-style curriculum.[48]

In 1930, an architecture program was reorganized at National Central University in Nanjing, formed largely from remnants of the first department at the Jiangsu Provincial Suzhou Industrial School, which opened in 1923 and then was amalgamated in 1927 into what soon became National Central; another program began at the Peking School of Fine Arts. By 1932, National Central had two graduates; Peking Fine Arts, five; and Northeastern, nine. But in the following year, both the Peking School of Fine Arts and Northeastern closed, the latter because of Japanese encroachment into Manchuria. The department at National Central in Nanjing was joined by architecture programs at both Beijing University and at Qinghua (Tsinghua).[49]

Journals and associations provided further elements of a professional infrastructure. *Hexa-gon* was founded in 1930 and two Chinese-language magazines, *Zhongguo jianzhu* (*The Chinese Architect*) and *Jianzhu yuekan* (*The Builder*) began publication in 1932. The *Journal of the Association of Chinese and American Engineers* had been started in 1920.[50] National registration of architects was finally required by the Ministry of Labor and Education in 1929, after much discussion; to register, an architect needed three years of experience after earning a college degree or had to pass an examination and show proof of employment in architecture.[51] Registration of architects and engineers had begun in Shanghai in November 1927. By 1931 fully twenty-eight of the fifty-one architects in the Society of Chinese Architects were American-educated; that number rose thirty-five of fifty-five members by 1935, and eight more were trained in foreign countries other than the United States.[52]

Foreign firms also became better established during the early Republican era, again especially in the thriving politically and economically stable treaty ports like Shanghai. There, the British firm of Palmer and Turner established a branch in 1912; two other notable firms were Spense Robinson and Partners and Atkinson and Dallas.[53] Foreign educational institutions and missionaries, especially the American-based, also became firmly ensconced—including Tsinghua College in Beijing, supported by moneys remitted in 1908 by the U.S. Congress from China's payments to the Boxer Indemnity Fund. Similarly, Lingnan University was founded as the Canton Christian College in Guangzhou (1909), followed by the Yale-in-China program in Changsha (1913) and both Ginling College in Nanjing and Yenching University (1918).[54] The immediate result was increased foreign influence and a concomitant modernization of China's secondary and tertiary educational system, in addition to the further proliferation of the ideologies that accompanied such innovations. To be sure, the changes were largely welcomed in the more tolerant atmosphere of the early Republican period and, as will be discussed later, the physical layout and architecture of these institutions was also to become influential. In addition, as time wore on, foreign technology—especially American building technology—also affected Chinese practice, notably when building programs increased considerably in scale and as the material conditions of construction became more difficult. Steel frames for high-rise buildings were introduced as early as 1916, for structures from eight to ten stories in height; by 1930, buildings were up to twenty-four floors high. Reinforced concrete was also introduced at around the same time, and it proved to be a very malleable and relatively economical material capable of giving shape to traditional as well as contemporary architectural designs.[55]

During the decade or so of full-fledged and largely uninterrupted architectural practice in China that was to follow its foundation as a profession, several developments occurred, more or less simultaneously. Change was largely determined by geography, as it was circumscribed within areas of strong Republican control and foreign concession interests. Both Chinese and foreign firms continued to proliferate and become better established, particularly in cities reflecting relatively high growth, development, and modernization, such as Shanghai, Guangzhou, Nanjing, and, to some extent, Beijing. Approximately fifty foreign architectural practices were to be found in Shanghai, for instance, a more than threefold increase from two decades earlier.[56] Prominent Chinese firms also began to emerge, competing successfully for a wide variety of commissions. The leader among these was Kwan, Chu, and Yang, mentioned earlier, where Song-sing Kwan (Guan Songsheng), a graduate of MIT and Harvard, joined Yang Tingbao and Chu Pin (Zhu Bing) from the University of Pennsylvania.[57] They designed the multistory art deco, or "moderne"-style, Sun Company Headquarters in Shanghai (1936), among many other commissions. Also noteworthy was Allied Architects, a firm established in 1932 by three University of Pennsylvania graduates: Chen Zhi and Tong Jun, both faculty members of Northeastern University, together with Zhao Shen (1898–1978).[58] Others, like Dong Dayou (1899–1973), who returned to China in 1930 with architecture degrees from the University of Minnesota and Columbia University, immediately set up thriving practices, as did H. S. Luke (Lu Qianshou, 1904–1992), who was British-educated and a collaborator with the well-established firm of Palmer and Turner. Their Bank of China Building (1936) became a prominent feature in the Shanghai urban landscape.[59]

Modern architecture, in the form of what became recognizable later as the International Style, also made its presence felt in China in the 1930s, primarily in the larger coastal cities, together with its virtual stylistic opposite, which echoed the National Rejuvenation Movement sponsored by the Republican or Guomindang government. The latter style was favored particularly in connection with plans for the national capital in Nanjing and only to a lesser extent in other cities slated for modernization, such as Shanghai and Guangzhou. For the time, however, these plans were not unusual, representing an amalgam of Beaux-Arts axial town-planning prin-

10   The Hong Kong and Shanghai Banking Corporation, Shanghai, by Palmer and Turner, 1921–1923.

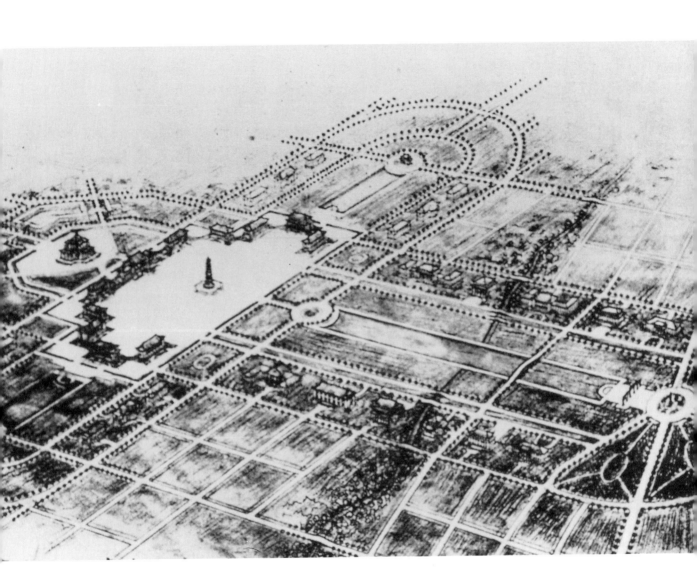

11   Plan for the northern extension of Shanghai, by Dong Dayou, 1933.

ciples similar to those produced by the earlier U.S. "city beautiful" movement, popular between the 1890s and 1910, together with some elements of the contemporaneous Euro-American garden city movement. The potentially less congruous and more interesting element was the further addition of traditional Chinese urban architectural expression, seen primarily in monuments and in prominent public buildings.[60]

In sum, then, the foreign concessions and other colonial holdings on Chinese soil provided a broad avenue for direct importation of foreign influences, including modern architecture and planning principles. In these matters, the transactions between China and the West were largely one-way. Foreign methods of city improvement and building were borrowed wholesale, with relatively little attention to local circumstances—certainly (and not unexpectedly) in jurisdictions under foreign colonial power. Western influence also dominated when the Qing government finally and belatedly entered into reform and when its few prominent architectural commissions were turned over primarily into foreign hands. Similarly, when the newly founded Republican regime set out to modernize its cities, officials followed modern, internationally available planning principles, often with an open disregard for the buildings that were already there. Moreover, this borrowing was also supported, at least when modern professional design practices first took shape, by foreign-trained Chinese architects familiar with modern Western building and largely unfamiliar with their own architectural traditions. Their Western orientation was exacerbated further by the nature of their commissions, which were often for modern building programs unknown in nineteenth-century China, undertaken for clients involved with modern institutions and new commercial enterprises.

Nevertheless, tensions between the forceful arrival of modernization and traditional ways of doing things also existed—and not just as something of a counterdiscourse beneath the discourse of those in power, to use Michel Foucault's terminology for a moment.[61] For one thing, thoroughgoing urban reform and modernization was only beginning to take place in China, despite the conscientiousness of early Republican efforts; as a result, patrons by and large had well-entrenched traditional views, or at least a profound uncertainty about the future and modern novelty. For another, much of the significant modernization was taking place only within the foreign-occupied territories and not in the remaining vast areas of China, which had remained politically fragmented and outside of Republican hegemony. And finally, as demonstrated by the trajectory of the sociocultural positions discussed earlier, the matter of Chinese "essence" was still very much in contention, especially in official and quasi-official circles. Certainly, the appeal of modernization, and all the architectural and urban improvements that went with it, was a necessary and important ingredient in anti-Qing sentiment, even if modernization itself was not inevitable for China's progress. As matters turned out, however, these pressures were only part of the story, particularly as the issue of national identity surfaced more strongly.

"I STILL DON'T KNOW WHAT ACTUALLY HAPPENED IN ARCHITECTURE. You know, the way buildings look!" interjected Wu Feng, between bites of his hamburger. It was lunchtime, and when they were working this intensely, they had the habit of eating early in the office to save time. "What do you mean?" replied Zhang Shaoshu, watching Feng eat and thinking to himself that it was just as well there were McDonald's all over, including just around the corner, or else Feng would starve.

"Well, I remember all those buildings with big roofs, like old hats, that were put on top of administrative centers, railway stations, and things," Feng went on, getting up and looking for something to wipe his hands on.

"What I think he means," interrupted Lu Hui, "is how did we come to grips with all those foreign stylistic influences when we were also trying to reestablish something of our own tradition."

"Yeah, that's sort of what I mean, although I don't think it was about style exactly," mumbled Feng, having found some paper and again beginning to eat.

"Well, as I said before, we tried to find ways of being modern and Chinese at the same time and of combining the old with the new," responded Shaoshu amiably.

"Which only takes us back to where we were this morning," retorted Feng. "And why can't I be Chinese and modern without being so schizoid about it?" he continued.

"Will you let him finish!" broke in Hui, uncharacteristically pointing at Feng with her chopsticks in a moment of exasperation.

"Take the Nationalists, for instance," Shaoshu continued calmly. "They were very interested in celebrating the past in their architecture and of making modern buildings at the same time.

Therefore, they incorporated well-known elements of traditional architecture—like the big roofs you are talking about—into their new projects."

"But how could they do that, it's so . . . so 'retro'!" Feng shot back, using another one of those new terms he had learned in Hong Kong. "Surely there were other ways?" he went on emphatically. As Hui had often noticed, Feng had little regard for what he thought were "backward moves," another one of his new phrases. "And, anyway, architecture is architecture and politics are politics, that's all there is to it!" continued Feng without much of a pause, trying to put an end to the conversation so they could all get back to work.

"I really don't think it's that simple," retorted Hui rather haughtily, also responding to Feng's impatience, as she continued to eat her lunch. "There were lots of experiments and they were not all about big hats, as you call them, nor as ridiculous as you make them out to be." Feng could be so self-centered and inconsiderate, she thought to herself, surprised by her own sense of disappointment.

FOUR ARCHITECTURAL ATTITUDES TOWARD MODERNIZATION

had emerged in China since the turn of the twentieth century, each notionally comparable, at least in part, with the trajectory of philosophical positions on culture discussed earlier, especially with regard to reconciling Chinese essence and modern or Western form; if anything, the differences between the two sharpened when the need for contemporary identity intensified. As elsewhere, though, the connection between the broad sociopolitical preoccupations of successive generations of reformers and conservers in China (and of their architectural counterparts) and the relative roles of tradition and modernization often remained relatively indirect.

Of considerable importance was the extent to which architecture did or even could unequivocally mirror politico-cultural reform. First, the meaning of a particular style or form of expression cannot simply be identified with a particular political point of view. Barbara Miller Lane gave a persuasive account of this kind of ambiguity when comparing fascist German architecture and its neoclassical counterpart in the federal architecture of the United States.[1] Second, time lags between the promulgation of political ideas and the invention, or adoption, of an appropriate architectural expression, and vice versa, also often make a precise determination of corresponding meanings impossible. It took some time, for instance, during the Progressive Era in the United States for an architectural equivalent to be developed—and that style then went on to be appropriated by other sociopolitical points of view.[2] Third, many technical exigencies in architecture often affect the shape and appearance of a building but have no relevance to any current sociopolitical discourse. Finally, even when a reasonably direct link can be traced between a program of sociopolitical reform and, say, a corresponding program of urban improvement in city building, as in China, architects still must deal with expressive problems and decide how best to represent that linkage, if they choose to do so and not simply pursue architecture qua architecture. Nevertheless, common themes and ideas about the appropriate role of traditional expression in modernization were spread widely and even unwittingly and were often manifest—sometimes quite strikingly—in emerging modern Chinese architecture.

The first and probably most obvious approach, especially in the foreign concessions, was to ignore the host tradition almost completely, striving instead for widely available contemporary architectural modes of design and construction. Such an approach implicitly conflated Western forms of expression with modernization, although not necessarily on the deep epistemological grounds suggested by, say, the May Fourth supporters, even though the town planning and urban renewal that was taking place in some parts of China did coincide with their call for applying scientific, rational principles of decision making and planning. More practically, traditional Chinese architecture was often deemed inappropriate for the new institutions, commercial enterprises, and even stately homes of a modern city. Shanghai in particular and, of course, Japanese Changchun (described earlier) and the British crown colony of Hong Kong led the way by virtue of their entrenched foreign interests and concessions, as well as rising market and other commercial pressures for urban development and modernization. But they were certainly not alone. Beijing was also beginning to have modern institutions and Nanjing, which had suffered considerable decline after the Taiping Rebellion, was being planned (as discussed later) as the national capital, according to the 1929 design of the Guomindang's National Capital Reconstruction Commission (*Shoudu jianshe weiyuanhui*). At that time, fully two-thirds of the area inside the walled city remained like "open countryside."[3]

Predictably, the main proponents of contemporary Western revivalist architecture were foreign architects. The Shanghai Club (1906) by R. B. Morehead has already been mentioned; to it could be added the slightly taller Jardine Matheson Company building (1920) by R. E. Stewardson.[4] Each had a strong neoclassical facade with a columnar double-height porch in front of the main rooms located at the center of the buildings. Both structures also had classical detailing around the windows, rusticated stonework at the base, and stepped-back top floors to better frame the porch of the main facade. The Shanghai General Post Office (1924) by Stewardson and Spence was also neoclassical in appearance, although more modern in layout and in the repetitive treatment of the tall window bays and pilasters along the main elevations.[5] The shapely tower at the corner entrance to the building was graced with a finely wrought cupola and classical statuary.

Several Chinese firms, including H. S. Luke and Bei Shoutong, with Song-sing Kwan (Guan Songsheng), also produced neoclassical work. For example, the Continental Bank Building in Beijing (1924), by Bei and Kwan, is certainly within the modern classical tradition, reflecting the Beaux-Arts training both architects received abroad.[6] Kwan, as already noted, graduated from MIT and then Harvard before being influenced by the Bauhaus, and Bei studied at the Technische Hochschule in Berlin. Indeed, to repeat an earlier observation, many returning Chinese architects probably found it easier to design in this Western tradition than to suddenly adopt a Chinese form of architectural expression that was almost completely foreign to them. Both Allied Architects and Kwan, Chu, and Yang, two prominent Chinese firms, displayed this architectural tendency, at least early in their existence, before experimenting with different forms of expression on the way to finding their own language.

Among the most prolific foreign firms and most steadfast proponents of evolving Western styles of architecture was Palmer and Turner in Shanghai, a firm originally founded in 1868. One of its earliest commissions in China was the Mercantile Bank of India (1916), which it rendered along conventional neoclassical lines.[7] This was followed by a prestigious commission for the Hong Kong and Shanghai Banking Corporation (1921–1923), prominently located on the Bund at the forefront of Shanghai's burgeoning commercial center.[8] In fact, this building was something of a tour de force of neoclassical detailing, which clad an otherwise fairly modern five-story steel-framed building. The plan of the building was roughly square, with an entrance and circular lobby at ground level, referred to on the outside by a large dome rising above the building's center. The protruding central bay had a Corinthian colonnade of double columns above a solid granite base, penetrated by three large arches. These combined with the Italian marble interior for a very imposing overall effect.

Palmer and Turner persisted in this strongly neoclassical manner through the middle to late 1920s with buildings such as the Shanghai Customs House (1925), another steel-framed structure, eight stories high and crowned by a four-faced clock tower. Doric columns formed the entrance, above which appeared a heavily corbeled cornice line.[9] But slowly the firm's style began to shift in the direction of art deco, or the so-called moderne: the change was signaled by the Sassoon House, a hotel of 1929. There, however, the relatively straightforward and undecorated vertical line of the building's base was crowned at the corner by a neoclassical tower.[10] More unabashedly moderne were the Metropole Hotel and Hamilton House twin towers complex (1933–1934), whose curved main facades were used to define a well-proportioned urban space, much as was being done elsewhere in the modern world at the time.[11] A similar approach to both architecture and place making was taken almost simultaneously by B. Flazer with the curved, symmetric stepped-back facade of Broadway Mansions (1930–1934).[12] The firm of Palmer and Turner was to continue with curvilinear plan forms in the organic layout of the large Embankment Building of 1933, although there the overall appearance was more strictly modern, as the strong horizontal bands of windows and balconies were accentuated.[13] At the end of this era, in the late 1930s, the commercial center of Shanghai along the Bund had well and truly become modern and high-rise, earning the city the sobriquet "the New York of the Orient."

In the hands of others, architecture in China pushed further in the direction of orthodox modernism and what was soon to become known as the International Style. One major influence in this movement was the émigré Slovak architect Laszlo (Ladislau) Edward Hudec (1892–1952), who produced a number of notable works.[14] The Zhou House (1930), for instance, was an overtly modernist project; the clean lines of the symmetrical facade of walls, windows, and balconies were offset by the asymmetrical alignment of the stairway and stair tower above the roof deck. The use of contemporary materials, expressed straightforwardly yet boldly, together with careful placement of asymmetrical elements, continued in Hudec's Woo (Wu) Residence and in the Grand Theatre of Shanghai, both built in 1933.[15] In these and other buildings designed by Hudec, the thoroughgoing modernist continuity of the layout, appearance, and material content was also very apparent, in marked contrast to the detachment of functional layout from questions of style then common in other architects' work. Hudec's twenty-two-story, steel-frame Park Hotel (1934), the tallest building in Asia when it was built,

12   Sassoon House, Shanghai, by Palmer and Turner, 1929.
13   The Metropole Hotel, Shanghai, by Palmer and Turner, 1933–1934.

14   The Embankment Building, Shanghai, by Palmer and Turner, 1933.

is particularly instructive, though once again a foreign architect did not monopolize a particular modern approach.[16]

The Hongqiao Sanatorium (1934) by F. G. Ede (Xi Fuquan) of the firm of Chang Ede and Partners, for instance, was also modernist and designed very much in the manner of Bruno Taut and other members of Der Ring in Germany.[17] Similarly, the Metropole Theater in Shanghai (1933) by Allied Architects certainly showed that firm's interest in modernism; and in form and function, its Victoria Nurses' Dormitory (1930) was without doubt one of the most modernist buildings of the period. There the reinforced concrete structure of the building was clearly visible, with protruding floor slabs edged in well-proportioned balcony balustrades. Indeed, at least at this juncture, Tong Jun of Allied Architects was an unabashed modernist. For him the plan of a building could "only be one thing: a logical and scientific arrangement of rooms according to the most up-to-date knowledge available [and] naturally the facade, a product of the plan could be nothing but modernistic."[18] A number of anonymous modernist buildings were also constructed elsewhere in China—for example, in Dalian—again in the orthodox expressive manner of German architects of the time.

A second approach to the matter of tradition and modernity, which in retrospect bears a striking resemblance to broader philosophical distinctions drawn earlier between *ti,* or essence, and *yong,* or application, was the so-called adaptive approach of such foreign architects as the American Henry K. Murphy (1877–1954) and the Canadian Henry H. Hussey, as well as such Chinese architects as Lu Yanzhi (1894–1929), Dong Dayou, and Lin Keming (1900–1999) and such theorists as William Chaund. As Murphy explained, "I decided that we must start out with Chinese exteriors, into which we would introduce only such foreign features as were needed to meet definite requirements, and . . . , as a result, our completed buildings really are Chinese."[19] In other words (to use the conceptual terminology of the likes of Feng Guifen), clearly the essence and body of an architectural work were to be Chinese, adapted in a foreign, presumably Western direction only as much as was absolutely necessary. In short, the balance struck between *ti* and *yong* very much favored the former.

Murphy went on to describe the essential features of traditional Chinese architecture to be preserved intact whenever possible. First was the "curving upturned roof," clad in clay tile of some color. Second was "orderliness of arrangement," which usually meant using rectangular

15 The Woo (Wu) Residence, Shanghai, by Laszlo Hudec, 1933.
16 The Grand Theatre of Shanghai, by Laszlo Hudec, 1933.

courtyards in building complexes, relying on axial planning, and striking a "feeling of balance" without being rigidly symmetrical. Third came "frankness of construction"; fourth, the "lavish use of gorgeous color," followed by "perfect proportioning," a quality that was often difficult to define precisely but that nonetheless must be striven for.[20] Architecturally, Murphy was committed to remaking Chinese architecture into what he termed "a living style," reflecting much the same change, he reasoned, as that of the classical architecture of the West, which had shifted in stance from the "rigidity of the Greeks" through the "elasticity of the Romans" to the "flexibility of the European renaissance."[21] Indeed, he saw much of his lifework in precisely those terms: as stimulating and propagating a Chinese architectural renaissance much like the one that had happened earlier in the West. The only real practical limitations he acknowledged were the number of full stories, or levels, that could be accommodated in adapted Chinese architecture, which he put at around two or three at the most, and the additional cost—an eighth or tenth of the total—that building the comparatively larger volume of space required might incur. This latter limitation, however, he clearly saw as being a small price to pay for continuing an architectural tradition.[22]

Although it is not entirely clear why Yale University's Foreign Missionary Society selected the New York firm of Murphy and Dana to design their Yale-in-China campus at Changsha, the choice probably had something to do with the principals' prior work in educational settings in the United States and their own backgrounds—Murphy graduated from Yale in 1899 and Richard Henry Dana, Jr., had begun teaching at Yale in 1908. In any event, in 1913 Murphy set sail for China, via Japan, to start work on the Yale-in-China commission, which was followed a year later by a commission to design further additions to Tsinghua College in Beijing (Qinghua).[23] In both cases a thoroughly Chinese style of architecture was considered, at least initially. The result at Changsha was a blend of East and West, with Chinese revival for the library and chapel but American colonial revival for the hospital and faculty houses; at Qinghua a Chinese style was finally rejected altogether in favor of a sober Western classical revival. By 1918, four buildings had been completed at Qinghua—the auditorium, science building, library, and gymnasium—all with a very high quality of construction. In fact, Zhuang Jun was employed as one of the superintendents of works and later worked for a time in Murphy and Dana's New York office. These additions relied heavily on past precedents. For instance, the auditorium at Qinghua was modeled after McKim, Mead and White's Columbia University Low Memorial Library (1895), which Murphy greatly admired, reflecting the idea then current that "Western functions and ideas" should be housed in a Western manner.[24] This stance was to change substantially, however, when he designed Ginling College in Nanjing, constructed between 1918 and 1923, and the Yenching University project in Beijing, built between 1918 and 1927, arguably the two crowning achievements of his career in China.

In Matilda Thurston, Ginling College's first president, Murphy found a client who shared his support for a more or less complete sinicization of the campus architecture; much the same attitude was expressed by the Yenching client group.[25] Ideologically, as noted earlier, a number of foreign institutional clients then operating in China appeared to be very much aware of the possible parallels between their mission and adaptive Chinese architecture. Certainly the antimissionary rioting that had taken place in Changsha in 1910 had sensitized foreign representatives to the symbolism involved in their architectural self-presentation in China. Originally, even Y. T. Tsur, the president of Qinghua University, had argued for the didactic value of a group of Chinese rather than Western buildings.[26] In 1924, representatives of the indigenous China movement in China such as Charles A. Gunn and J. V. W. Bergamini argued for Chinese architecture as a matter of mission policy.[27] Certainly Murphy, who always listened attentively to the wishes of his clients, would have been influenced by this general view voiced with increasing force, even if his own visit to the Forbidden City in Beijing in 1914 had not left him committed to a "living Chinese architecture."[28]

The Ginling campus was an orderly layout of two- to three-story buildings in adaptive Chinese architecture on the flat area at the foot of a hill that provided the necessary seclusion for dormitories, maximum access to sunlight, and shelter from inclement weather. Reinforced concrete, a most modern material, was used extensively, including in the conformation of the *dougong,* or Chinese system of brackets, at the eaves line of the roofs. This favoring of the Chinese essence, or "truth" quality of buildings, over a form that might have followed rationally from function, as well as the sharp separation of form from the modern means used to produce it, clearly demonstrated how the *ti* and *yong* distinction in Chinese thought might be embodied in architecture. Murphy himself appears to have shown little appreciation of parallels between his adaptive architectural approach and sentiments expressed during any of China's cultural

66

17   Ginling College, Nanjing, by Henry K. Murphy, 1918–1923.

18   Building on the Yenching Campus, Beijing, by Henry K. Murphy, 1918–1927.

19   The Peking Union Medical College, Beijing, by Henry H. Hussey, 1916–1918.

67

reform movements—though he was certainly familiar with the events of May 4, 1919, if not personally then through his friendship with Hu Shi and Lin Yutang, two of the May Fourth Movement's staunchest supporters.[29]

The Yenching campus commission involved some sixty buildings, again all in "adaptive Chinese architecture" and built in "enduring concrete."[30] Rectangular courtyards were deployed throughout; the remainder of the site, adjacent to Qinghua on the northwestern outskirts of Beijing, was imbued with Chinese characteristics.[31] The most prominent architectural feature in the whole composition was a water tower in the form of a thirteen-story Ming dynasty pagoda, set slightly off-axis at the end of a long lake. Also of note was the chapel, intended by Murphy "to be the purest modern example of Chinese architecture in China," whose appearance would "minimize the differences between Western education and religion and those of China."[32] As the Yenching project drew to a close, Murphy threw in his lot with the Guomindang regime; he was retained in 1928 as the chief architectural advisor for the National Capital Reconstruction Commission in Nanjing, having finished a plan for Guangzhou a year earlier. In both cases he pressed forward his ideas for the use of adaptive Chinese architecture, even drawing up proposals to show how a modern roadway could be built on top of Nanjing's 34-kilometer wall, which thus could be saved from destruction.[33]

For a short time Murphy's foreign architectural rival as chief proponent of a sinified contemporary architecture was Henry H. Hussey, originally from Toronto. Hussey's main commission was the Peking Union Medical College (1916–1918), built with funds donated by the Rockefeller Foundation.[34] Although Charles A. Coolidge, the architect of Harvard's Medical School, had been originally asked to design the project, the firm of Shattuck and Hussey, with offices in Beijing as well as in Chicago, was finally chosen because it had a lower bid and was more familiar with local conditions.[35] Hussey's plan divided the college functionally into a number of compounds and courts entered through gateways and walkways, some of which were elevated above the grade of the open courtyard below. All components were rendered in a Chinese architectural style, reminiscent of some of the few remaining buildings on site surviving from the Qing dynasty. The entrances of the hospital and the medical school, for instance, had traditional upturned Chinese tiled roofs, and the overall proportions and articulation of both buildings were more or less consistent with traditional Chinese pavilions, even if on a considerably larger scale. As in Murphy's work at Changsha, the exceptions appeared in the north and south residential compounds, where dormer windows and other architectural devices betrayed a stronger Western style. Hussey eventually ran into logistical and budgetary problems, leading him to quarrel with the College Board and to leave the project before it was completed. Many years later, in retirement he took up residence in Beijing in a traditional courtyard house.[36]

At the forefront of the revival of interest in Chinese architecture by practicing Chinese architects, which later coincided with the expressive interests of the National Rejuvenation or New Life Movement of the 1930s, was the work of Lu Yanzhi, widely regarded as one of the country's most talented young architects.[37] With the death in 1925 of the Republican leader Sun Yat-sen, widely regarded as the founder of modern China, this new course of events could be symbolized in the form of several memorials to Sun. These included his mausoleum, which was to be constructed on the Purple Mountain (*Zijin shan*) on the outskirts of Nanjing, close by the much earlier Ming Tombs.

The competition for the mausoleum was won by Lu Yanzhi, another American-trained architect who had earned a degree from Cornell University in 1918; he worked in Murphy's office from shortly after his graduation until 1921. Lu's winning entry was a bold axial arrangement of gateways and traditionally styled pavilions with prominent blue-tiled roofs, located at various points along a broad, steeply ascending stairway. At the top of the hill was the mausoleum itself, also in an ostensibly traditional form. The overall composition was fittingly monumental and a clear adaptation of planning and architectural principles that alluded strongly to the past architectural monuments of ancient China, as well as to Lu's formal Beaux-Arts education. Some inspiration was drawn from Paul Cret's Pan American Union (1907) in Washington, D.C., with its tripartite neoclassical composition.[38] Furthermore, the sunken crypt within the mausoleum itself must be seen as a reference to Napoleon's Tomb in the Invalides in Paris, if not to much earlier Roman practice. Chinese influence was less marked: there was little to no deployment of the sophisticated enframing devices and ocular systems of composition found in the western Qing Tombs, although the unfolding view, as one ascends the enormous staircase segments, was clearly designed to be traditional in its effects. On the whole, the site-planning strategy appears as a not entirely self-conscious merger of Western neoclassical and Chinese traditional principles.

20 The Sun Yat-sen Mausoleum, Nanjing, by Lu Yanzhi, 1925.

Lu Yanzhi went on in 1926 to design the Sun Yat-sen Memorial Auditorium in Guangzhou, near the leader's hometown; its plan took the form of an octagon, with three extended porches and a seating capacity of 4,700. The prominent curved roofs, with blue glazed tiles, and the pillars of stone around the outside gave the appearance of a palatial traditional Chinese style, although modern methods of construction were used.[39] Unfortunately, Lu died of cancer and the building was completed by Li Jinpei (Poy G. Lee), a graduate of Pratt Institute, who in 1931 designed the Guangzhou City Hall in a traditional Chinese manner. In 1933, Dong Dayou took a similar approach to designing the Shanghai City Hall, using traditional forms that included a raised stone base, a broad stairway with the bas-relief of the "Spirits Way" down the center, and Chinese upturned tile roofs.[40] Overall, the massing of the city hall was divided into three parts; a

21   The Shanghai City Hall, by Dong Dayou, 1933.

prominent central building extended symmetrically on both sides. Dong, who also briefly collaborated with Murphy on the Nanjing plan, was appointed as chief architectural advisor to the Greater Shanghai Reconstruction Commission, creating the strongly axial plan mentioned earlier. It culminated in a monumental center in the northeast of the city.[41]

But by far the most ambitious formal architectural and planning undertaking of the Guomindang government during its "Nanjing Decade" was the creation of a new national capital. For a decade or more the brainchild of Sun Yat-sen, the new Nanjing was to become an exemplar for the future modern China—harking back, on the one hand, to past glories by invoking commonly held references to an imperial style of architecture and city building and projecting forward, on the other, by providing a functionally efficient, well-appointed, and well-serviced city. Moreover, Nanjing was the best place for such a venture, well within Nationalist-controlled territory, free from the congestion of overbuilding (indeed, as noted earlier, still largely agricultural), and in dire need of substantial renovation and revitalization. Having suffered almost complete destruction when the Qing army crushed Taiping opposition in 1864, the city—with a population of around 370,000 by 1927—had no street lights, no sewers, and no administrative government.[42] Taking on such a project would be less expensive in Nanjing than in, say, Beijing, and there the payoff for demonstrating a new start for the nation would be substantial. Although the project was overseen by the National Capital Construction Committee, which included high-ranking Guomindang officials as well as Chang Kai-shek himself, the real planning work fell to the National Capital Planning Office (*Guodu sheji jishu zhuanyuan banshichu*); it was formed in November 1928, led by Yin Yiming, a Harvard-trained engineer.[43] Indeed, considerable use was to be made of such American consultants as Ernest P. Goodrich, an engineer, and Henry K. Murphy, along with American-trained architects and engineers. This reflected in part a wish to legitimate the process in foreign eyes and in part these consultants' sympathetic viewpoints (at least in Murphy's case) about architecture. The planning office also examined other models for building national capitals, ranging from Paris, where, as in Nanjing, modern building took place within an already well-established city, to Washington, D.C., where, as in Nanjing, underdeveloped sites were available. Other international models were also consulted, including Canberra and New Delhi.[44]

The planning office first attempted to arrive at an acceptable proposal for the new capital's administrative center on Purple Mountain through a design competition. The first-ranked submission, by Huang Yuyu (an engineer in the planning office) and Zhu Shenkang, was noteworthy for combining modern Beaux-Arts axial planning and, in places, a traditional Chinese unfolding of major urban spaces, as well as for its sinified architectural proposals.[45] Curiously, the southern end of the proposal was anchored by a large circular figure to house the proposed airport, a design that clearly had much more to do with satisfactorily completing the overall Beaux-Arts and traditional axial arrangement than with the actual requirements of a modern airport. The planning office judged this proposal to be too expensive and too impractical to build on the higher slopes of Purple Mountain.

The plan finally published by the National Capital Planning Office late in 1929 was broad in scope, dividing Nanjing into specific zones according to modern principles of city planning. It located the central administrative zone on Purple Mountain, below Sun Yat-sen's mausoleum and the Ming Tombs, thereby creating a direct symbolic relationship back to past glories and to the founder of modern China, and proposed an architectural style that was to be both modern and classically Chinese at the same time. Major institutional and other buildings were to feature large, upturned tiled roofs on columns that crowned buildings otherwise contemporary in layout, fenestration, and materials. The Ministry of Railways, one of the relatively few completed projects, epitomized this approach and what sometimes became referred to awkwardly as "Chinese Renaissance" architecture (a term that recalls Murphy's aspirations). Designed by Robert Fan (Fan Wenzhao, 1893–1979), a 1921 University of Pennsylvania graduate, its buildings were arranged symmetrically by overall height and volume, on a pronounced raised base (*xumizuo*); they had large, well-proportioned upturned curved roofs, supported in a classical manner on painted columns, but relatively plain concrete exterior walls and large Western-style glass windows. It was, in the words of contemporary observers, "a modification of the classical Chinese style."[46] Ground was broken in 1929, but implementation of the overall plan had barely gotten under way when it stalled—both because of the worldwide economic depression, which caught up with China in 1931, and because of the Guomindang's need to spend its money on fighting the Communists as well as on other pressing public works and infrastructure projects.

As one might expect in a country as large and diverse as China, strong regional styles emerged from time to time, including during the modern period of interest in an adaptive Chinese architecture. The work of Lin Keming in Guangzhou is notable in this regard, particularly the buildings he designed for Zhongshan University—now the South China Institute of Technol-

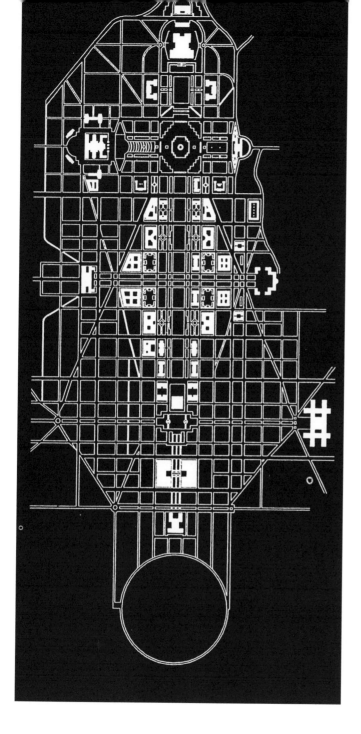

22   The first-place plan for Nanjing's central administrative area, by Huang Yuyu and Zhu Shenkang, 1928.

ogy—between 1930 and 1935.[47] The College of Law and the Geology, Geography, and Biology Building, for example, both had double tiers of traditional Chinese upturned tiled roofs and were placed on a raised base, with prominent stairways at the center of the main facade. The pilasters and columns also incorporated traditional decorative motifs and used brackets (*dougong*) under the eaves. The bracket system is even more prominent in the upper-story gallery of the College of Sciences Building of 1933, which includes a traditional balustrade and latticework screens above the windows and doors.

Lin was educated first at Peking University and then in France, where he worked with Tony Garnier; he returned to China in the 1920s. Throughout his career he remained mindful of China's traditional architectural legacy and the appropriateness of adapting it for modern use. In fact, later in life, he explicitly referred to Mao Zedong's thesis on the subject and the need to absorb the *jinghua,* or the quintessence of Chinese culture and tradition.[48] In designing the Zhongshan campus, Lin was joined by Zheng Xiaozhi, who completed the College of Humanities in 1934, and by others (including Guan Yizhou and Yu Qingjiang) who all worked to some extent in the so-called southern or Lingnan style. That style, which began evolving around the Pearl River delta and much of Guangdong province in the middle of the nineteenth century, subsequently went through various phases of blending traditional Chinese and Western influences.[49] The buildings of the Lingnan University campus constructed between 1910 and 1917, across the river from Zhongshan, showed ample evidence of this blending, especially in the work of such foreign architects as Jas R. Edmunds, A. S. Collins, and the firm of Stoughton and Stoughton.[50]

One of the earliest commentaries about how architecture in China should relate to the broader cultural discourse, particularly to the ideology of the May Fourth Movement, was written by an architect from Guangzhou with the anglicized name of William H. Chaund,[51] who argued that China had for too long overlooked architecture as a progressive discipline. In "Architectural Effort and Chinese Nationalism," published in the *Far Eastern Review* (1919), Chaund asserted that there was indeed an inherent correlation between a nation's spirit or tradition and its architecture. As he put it, "a building must express the life, tradition, national spirit and dominating ideal of the period in which it is built." His concern was that China was unprepared to face the massive construction problems facing it; moreover, while it was open to the "stimulating influence of Western achievement," it must "select and adopt only that which will fulfill its requirements and provide it with strength"[52]—again the familiar refrain of balancing *ti* and *yong*. Like Murphy, Hussey, Lu, Lin, and others interested in an adaptive Chinese architecture, Chaund strongly emphasized architectural essence. "The outstanding idea is this," he declared: "the sum total of our architectural development must be distinctly national in character and joyously Chinese in spirit."[53]

The third approach to tradition and modernity shifted the balance between "essence" and "application" further away from traditional forms, as these merged with a modern Western neo-classical tradition learned by many Chinese architects educated abroad during the first three decades of the twentieth century. Certainly among the most prominent proponents of this

23   The College of Sciences on Zhongshan campus, Guangzhou, by Lin Keming, 1933.

merger was Yang Tingbao, who returned to China in 1927 to practice with Kwan, Chu, and Yang. He had studied at the University of Pennsylvania with such classmates as Louis Kahn, Norman Rice, and Eldrege Snyder and then had worked for Paul Cret between 1924 and 1926.[54] From Cret (1876–1945), himself an 1896 graduate from the École des Beaux-Arts who had joined the Penn faculty in 1905, Yang learned an appreciation of classical traditions, a respect for architectural history, and a high level of competence in delineation.[55]

However, Yang was to start off slowly in the direction of an architectural merger between East and West. His first building in China, the Shenyang Railway Station (1927), was an elegant structure with a large, semicircular vaultlike space over the main waiting hall, owing more to Western railroad stations of the time than to any traditional Chinese influence. If anything, the light colonnaded front porch and the expansive glazed end of the waiting hall's vault showed off new Western technology and building materials to advantage.[56] But Yang was to change his approach in his project for Qinghua University in 1930 and in the Nanjing Central Athletic Complex of 1931; there the roofscape and latticework on the corner towers and other details of the main stadium had a distinctly Chinese character, though the massing, symmetry, and window and door openings were of a modern neoclassical style popular in the West.[57]

Yang's design for the Nanjing Central Hospital, which followed in 1933, had a similar architectural character. It was composed of a long, simple, four-story massing that ran parallel to the frontage road; two towers rose symmetrically at points a third of the distance along the length of the building, at which further extensions protruded out toward the street. The vertical proportions of the fenestration alternating with the brick-encased steel columns along the facade, as well as the squared-off tops of the towers, gave the building a moderne feeling overall. The traditional Chinese elements were to be found in the building details, such as the gateway, the protruding brackets of the entrance canopy, and the bracketed semiopen enclosure along the top of the building between the two towers.[58] In comparison to earlier buildings, both the overt Western and Chinese influences were more refined and less immediately present, giving the project a very modern yet culturally well-grounded appearance. This grounding is perhaps not surprising, given that Yang was commissioned to survey and restore major historic buildings in Beijing, including the Temple of Heaven, from which he acquired a knowledge of traditional building techniques.

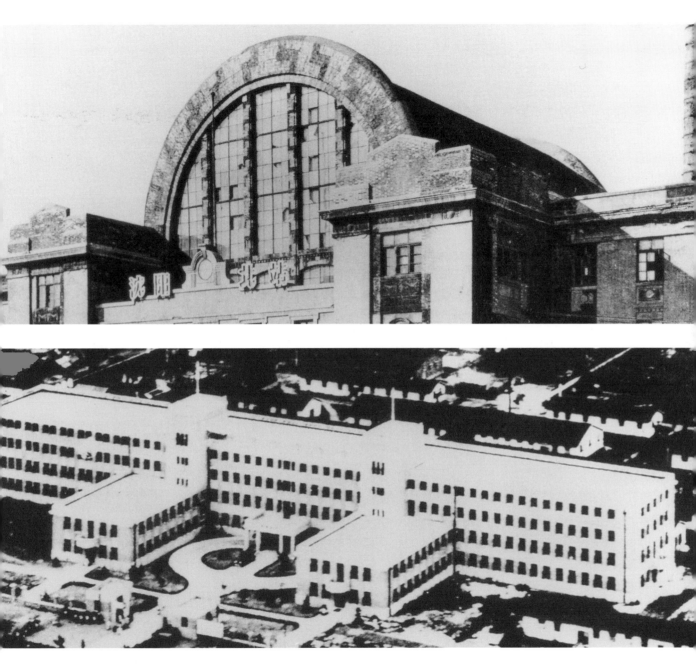

24 Shenyang Railway Station, by Yang Tingbao, 1927.
25 Nanjing Central Hospital, by Yang Tingbao, 1933.

26 The Bank of China, Shanghai, by Palmer and Turner in collaboration with Lu Qianshou, 1937.

Much later, in 1947, Yang Tingbao was to design a self-consciously traditional Chinese building complex for the Social Sciences Institute of the Academia Sinica in Nanjing, followed by an International Style modern house for Sun Fo (Sun Ke), in the same city.[59] In retrospect, both buildings represent stylistic extremes for Yang, illustrating the architectural poles that his idea of merger might be expected to span. They also demonstrated the continuing tension in Chinese architectural identity and the lingering idea that prominent institutions, at least, should be sinified in their expression.

Other attempts to effect a successful merger between prevailing Western architectural styles and the Chinese traditions were to be found in the YMCA building in Shanghai of 1931 by Li Jinpei, Fan Wenzhao, and Zhao Shen (before he joined Allied Architects) and in the Sun Company headquarters, mentioned earlier. Both buildings were relatively simple structures with a modest level of Chinese detailing, typically around windows and at the entrance.[60] The Ministry of Foreign Affairs in Nanjing of 1933 was an expressive attempt by Allied Architects to develop a new modern Chinese architecture without a curved roof. In appearance, it was a merger between overall Western site organization, building compositional principles, and interior layout and distinctively Chinese architectural elements, such as a decorated pedestal base for the building (*xumizuo*), an entablature and porch with *dougong,* and a south-facing main facade.[61] Xi Fuquan and Li Zhongshen followed much the same approach in their design of the National Hall in Nanjing of 1937 to 1939, giving something of an official stamp to this merger of moderne with Chinese characteristics.[62] Even Palmer and Turner in the Bank of China in Shanghai of 1937, another prominent official building, were to bow to the need for a new Chinese architecture. This seventeen-story tower had a traditional Chinese-gate-like proportion and massing crowned by a pyramidal upturned roof replete with *dougong*; other traditional Chinese details were scattered throughout an otherwise modern facade.

In all these cases, the building materials and techniques were distinctly modern and of Western origin, including steel frames and the ubiquitous use of reinforced concrete even for traditional Chinese detailing.[63] Probably unknowingly, the Chinese architects seem to have followed the advice of Walter Taylor (b. 1899), an architect who studied at the Harvard-Yenching School of Chinese Studies and later taught at Columbia University, who inveighed against too singular an interpretation of Chinese architecture. As he put it, "we cannot carry on in a foreign 'rut' and we cannot go off into a Chinese 'ditch.'"[64]

Although often not in the hands of architects per se, such middle-ground mergers also occurred in the burgeoning residential quarters of larger cities. In Shanghai, for instance, *shikumen* lane or *lilong* houses began to emerge before the turn of the century, first as a more tightly clustered version of the traditional Chinese courtyard house and then, during the early twentieth century, as something of a cross between the traditional courtyard house and Western terrace housing.[65] Similar developments also occurred in other places, including Beijing, where courtyard lane houses were adapted to accommodate smaller families and a slowly modernizing lifestyle. As the availability of urban land declined, property values increased and, with them, residential densities. The terrace house offered a compact form with a relatively small street frontage, whereas the courtyard house provided a customary arrangement of rooms and enclosed ample outdoor space. These two housing types combined rather easily, resulting in dense low-rise residential precincts with clusters, or rows, of attached houses served by narrow lanes opening onto a main street. The houses themselves were usually two (though possibly three or more) stories high and one to two rooms wide, with a courtyard behind an enclosing wall and gate at the front; sometimes they had a small yard toward the rear.

Built primarily by Chinese and Western real estate developers and other property speculators, such as industrial firms, in places like Shanghai this form of housing—with various enlargements, contractions, and other embellishments—served the needs of a broad spectrum of the urban population, ranging from workers to members of the emerging middle class. In Shanghai alone, several hundred thousand *lilong* houses were constructed during the early part of the twentieth century, leading to a succession of styles that culminated in the more commodious and "suburban" garden *lilong* houses of the 1920s and '30s.[66] In addition to commingling housing types, the decorative programs of many residences also represented in their materials and motifs a merger between China and the West. Thus, while the term *shikumen* refers to the traditional stone gate structure that often graced the lane entrances of residential complexes in Shanghai, the use of Western, usually Italian, floor tiles became something of a popular rage during the 1920s and '30s.

27 *Lilong* housing, in Shanghai.
28 A lane within the Forbidden City, Beijing.

The fourth approach to tradition as China increasingly became modern was not so much a specific manner of practicing architecture as an attempt to set the record straight by thoroughly understanding traditional Chinese architecture and taking all steps necessary to conserve and document its presence. Furthermore, this archaeological activity was meant to inspire a sense of pride and value in China's architectural legacy, corresponding to the nationalistic mood then emerging, and to yield insights that could be applied to contemporary design problems—to accurately restore, in other words, the pursuit of *ti* (essence) as a central concern in Chinese architecture. Clearly the leader of this approach was Liang Sicheng, mentioned earlier as the founder of the architecture program at Northeastern University.[67] Leaving Manchuria in 1931

83

during the Japanese takeover, Liang Sicheng took up a post at the Society (later Institute) for Research in Chinese Architecture (*Zhongguo yingzao xueshe*) established in 1930 by Zhu Qiqian (Chu Ch'i-ch'ien, b. 1872), who in 1915 had been minister of the interior. Zhu's interest in Chinese traditional architecture was sparked when he supervised the repair of palaces and other public buildings; he also acquired a copy of the Song dynasty manual *Yingzao fashi,* written by Li Jie (Chieh), an official of the Imperial Court, which he then attempted to decode (despite its opacity) with the help of the oral tradition of the craftsmen working for him at the time.[68]

The central question Liang set himself for his research was to determine the stages of Chinese architectural evolution. He had learned earlier from his studies in the United States, as well as from his familiarity with the prevailing knowledge (or the lack thereof) in China, that very little was known on the subject.[69] The major Western texts then in use, by Osvald Sirén and by Ernst Boerschmann,[70] he regarded as being riddled with mistakes and interpretive misunderstandings. Appreciative of the Western practice of direct field observation, Liang set out to augment what documentary evidence he could find, in the form of manuals and other drawings and descriptions, by photographing, measuring, and taking notes on major surviving traditional buildings and traditional artifacts.

Liang was joined at the Institute in 1932 by Liu Dunzhen (Liu Tun-chen, 1897–1968), who graduated from the department of architecture of the Tokyo Institute of Technology in 1920 and had become a professor at National Central University in Nanjing in 1927.[71] They shared the responsibility for directing and organizing restoration, fieldwork, and other archival activities. Although they worked closely together, Liang generally concentrated on research methods, whereas Liu took care of manuscripts. One of the aims of the research group—working under the highly defensible assumption that the first Chinese buildings were fashioned from timber—was to discover the oldest surviving wooden structure. After several expeditions, in 1937 they discovered a Tang dynasty wooden structure in the main hall of a temple complex in the Wutai-shan area, north of Beijing.

Throughout, Liang and Liu's interest in tracing architectural developments from their origins was consistent. In time, as he mastered the complex grammar of various Chinese traditional constructive systems, Liang became critical of his contemporaries' use of traditional Chinese architecture in modern buildings. For instance, though respecting Lu Yanzhi in many ways, Liang commented on his Sun Yat-sen Memorial Auditorium: "Except for giving the mausoleum hall a seemingly Chinese appearance, [Lu] lacked understanding of the old style, in terms of layout, structure, and details, resulting in a series of mistakes in proportions."[72] In fact he probably could have made the same sort of comments about Murphy's, Hussey's, or Dong's work, which, in the end, was more about creating the appearance of traditional Chinese architecture than replicating it. Until Liang completed his *History of Chinese Architecture* in 1943, with a companion English-language edition titled *A Pictorial History of Chinese Architecture* (published only in 1984), there was no thoroughgoing contemporary account of what actually constituted the classical Chinese architectural tradition.[73]

Liang himself was rarely involved in new works of architecture. One exception was the Central Museum in Nanjing of 1937, a project on which he served as a consultant to Gin-djih Su (Xu Jinzhi) and Li Wei-paak (Li Huibo). It took the form of a very traditional-looking Chinese pavilion with a classical roof structure, *dougong*, and a raised platform with broad stairs as a base.[74] With the Japanese partial occupation of China in 1937 and the beginning of the War of Resistance, Liang and his colleagues moved the Institute for Research in Chinese Architecture first to Changsha in central China, then to Kunming and nearby Chongqing (Chungking) in the southwest. Research expeditions continued throughout this period, mainly into Sichuan province, and Liang continued to write for both English and Chinese publications.

In 1938, the Guomindang administration of the Nationalist Government shifted its capital from Nanjing to Chongqing to avoid occupation, devising construction plans, moving many industries from coastal areas to unoccupied hinterlands, and prosecuting the War of Resistance against Japan. At the time, the issue of how best to deploy tradition in modern architecture in China was not resolved. The idea that some elements of both tradition and modernity should be included generally held sway, although the balance often depended on where and for whom building was taking place. Buildings of Guomindang officialdom presented one extreme: they were clearly designed to project the grandeur of a traditional mode of expression, while also suggesting a modern way forward by using modern building materials and organizational plans. At the other extreme commercial buildings, especially those involved in foreign trade, reflected the dominant overseas architectural tastes. As the grand nationalistic plans for Nanjing, Shanghai, and Guangzhou fell on hard economic times, the architectural conditions of the New Life

Movement shifted, falling into a gradual transition from Western neoclassicism through moderne and art deco to the International Style, especially in the more thriving commercial centers.

The Chinese architectural profession certainly became well-established during this period of roughly forty years, primarily through a first generation of foreign Beaux-Arts-educated architects who finally had the means at their disposal to begin fostering an authentic modern Chinese architecture. Indeed, it can be argued that their Beaux-Arts training equipped them well for this task, for the axial, symmetrical composition and hierarchical disposition of building elements that it at least superficially emphasized were also common features in classical Chinese architecture. As important, though, the habit of distinguishing the expressive "figure" of a building from its "form," or spatial organization, helped them render architecturally the distinction between traditional "essence" and modern "use" that was so much a part of the broader cultural debate in China. Happily, the fledgling system of architectural education, by now strongly rooted in the Beaux-Arts tradition with the beginning of a Bauhaus influence, continued, in spite of the Japanese occupation, through the strategic merger of the faculties of Peking University, Qinghua, and Nankai in Tianjin into the Associated University of Chongqing, as well as the relocation there, by 1940, of Nanjing's National Central University. In addition, some existing firms such as Kwan, Chu, and Yang, remained in practice in Chongqing, although under beleaguered circumstances.

*"**DIDN'T ALL THAT STUFF ABOUT TRADITION AND MODERNISM** come to a head after the war?" asked Wu Feng, although not really wanting to prolong the discussion. When Shaoshu went off on a tangent there was no stopping him.*

"Which war?" responded Lu Hui, looking genuinely puzzled.

"The civil war, of course!" exclaimed Feng, wondering how she could be so obtuse.

"You mean after liberation!" replied Hui, knowingly.

"Yes, I suppose I do," Feng went on without skipping a beat. "She has always been a good socialist girl," he thought to himself smugly.

"Yet another period of foreign intervention," intoned Zhang Shaoshu in a somewhat superior manner. He did, after all, pride himself on being the intellectual of the group.

"What foreigners?" Feng blurted out without thinking.

"He means our Soviet comrades," Hui said tartly, seeming to read Feng's mind.

"You mean former comrades, don't you?" shot back Feng. "And what good did they do for us, eh?" he went on, more to get a rise from Hui than out of any sense of conviction.

"Anyway, Hui is right, the Russians were invited over to give us a hand," Shaoshu continued, as if there were no disagreement between them. "Replacing the Americans, you might say."

"Different strokes for different folks," interrupted Feng in a singsong tone.

"Why are you always so cynical? Let him go on," broke in Hui rather angrily.

"Oh, I love it when you're mad!" Feng joked, pursing his lips together in a mock kiss for further effect.

"Please, you two! Can we be serious for a moment?" Shaoshu was beginning to get impatient with his partners' antics. "The fact of the matter is that first they gave us socialist realism and then they turned around and gave us industrialized building," he continued, regaining his composure.

"So much for the modern world!" Feng retorted predictably.

"Well, there was a bit more to it than that," replied Shaoshu. "Some of those postwar buildings with the big roofs were really out of proportion, like imperial palaces. Look at that one out on the west side of town in Beihai—and that was a dormitory, if you can believe it," he added for emphasis. By now the air conditioner in the corner was beginning to wheeze and rattle as it always did at this time in the early afternoon when it was still hot.

THE "BIG ROOF" CONTROVERSY in China, during the 1950s, took some years to

unfold. With the end of hostilities with the Japanese, some normality returned to life, institutionally speaking, though China would never be the same again. In 1946, Liang Sicheng was appointed by the Ministry of Education under the Nationalist Government to establish and head a new department of architecture at Qinghua University (created partly at his own urging) and to travel to the United States in order to study current architectural educational practices there. Quite apart from Liang's stature in the architectural community, this ministerial appointment was perhaps predictable, given the Nationalist Government's architectural ambition to produce modern buildings with Chinese characteristics and Liang's scholarly interest in China's heritage as a point of departure for contemporary architecture.

In any event, Liang set sail late in 1946, having dispatched Wu Liangyong (b. 1922), his assistant at Chongqing, and three other close colleagues to Beijing to start the new school.[1] Wu himself would later travel to the United States, at Liang's insistence, to study architecture and urban design at the Cranbrook Academy of Art between 1948 and 1950 and to work in Eliel Saarinen's office; in 1950 he returned to teach at Qinghua. A student of both Yang Tingbao and Liu Dunzhen at the National Central University in Chongqing between 1940 and 1944, Wu was one of the first of the second generation of Chinese architects to become involved in reshaping architectural education in China under Liang's tutelage.[2]

Also in 1946 a new plan for the Shanghai metropolitan area was undertaken; the architects actively participating were Lu Qianshou, Fan Wenzhao, Zhuang Jun, Mei Guozhao, and Songsing Kwan. In Nanjing, Yang Tingbao continued to practice in a modernist idiom, completing designs for the Nanjing Railway Station (Xiaguan) in 1946, as well as those for his own home and the residence for Sun Ke, mentioned earlier, a couple of years later.[3] The Shanghai metropolitan area plan, also known as the Master Plan for Greater Shanghai, embodied modern town-planning principles, similar to those devised earlier by Sir Patrick Abercrombie for London, including a system of greenbelts, radial transportation corridors leading away from the center of Shanghai to the west, and numerous satellite communities to decentralize population and reconcentrate employment opportunities.

Yang's residence for Sun Ke, completed in 1948, was placed at the end of a driveway on a secluded site, with two wings of rooms extending into the landscape facing south. Its rational modern architectural expression extended from the plan, with articulated volumes of white stucco, expansive areas of fenestration, broad protruding roof overhangs, and registration of the juncture of the two wings in a curvilinear two-story balcony to the south. Although generally modernist in the spatial flow of its layout, the plan also subtly incorporated traditional characteristics. Apart from the southern orientation and the implied "courtyard" beyond, the entry sequence followed a zigzag pattern to the main rooms, retaining an ample sense of protocol and propriety for the residents.

By the 1940s, the four architectural attitudes of the previous era had been reduced to two expressive doctrines: one overtly modernist and the other continuing to incorporate traditional-looking Chinese characteristics into modern programs. To be sure, architectural production in many of the treaty ports still followed a variety of overseas trends, including the popular "moderne," or art deco, style in institutional and commercial settings. Nevertheless, the lines among Chinese architects were becoming more sharply drawn between those retaining sinified forms of expression and those favoring the new International Style. While the former represented a continuation of Nationalist architectural ambitions, the latter was introduced gradually during the 1930s, principally in Shanghai construction and more forcefully through architectural education and the infusion of Bauhaus principles into school curricula.

In the late 1940s, Huang Zuoxin (Henry Wong, 1915–1975) was asked to form the Faculty of Architecture at St. John's University in Shanghai, a missionary school founded by Americans.[4] Having first studied in London at the Architectural Association, Huang followed his former teacher—Walter Gropius—to Harvard in 1937, continuing his studies at the Graduate School of Design and acting as a teaching assistant. At St. John's, Huang drew on his Harvard experience, integrating Bauhaus concepts of function, technology, economy, and modern art into the new faculty's professional program. He also invited like-minded architects, such as the German Richard Paulick, to join in this educational enterprise. Paulick, a principal in Gropius's office in Dessau, later taught and, with his brother, opened a practice also known as "Modern Homes," and headed up the works committee for the Shanghai master plan.[5]

After World War II, the influence of the modernist functionalist program at St. John's gave considerable support to earlier, more tentative modernist teaching at other institutions, including Hangchow (Zhijiang) University (founded in 1938), as well as to the nascent modern practices of young graduates. It also provided a deeper theoretical underpinning to prior work by the likes of Fan Wenzhao and Xi Fuquan in Nationalist China; though contemporary architects would not use exactly these terms, "form following function" located *ti* and *yong* beyond matters of any particular traditional circumstance, much as it had done to similar concerns in the West. Indeed, Fan Wenzhao had been highly critical of Western-style buildings with Chinese-style roofs, calling them an "abomination," and Zhuang Jun had expressed similar sentiments in advocating "universal functionalism."[6] In effect, for them modern use became the essence of form.

But national politics were about to overtake architectural developments. The civil war that had begun had in effect ceased from 1937 until 1945, when both forces contributed to the War of Resistance against Japan and managed to defend the north and southwest of their country. Despite efforts by the American General Marshall to mediate between them, conflict broke out again in earnest in 1946, with the People's Liberation Army clashing with Nationalist troops in Hubei and Hunan.[7] Though they suffered setbacks in early 1947, the Communists, under Mao Zedong, soon gained the upper hand in the escalating civil war, as spiraling economic inflation continued at a catastrophic rate, in spite of American aid that had poured into the country since early in the 1930s; and the general populace continued to become disaffected with life under the Guomindang regime. In 1948 the Nationalist army was routed in the north, followed by the fall of China's major cities to the Communists in 1949—Beijing in January, Nanjing in April, Shanghai in May, Guangzhou in October, and, finally, Chongqing in November.

Almost immediately with the ascendancy of the Communists came a strong Russian Soviet influence. Mao Zedong traveled to Moscow in 1950, securing pledges for massive amounts of foreign aid. Like the Americans before them, the Russians gained influence over the development and modernization of China. Some 11,000 Russian advisors spread out into many walks of Chinese life, bringing especially technical expertise to areas where China lagged behind the West; more than 37,000 Chinese received some form of training or education in the Soviet Union, again primarily in technical areas.[8] These exchanges encouraged the reorganization of schools and universities throughout China, with an emphasis on fewer and more specialized institutes. These changes affected the study of architecture. At the end of the Nationalist era, there were ten university departments of architecture in China, including Qinghua's, Peking University's, and the reformed department at National Central, headed by Yang Tingbao in 1949. By 1952 these schools had been consolidated and strengthened, as the humanities were separated from scientific and technical subject matter. Consequently, Peking University's department of architecture merged with Qinghua's in Beijing; National Central's department became a part of Nanjing Institute of Technology; and Zhongshan was incorporated into the South China Institute of Technology. The program at St. John's University, for its part, was dissolved in 1949; its faculty, together with architecture faculties from Zhijiang University, the Hangzhou School of Art, and construction engineering at Tongji, was reconstituted into the Faculty of Architecture at Tongji University. Shortly after its formation, the faculty moved into a new building that symbolized their modernist Bauhaus architectural stance;[9] it was designed by Ha Xiongwen and Huang Yulin, a recent student of Huang Zuoxin.

29 Faculty of Architecture building at Tongji University, Shanghai,
by Ha Xiongwen and Huang Yulin, 1953.

Many practicing architects became teachers. For example, Chen Zhi took a position in Tongji University's department of architecture in 1952, having taught at Zhijiang University between 1938 and 1952, and Tong Jun joined Liu Dunzhen and Yang Tingbao at Nanjing. Xia Changshi, who in the late 1930s joined the faculty at the South China Institute of Technology with a doctorate from Tübingen, promoted Bauhaus design principles learned during his studies in Germany, giving his host institution in Guangzhou a distinctive character.[10]

Professional practices also became gradually nationalized over much the same period, as city- or province-based design institutes were formed. Thus Zhuang Jun closed his office in 1949 to join the North China Architecture and Engineering Company, moving in 1952 to the new East China Institute of Architectural Design and Research in Shanghai. Likewise Zhang Bo (1911–1999)—another prominent member of China's second generation of architects, having graduated from National Central at Nanjing in 1934—became the chief architect at the Beijing Institute of Architectural Design and Research. Before this posting he worked as a junior partner in the office of Kwan, Chu, and Yang.[11] Lin Keming joined the Guangzhou Institute of Design; some, like Yang Tingbao, entered design offices closely affiliated with their academic posts. One result of this nationalization is that today there are about fifty-six major design institutes in China, all quite large in comparison with their Western counterparts.[12] Other institutional forms of professionalism revived in the early 1950s as well: the Architectural Society of China was created by Liang Sicheng and others in 1952, and *Architectural Journal* was founded in 1953.

The Russian influence extended beyond technical advice and into the cultural realm. Socialist realism, then prevalent in the art and architecture of the Soviet Union and embedded in Marxist thinking, perhaps not surprisingly was seen in China as an appropriate way of celebrating the socialist revolution and a newfound sense of nationalism. Some prominent buildings, like the Soviet Exhibition Hall in Beijing of 1953, were even designed by Russian architects (in this case Sergei Andreyev).[13] Still standing today, the exhibition hall terminated the axis of a major street; the tall, towerlike structure, adorned with socialist realist statuary, rises above the main crossing of two sections of the exhibition space at the entrance to the building. Two lower wings formed a curvilinear neoclassical colonnade around the base of the building, symmetrically arranged around the central tower. The impact of the complex was unmistakably monumental, visually underscoring the new Soviet presence in China.

30   The Soviet Exhibition Hall, Beijing, by Sergei Andreyev, 1953.

31 The Friendship Hotel, Beijing, by Zhang Bo, 1954.

To satisfy Russian urging, if not demands, that their model be followed, the governmental center of the new capital in Beijing was located on Tiananmen Square, along the north-south axis of the Forbidden City.[14] The square itself was substantially modified: the elongated T-shaped open area that had existed outside the main gate of the imperial complex for centuries was changed into the vast paved area of today, much like Red Square in front of the Kremlin in Moscow. Though Liang Sicheng was vice director of the Beijing City Planning Commission, almost all his recommendations were ignored; he and his colleague Liu Kaiqu had a rare success in 1951, persuading the Communist Party that the Monument to the People's Heroes in the center of Tiananmen should take the form of a stone memorial *stele,* traditionally used for such a purpose throughout China.[15] Liang, wishing to preserve the old character of central Beijing, had argued that the government center should be located to the west rather than on the north-south axis south of the Forbidden City. But the Communist regime was far more interested in promoting heavy industry throughout the nation and continued to focus on transforming cities, including the historic capital, into production-based economies. Thus Beijing should become an industrial city as well as a political center, an attitude that was officially reiterated in Beijing's city plans of 1954 and 1957.[16]

The influence of Soviet architectural theory and an advocacy of "socialist content and national form," or "cultural form and socialist content" as it was alternatively phrased—both expressing the by now familiar conjunction of "essence" (*ti*) and "application" (*yong*)—were not alone in pushing the new Chinese architecture of the early Communist period in the direction of monumentality, formalism, and a renewal of strong traditional forms such as large, upturned tiled roofs. An "academic school" was predominant among Chinese architects and educators at the time. Some, like Liang Sicheng, had even been made responsible for proposing and developing a new national style—although in fairness to Liang, he was, as he put it, against buildings "wearing a Western suit and a Chinese skullcap."[17] Nevertheless, works such as Zhang Bo's Friendship Hotel in Beijing (1954) were clearly revivalist in style.[18] E-shaped in plan, with a more or less straight facade running along a main street, the hotel was symmetrically organized in five to six stories of guest rooms, conference rooms, banquet halls, and the like. Sections of an upturned gable-and-hipped roof connected to stair turrets crowned with traditional roofs, and a larger classical pavilion-like structure was located over the central bay at the hotel's entrance.

Inlaid and glazed brickwork and other Chinese decorative motifs further accentuated the revivalist composition, which was otherwise Western neoclassicist in overall arrangement, much like some of the buildings from the 1930s described earlier.

Another underlying cause of the swing toward a new national style was quite simply the "prevailing feeling of pride which came from national liberation and economic revival," as Zhang Qinnan, a contemporary observer, put it, and the end of special privileges for foreigners.[19] If nothing else, the Communists had cleaned up most cities, gotten essential services back in operation, and brought under control the ruinous inflation that had crippled the country for the past decade. The modernization that was now being undertaken in China relied largely on the nation's centrally planned, socialist economic system, which eventually included the public ownership of private property. As Zhang noted, "It was only natural that architects then attempted to express this social progressiveness through architectural monumentality, which soon led to the proliferation of the 'Big Roof.'"[20] Furthermore, the launching of the First Five-Year Plan in 1953 called for national building;[21] with the end of the Korean War came unprecedented opportunities for construction.

A deeper explanation of the emphasis on "socialist content and cultural form" turns on Marxist thinking about socialist realism, and more specifically Mao Zedong's own brand of aesthetics and the role of art in his political revolution. As early as 1942 he had declared that "man's social life constitutes the only source of art and literature" and argued for a particular treatment of that source: "life as reflected in artistic and literary works can and ought to be on a higher level and of a greater power and better focused, more typical, nearer the ideal, and therefore more universal than actual everyday life."[22] While thus separating content and form, he also demanded both "popularization" and "elevation" on the formal side of the equation—that is, both simple, plain, and readily accepted characteristics and a "polished representation, less likely to win the ready acceptance of the masses."[23] There was no real contradiction, for the elevated representation was needed to uplift the people and create solidarity, as well as to appeal more immediately to the better-educated and cultivated party leadership—the cadres. An artwork is more than mere propaganda: according to Mao, its social effect depended on artistry as well. As he put it, a "poster and slogan style" was not enough.[24]

When applied to architecture this line of argument rather quickly led toward content that was emblematic of national struggle, rendered in a manner that was uplifting and gauged to evoke solidarity through a common sense of purpose and pride. It was also literal, to the extent that the shape and appearance of structures were to be familiar and somehow ingrained in the culture. From this position, it was only a small step to monumentality and architecture with more than a passing resemblance to the past, much as the Nationalists had favored almost twenty years earlier. But there was a fundamental theoretical difference in denotative intent, turning on the distinction between popularization (the Communists) and out-and-out celebration of past glories (the Nationalists). The Communists had to resurrect an architectural past only to render their vision of the built environment locally familiar, not to engage in backward-looking historicism and glorification of a repressive feudalism that they found abhorrent. In the words of Mao's other forward-looking treatise on cultural theory, it was necessary to separate the *jinghua* (quintessence) from the *zaopo* (sediment);[25] and part of this quintessence could be the nonexploitative creations of China's people, including elements of its building tradition.

This euphoric situation did not continue for long, as economic conditions began to worsen and a more sober mood began to settle on Communist Party deliberations. No less a figure than Zhou Enlai (1898–1976), the nation's premier, inveighed against unnecessary waste at the First National People's Congress in 1954. In his address he singled out building, among other sectors, declaring that "more than a few cities, institutions, schools, and businesses have undertaken some overly lavish construction, willingly exhausting the limited resources of the country."[26] Zhou's statement was no sudden autocratic and pernicious attack on the architectural establishment but rather a logical outgrowth of the Communist Party's stance on economic development. From the outset, the means of production (i.e., heavy industry) had clearly been given priority over the means of subsistence, including most urban accommodations and services. When times were bad, leaders argued, every effort should be made to avoid fighting over scarce resources, which must be directed toward the means of production—even if cities and people's livelihoods suffered as a consequence. During the previous four years, the government of the People's Republic of China had enjoyed considerable success with this approach; Zhou was, in essence, calling for renewed efforts in the same direction, which appeared to be in the long-term interests of the nation. This policy was referred to as "production first and livelihood second."[27]

In concert with this policy and the need to deal with the economic downturn, the sixth session of the board of directors of the newly re-formed Architectural Society of China, in October 1954, began to address the premier's concern. "Function, economy, and appearance when circumstances allow" became the new watchwords, sharpening, in the national interest, the previous focus on socialist content and cultural form.[28] This shift in the balance between aesthetic considerations and functional economy was also probably further emphasized when the *People's Daily* in China published the Soviet Premier Khrushchev's speech of January 1955 on the need for an industrialized approach to all building in order to improve quality and, at the same time, reduce unit costs. By now China's Russian patron was abandoning socialist realist monumentality, except for exceptional buildings, in favor of a wholesale commitment to standardized construction methods and factory-produced materials, especially for housing, factories, and other utilitarian buildings.[29] The charge can also be seen as consonant with Mao's aesthetic doctrine, now that times and therefore social reality had changed. Clearly, however, the interest in "elevation," which had afforded architectural scope for direct references to traditional architecture, had lessened—or, rather, been displaced, as the stamp of architectural quality and formal ambition became the acquisition and perfection of modern industrialized building methods.

The buildings that contributed most to Zhou Enlai's concern and to this retreat from a monumental or formalistic national style were mostly constructed between 1952 and 1955 and incorporated a literal borrowing of traditional Chinese architectural motifs, including large, upturned tiled roofs, at an extensive scale. They were all very big, somewhat outlandish, and very conspicuous. For instance, the Chongqing Great Hall of the People, designed by Zhang Jiade and built in 1952, consisted of a huge central auditorium, circular in shape, flanked by two four-story wings of offices and hotel accommodations.[30] The central part of the main facade was a reproduction of a traditional city gate flanked by octagonal pillars, and the steel-framed dome over the central auditorium space had three layers of eaves, like the main hall of the Temple of Heaven in Beijing. Situated on a prominent site, the building complex was entered through a traditional *pailou* gate into a courtyard, where a flight of 128 broad steps led to the auditorium's main entrance. Similarly, the Di'anmen Government Dormitory of 1954 and the Beihai Government Offices of 1955, both in Beijing and both designed by Chen Dengao, were very large, symmetrically arranged buildings of five and eight stories, respectively, towering above the traditional one- and two-

32   The Beihai Government Offices, Beijing, by Chen Dengao, 1955.

story urban tissue of the capital.[31] The Beihai Government Offices looked like a segment of the old wall with office windows punched in along its length and with a grand gate-tower-like structure at its center and two smaller towers at its ends, all topped by traditional Chinese pavilion roofs with single and double eaves. Such a reference was almost as unmistakable at the dormitory, which was similarly composed of central and flanking entrance towers. Moreover, the residential scale of the building was almost completely subordinated to expression of the walled facade and traditionally decorated, elaborate balcony protrusions. The Sanlihe Government Office complex (1954) by Zhang Kaiji was, if anything, even more monumental, constructed in the manner of a traditional walled precinct with gateways and defensive towers.[32] The relatively unadorned yet well-proportioned masonry facades, rising to a consistent height of six stories with rounded archways providing entrances to inner courtyards, also lent a certain solemn, almost "imperial," appearance to the complex. Zhang's earlier Central Cultural College in Beijing (1951) had many of the same architectural characteristics.

On the side of the "Big Roof" controversy favoring less flamboyant and traditional design, the production of housing in China quickly became the architectural model to be followed, including fittedness to prevailing Chinese conditions. When the state's early economic plans emphasizing heavy industry gave rise to acute housing shortages, China turned to the Soviet model for potential relief. This model was an industrialized building system that emphasized construction speed, low cost, and labor savings—a promising approach when scarce construction resources and labor were required elsewhere.[33] Basic features of the system were design standardization, mass production, and systematic construction. Standardized design, in turn, meant a standard dwelling unit or module made up of standard building components; various combinations of these units formed buildings, which were then placed together to create residential areas. The core of the system was the standard dwelling unit, which was first built in 1952, under the guidance of Soviet experts in northeast China. By 1953, fully 34 percent of all housing construction employed this approach, as the Ministry of Urban Construction was placed in charge of its deployment.[34] The Soviet standard for each unit was 9 square meters of livable space per person, far above the national Chinese average, which at the time was about 4 square meters. Nevertheless, in a period of improving economic conditions and general optimism, the larger area remained the official standard, with families sharing apartments in the hopes that the situation would get better.

In general, these housing units took the form of three or more stories of walk-up apartments constructed in concrete and masonry as rectilinear blocks, with access along the length of the block to each group of apartments offered via stairways or internal corridors. Sometimes an aesthetic program of socialist realism was employed, as pitched gable roofs and other motifs were added to the standardized units, before economic constraints mandated a more utilitarian architecture. The Di'anmen complex in Beijing mentioned earlier exemplified this socialist realist style. More often than not, though, housing was functional, well-built, and, as in the case of

33 Standardized, industrialized housing production.

34   An interior street of the Broadcasting Work Unit, Beijing.

the Broadcasting Work Unit near Beijing's second ring road in the southwest, without much in the way of architectural rhetoric, whether socialist realist or functionalist. There, spacious apartment buildings three and four stories high, with pitched roofs, were set out in a largely self-contained garden compound; interior streets and courtyards, as well as accommodations for social and community services, were all walled off from neighboring public thoroughfares. The early Communist mandate that each work unit, or enterprise, be responsible for its own employees (given the shortage of direct state support) had certainly pushed urbanization in this direction. But something of a continued spatial adherence to the traditional "household" compound can also be seen there, including a favorable southern orientation for units, a strong sense of enclosure, and the inclusion of entrance and other secluded spaces necessary for inhabitants to maintain decorum and propriety.

Soviet influence also extended to the use of perimeter-block residential area layouts: housing was aligned along streets, usually with a strong axial arrangement, and public buildings were located at the center of the residential area. The overall appearance was of distinct formalism, such as that amply displayed by the residential area attached to the Number One Automobile Plant in Changchun, constructed in 1955. Changchun's location—in northern China, in an area once controlled and thus directly influenced first by Russia and then by post–Meiji Restoration Japan—may also have had something to do with the layout, although the perimeter-block arrangement was commonly used elsewhere in China and favored by architects such as Yang Tingbao, who believed that it conveyed a sense of urbanity.

But over time, widespread dissatisfaction with the Soviet-style standard housing design grew; though by no means abandoned, it began incrementally to be adapted and modified.[36] One problem was the inner corridor design of the original model, which was often poorly suited to China's climate and living conditions. For this among other reasons, the Ministry of Urban Construction promulgated six geographical versions, providing separate designs for the northeastern, northern, northwestern, southwestern, central and southeastern regions. Another problem was the economy's failure to catch up with the housing's originally inflated space standard; units were therefore reduced substantially in size so that each family could enjoy a separate dwelling.

In addition, by 1955 the architectural community had become more vocal in criticizing the waste involved in nonproductive building and turned their backs on what they saw as superficial excesses in housing architecture. A debate also erupted over whether to use perimeter-block arrangements in general residential area design or a climatically and culturally more compatible design—north-south orientations of apartment blocks in parallel rows with adequate open space between them. Although the arguments in its favor were not entirely convincing, especially when housing density in areas with scarce land resources was considered, the uniform structure of parallel housing blocks finally won out. For the next several decades, any pretense to architectural formalism vanished almost completely from China's housing, as economic conditions worsened and housing continued to be a low priority on the national economic agenda.

At the same time, the "Big Roof" style and the predominance of an academic school of thought, particularly as represented by Liang Sicheng, began to be actively denounced. Three hostile articles appeared in the *Architectural Journal* in 1955. In "How Has Mr. Liang Sicheng Twisted Architecture and Cultural Form," Niu Ming charged that "the perspective and approach of Mr. Liang's study of Chinese architecture is bourgeois and idealist, neglecting its economic appropriateness and scientific achievements." Moreover, "in studying Chinese architecture, Mr. Liang treats its components as signs and characteristics, and does not pursue their essence. Hence, in using the same approach in discussing new architectural creations, he can only vaguely say that 'it is an integral part of our lives' and fail[s] to deliver any mere substantial arguments." Niu concluded that Liang "only notices the importance of decorative quality and does not pursue the reality that produced this phenomenon, hence inevitably following the path of formalism."[37] Niu was also careful to point out differences between party, class, and socialist realist art and what he saw as revivalist sentiments of formalism and revivalism. In a self-repudiatory critique in the same issue, Wang Ying posed a rhetorical question along much the same lines: "Today we have thousands of new building materials, scientific structural techniques, and mechanized and industrialized building methods. Many elements from our historical architectural heritage are not appropriate under these new circumstances. Why do we have to force the inheritance, subjecting technology to art, and build architecture on fake structures and redundant decorations?"[38] And finally Liu Huixian, in an article titled "The Poison of Formalism and Revivalism," railed against wasting money on decoration, subordinating function to appearance, and forcing ancient forms onto today's technology and zeitgeist.[39]

In hindsight and from a certain Western perspective, much of this rhetoric may sound familiar. References to the zeitgeist, to the promise of new technology, and to form following function are certainly reminiscent of European avant-garde modernist calls, heard much earlier in the century, for an architecture befitting a new social and technological era. Then, too, a need for economy and even frugality encouraged parsimony in matters of utility and material composition. Such references also seem to correspond to the Marxist embrace of modern architecture in the everyday life of the Soviet Union, albeit to a lesser degree. Undoubtedly, the groundwork already laid in architectural education (at St. John's University) and in practice (in Shanghai and elsewhere) had prepared the way for a much broader application of orthodox modern architectural principles in China. Nevertheless, a longer historical view also suggests that the Chinese were operating dialectally within their own rhetorical and evolving theory of contemporary architecture.

As his distinction between *jinghua,* or quintessence, and *zaopo,* or sediment, was being applied, Mao Zedong's admonition to look first at the "objective facts" of the times and his warning against too slavish an appropriation of Western methods were being heeded. Indeed, a widely held suspicion about what may be regarded as the formalistic excesses of Western modern architecture was to grow substantially during the coming decade in China. Moreover, the crude binary formulations of "essential traditional principle" and "practical modern function" set out in the nineteenth and early twentieth centuries no longer held. The socialist cultural program made ideas about tradition more than simply a reference to national identity; it had moved forward by asking how the past can be seen to guide the present and near future. The answer to that question clearly involved actively confronting contemporary socioeconomic circumstances based on a historical understanding of how they came about. It would take practical wisdom to deal constructively and progressively with these circumstances, as well as requiring artistry to give a form to this impetus that could elevate architectural production.

In short, matters of "essence" and "form" were becoming much more closely intertwined. Concern with appearance, and Chinese qualities in particular, had not vanished entirely from the architectural scene; but in these circumstances, architects could no longer rely on and had far less use for stylistic principles that were overtly traditional, as distinct from spatial-organizational. Moreover, as economic conditions worsened, the imperative—political, professional, and otherwise—to objectively adapt to those cultural realities was becoming that much stronger. It is in this context that by the mid-1950s, "revivalism" and "formalism" per se had become, as one commentator put it, "terrifying crimes for many architects."[40]

"IT JUST GOES TO SHOW YOU—when function and cost overcome how the building looks we end up with all those dreary modern buildings we still have around us today," proffered Wu Feng. "You know what I mean," he went on, countering Lu Hui's quizzical look, "slab after slab of six- or seven-story concrete buildings, all the same, all facing north-south, all falling apart. So much for individual expression!"

"Still, some of the modern buildings aren't that bad," replied Hui.

"True, some of that stuff over in the diplomatic area is pretty good," agreed Feng, quickly recalling the compound near where he had once lived. "Also, there's something a lot more honest about form following function than those reinforced concrete dougong." He continued soberly, "Perhaps we are trying too hard to make something different all the time," going back to the drawings spread across the conference table to begin sketching again.

"I didn't think I would ever hear you say that!" mocked Hui, aware that Feng's stance was somewhat self-contradictory, as he both advocated individual expression and admired a great deal of modern work that was far less formalistic than revivals of any kind, including many of the postmodern projects that were being thrown up in the city. Yet she also found Feng's position admirable. "Somehow Feng's sense of what counts never abandons him, in spite of all his posing," she thought to herself.

"But form following function doesn't necessarily wipe out the dougong, you know," broke in Zhang Shaoshu.

"What are you talking about?" shot back Feng, annoyed at the interruption now that he was finally getting back to work.

"What you just said," continued Shaoshu. "What if the function was to express a sense of national architecture, or to remind people about who they are? After all, your definition is very

Western. It's not as if a spirit of the times is necessarily so transferable, or that what happens in one place should happen elsewhere."

"You know your trouble?" said Feng in a warning tone. "You think too much about this stuff and, in the end, get nowhere." But even as he spoke, he realized that, as usual, he had gone too far. Shaoshu had a point. Many of these terms were so slippery: that was why he preferred to just design and be done with it.

"I'll ignore that," Shaoshu went on amiably, by now used to Feng's sudden tacks. "In the end we have to find the right balance. Formal aspirations can never be quite so straightforward."

"Look at that poor guy limping along down the lane," Hui thought to herself, now looking out the window and not concentrating on the conversation going on behind her. "He can't be more than in his mid-fifties, and look what's happened to him. He probably makes his living begging—like all the others out along the posh streets, where there are lots of foreigners."

"Part of the 'Lost Generation,'" Feng said softly, but with a tinge of sadness in his voice, as if in answer to her unspoken thought.

"Yes," she murmured to herself, aware of Feng's sudden presence very close behind her—though this time, to her surprise, without her usual feeling of annoyance.

STRUGGLES WITH MODERNISM in Chinese architecture became more pronounced during the late 1950s. In 1956, the *Architectural Journal* declared, "We need Modern Architecture." Others immediately objected, arguing that modernist architecture was not socialist but functional, a mode of building in which technology had supplanted art.[1] During 1957, the same influential magazine extensively covered the work of both Mies van der Rohe and Walter Gropius. Indeed, they were the only architects given monograph-like treatment during the 1950s.

Functional planning and the introduction of industrialized building techniques were becoming more commonplace in practice. One influential building of the time was the In-Patient Department of the Beijing Children's Hospital (1955) by Hua Lanhong, a reinforced-concrete-framed structure with uniform open bays; a driving force behind the design was an ostensibly highly functional layout.[2] Chinese-like detailing was limited to the nevertheless functional lattice balustrades along open corridors. More generally, the objective realities of China's relative poverty put the focus on constructing dwellings with minimum space standards and few material comforts, and on experimenting with mass production techniques adapted to local conditions. Certainly architects' attention to function, technology, and economy was also making its presence more thoroughly felt, even though some—careful to avoid falling into the trap of revivalism—were reluctant to entirely abandon aesthetic and nationalistic expressive considerations.

Probably the most prominent example of orthodox modern architecture built during the 1950s was Yang Tingbao's Peace Hotel in Beijing, designed in 1951 and completed in 1953.[3] It was an eight-story-high rectangular block, with rooms organized in modern layouts; access to them came from a central corridor along the length of the building, which terminated at one end with a tower containing a fire stair, in which the stair risers and landings were prominently expressed. Likewise the reinforced concrete frame of the building was not disguised, and the straightforward concrete paneled facade was fenestrated with a regular pattern of glazing that emphasized the material characteristics of the building and its functional layout. Even at the entrance and on the interiors the usual Chinese architectural motifs were absent, although the site retained several trees and older buildings related to the octagonal special function hall, which projected to the west of the main building and helped form a well-scaled courtyard.

Shortly after its construction, the hotel was acclaimed for its progressive functional and economic merits, as well as for the simplicity and elegance with which it created an inviting precinct within the site. But a few years later, the building was sparking considerable controversy, which focused especially on whether it presented an alternative to revivalist architecture, in the service of a new modern style. In short, it became a rallying point for modernists in the ongoing debate during 1956 and 1957, which centered on the connotations of modernist architecture's "boxlike" form and its strong emphasis on concepts and terms such as "functionalism" and "structuralism."[4] Those opposing the modernists had nagging suspicions that these were, in fact, concepts and terms associated with the capitalist West, even though on its face nothing could be more proletarian in orientation than "functionalism" or "structuralism."

These years also witnessed the Hundred Flowers Movement, inaugurated by Mao Zedong on May 2, 1956, on the heels of Zhou Enlai's proposed reforms and calling for criticism, expressions of opinion, and suggestions about China's modern progress;[5] in February of the same year, Nikita Khrushchev criticized Stalin during the Twentieth Congress of the Communist Party in the Soviet Union. Although slow in coming, "big character" posters at Beijing University, to-

35   The Peace Hotel, Beijing, by Yang Tingbao, 1951–1953.

gether with numerous articles in the press, complained openly about repression, bureaucracy, and corruption. Clearly taken aback by this outpouring, which rose to particularly high levels during April and May of 1957, the Party launched an anti-rightist campaign, abruptly ending the movement. Architecture was not excluded from this backlash. The *Architectural Journal,* for instance, devoted the entire September 1957 issue to attacking Hua Lanhong, designer of the Beijing Children's Hospital and a visiting faculty member at Qinghua, and Chen Zhanxiang; it included critical articles by Liang Sicheng, Wu Liangyong, and Zhang Bo.[6] Hua and Chen were branded as rightists for criticizing the government's planning policies as conservative and unresponsive and for suggesting that living standards and the quality of life were better in China before 1949. In the October issue, Hua was also accused of self-aggrandizement for claiming that his Children's Hospital was the only building in the country worthy of international notice. One critic even went so far as to take him to task for including too many windowless rooms and for making it necessary to transport corpses through the dining services area of the complex.[7]

Similar political sentiments also affected architectural education. Thus the prominent department of architecture of the Nanjing Institute of Technology called for "replacing white flags with red flags in the research and teaching of architectural history."[8] This apparently signified an internal revolt against no less a figure than Liu Dunzhen, director of the department's Architectural History Unit. According to the critics, architectural history as then taught was guilty of "favoring the past and neglecting the present, of coming from primarily personal interest, and of being history for the sake of history and research for the sake of research."[9] Also attacked was the content of the courses: 90 percent of the material was on ancient history, "approached [not] from the perspective of present needs and seldom using a Marxist point of view to analyze history, and hardly relating to production and reality."[10] In short, the prevailing methodology of architectural history, which was similar to that at other schools, was roundly denounced as being fundamentally bourgeois, arcane, and "primarily a genre of connoisseurs."[11] By this time, the socialist use value of architecture, as well as knowledge of how it played into issues such as class struggle and present-day economic realities in China, was becoming pronounced, as questions about both appropriate cultural content and material and technical application began to be asked more directly.

In the national sphere, matters of political alignment had cleared up appreciably with the promulgation, in February 1958, of the "Great Leap Forward." Frustrated by what they saw as a lack of productive economic progress, in spite of earlier calls to action, Mao Zedong and others called for still further efforts in heavy industrial production—or, in Marxist parlance, an even greater emphasis on the means of primary production. Under the slogan of "more, quicker, better, cheaper" (*duo kuai hao sheng*), production quotas throughout the country were raised considerably and the entire population was mobilized. Farmers were pulled off the land and put to work on major public works projects, steel—often unusable—was produced in backyard furnaces, and the people's commune came of age in a further attempt at social reform in the direction of real communism. Overall, the National People's Congress was looking for 20 percent increases in the production of coal, steel, and electricity over a three-year period, with the goal of surpassing British production levels in similar sectors within fifteen years. Indeed, at the end of the first year, official figures describing production increases were impressive. The national income accumulation rate, for instance, rose from 24.9 percent in 1957 to 33.9 percent in 1958; the number of large and medium-sized projects completed in 1958 exceeded the forecast of the original plan by a whopping 39.8 percent. But unfortunately, this dramatic shift and gross imbalance in economic production also sowed the seeds for later disaster, as the ratio between agricultural workers and industrial laborers decreased from 12.8:1 to 3.5:1 and urban populations began to fluctuate wildly.[12]

No doubt spurred on by these events, in October 1958 the Ministry of Construction hosted a conference on architectural history, attended by members of the leading teaching and professional institutions. During the proceedings, conference-goers "sharply renounced bourgeois and unrealistic thinking in the field of architecture history"; they also resolved to produce, collectively, three texts by the following year—the tenth anniversary of the People's Republic of China.[13] Both Liang Sicheng and Liu Dunzhen, formerly of the Institute of Chinese Architecture, delivered self-critical addresses. As Liang described it, "the Institute's methodology was formalist and revivalist, coming from the United States." Moreover, after speaking about the role of the Institute in archaeology, he declared that "the spectre of the Institute is still with us, and our minds have yet to be reformed."[14] Liang seemed to recant his position of the early 1950s: "I wanted to give a revivalist tone to Beijing's architecture. I stood on the grounds of the bourgeoisie and objected to the proletariat. . . . My investigations only talk about buildings and not people, only temples and not housing. . . . The study of history is to aid practice, to use the past as lessons for the present. Otherwise they have no use."[15] Liang also invoked Mao's concepts of *jinghua* and *zaopo*, observing that the deeper architects' involvement in practice, the more they learn. Apparently, even China's leading architectural historian was questioning the relevance of more theoretical deliberation and the role of tradition in a modern world, as leading habitually in the direction of formal revivalism.[16] Liang Sicheng, like many of his colleagues, was moving toward making much less of a distinction, if any distinction at all, between the architecture of a presumed realm of high culture and the buildings of a more popular sphere.

In the middle of 1959, the Ministry of Construction, together with the Architectural Society of China, took on directly the question of architecture as art during a conference about the seemingly prosaic topic of residential architectural standards. As Zhang Qinnan explained, there Liu Xiufeng, the minister of building engineering, "emphasized that the basic principle of socialist architecture should be the embodiment of a maximum concern for the human being: which he clearly saw in socially progressive terms and, hence, [as] practicality, economy or affordability and the superiority of socialism to care for people."[17] Liang Sicheng did not disagree, though he made a case for both architectural tradition and innovation. He called the prevailing doctrine of function, economy, and appearance where circumstances allow "itself dialectical," stating that "this is first manifested in its order. We undertake architecture first for some function." Here "socialist architecture demands that we meet the functional demands of people with the most economical means. Hence function becomes the premise of economy."[18] Liang then proceeded to argue that "economy" is included almost tautologically, speculating that if the Party's earlier demand for appearance and aesthetic qualities were now redundant, then function would suffice; furthermore, the beauty of architecture would immediately become manifest if function and structure were given reasonable consideration.

More interesting was Liang's proposal for achieving an appropriate appearance. Beginning with the observation that "tradition and innovation are two sides of a contradiction"—whose dominant side, consistent with progressive socialist rhetoric, is innovation—he argued that it was necessary to set "innovation on the foundations of tradition." He concluded, again swerving away from revivalism, that "in the process of innovation, we break some of the old, and raise the new."[19] Others at the conference made similar points, although perhaps not with the same philosophical elegance and, admittedly, drawing on few supporting examples. Yet they agreed that the "art of architecture" did matter and, despite their strongly left-leaning progressive stances, that the Chinese architectural tradition could have a positive role to play, if only in providing the starting point from which to move forward.

Actual architectural production during the late 1950s was eclectic, further illustrating both the difficulty experienced by the Chinese architects, as they attempted to effect in practice what theory and perhaps a sense of duty required, and the uneasiness they felt about moving collectively in a formal direction determined in advance. For example, the imposing Main Building on the Qinghua campus, designed by Guan Zhaoye and others from the faculty, was unabashedly neoclassical in composition; it also showed a strong Soviet realist influence (no doubt

36   The Main Building on the Qinghua campus, Beijing, by Guan Zhaoye and others, 1957–1959.

for political reasons) in the predominantly vertical proportions of the fenestration and in pi-lasters wrapped by a strong horizontal cornice line at the top, as well as in the long rectangular columns of the entrance portico and the colonnaded links between various segments of the building complex.[20] The overall plan was symmetrical, with two wings defining a paved and for-mally landscaped forecourt and an equally formal landscape at the back around the semicircular bulge of the three-story main auditorium. The Soviet influence was only to be expected; in fact, a number of the Qinghua architecture faculty, including Zhu Changzhong and Wang Guoyu, graduated from the Moscow School of Architecture. The Beijing Telecommunications Building (1958) by Lin Leyi (1916–1988), a 1948 graduate of the Georgia Institute of Technology in the United States, was similarly symmetrical and neoclassical in composition; it had a four-faced clock tower over the central portion and a protruding central bay, also with strong vertical pro-portions.[21] Like the main complex at Qinghua, the building had a sober masonry and concrete composition, relatively unadorned and relatively expressive of both the structure and the build-ing program. Eclecticism could also be found in Zhang Bo's Qianmen Hotel in Beijing (1956), with a composition and plan not too dissimilar from his earlier Friendship Hotel and yet without the traditional profuse Chinese decorative program.[22] The central bay of the front facade rose the equivalent of nine stories above the street, with a grand story-and-a-half-high entrance lobby, reception area, and function room protruding from the front portico, running through the building, and terminating in a semicircular apselike enclosure in the rear courtyard. That court-yard was framed by two wings of the hotel, much like the back of the Main Building auditorium at Qinghua. At a detailed level, however, traditional Chinese detailing could be found in the tiles and brickwork of the building's major elevations.

The culmination of architectural production during this era was undoubtedly the "Ten Great Buildings" designed to celebrate the tenth anniversary of the founding of the People's Republic in 1959, and also understandably intended to demonstrate China's new socialist architectural approach and to express its modern achievements. All ten buildings were designed by members of the Beijing Architectural Design Institute, in collaboration with other institutions, principally the Beijing Planning Bureau and the Ministry of Construction.[23] Far from representing any single architectural style, the buildings placed on display the various expressive preoccupations of the past decade or so. In speaking about the projects, Liang Sicheng carefully distinguished what

37　The Beijing Telecommunications Building, by Lin Leyi, 1958.

was by then often referred to as "cultural form" from eclecticism: eclecticism, by which he no doubt meant earlier forms of revivalism, was plagiarism of bits of an ancient heritage simply patched together, whereas cultural form—the heterogeneous architectural quality of the ten projects—drew directly on and further developed past tradition.[24]

The projects certainly were reasonably representative of where practical architectural thinking stood in China, which was far from any one stylistic orthodoxy—again, in spite of left-leaning theoretical pressures toward an architecture of progressive social reality. Also, because these celebratory projects were sponsored by those at the highest levels of government, they were spared many of the emerging parsimonious constraints of other building. In the end, the display of Chinese modernism—if it can be called that, strictly speaking—appeared mainly to reflect a mode of architectural reasoning conducted over a decade, focused on sorting out cultural essences, including past Chinese traditions and foreign influences, along with various other functional exigencies and material or structural implications. Liu Xiufeng described the thematic common denominator in terms similar to Liang's: it was a quality "metamorphosed from Chinese tradition" through contemporary material and technical circumstances, as well as foreign influence, and was, in Maoist terms, "digested into something that belonged to the Chinese."[25]

Three of the ten projects actually subscribed to the "Big Roof" tradition, at least in the dominant aspects of their appearance. Three others were primarily socialist realist, and another three were more or less modern. The last project, the State Guest House—removed as it was from the public eye—received little architectural attention. Yet all the projects to some degree included elements of expression that had been a part of architectural thinking and discussion during the past decade, particularly on the relation between modern architecture and the use of Chinese tradition.

Of the "Big Roof" projects, the Beijing Railway Station, on which Yang Tingbao worked, arguably included in its design the most superficial use of large-scale traditional Chinese elements.[26] The two towers at either end of the front elevation of the main hall, as well as two smaller towers at the ends of the main facade, were crowned by pyramidal upturned tiled roofs with traditional eaves detailing. The documentation available from various stages of the design process suggests that a commitment to using traditional Chinese architectural elements was not originally part of the plan.[27] Much of the remainder of the project was modern, including the curved concrete roof shell over the main hall, with a thin strip of clerestory windows between it and the main vertical structure below. Five smaller concrete shells on the concourse covered the links over the railway tracks that provided access to the platforms through enclosed unadorned stairways. Indeed, the front facade of the building bore similarities to Yang Tingbao's Shenyang Railway Station of 1927 (see figure 24), which strongly resembled many railway stations abroad. The large plaza in front of the Beijing station, though broader, did not break entirely with the traditional spatial continuity of the urban street.

Of the two other buildings showing the most traditional influence, Zhang Bo's People's Cultural Hall was the more architecturally rigorous. Its three major building components accommodated an auditorium and meeting and function rooms, linked asymmetrically together in plan and elevation by two halls with offices above.[28] The dominant element of the design was a tower, again containing offices, rising some fourteen floors at the center of the overall horizontal composition. The square columns, the pilasters, and the checkerboard pattern of deep window reveals on the facades of the tower were all functionally well integrated into the building's architecture and were modern in expression. While the roofs and cornices along the top of the building, including a double-eaved glazed tiled pyramidal capping of the tower, were all of a traditional Chinese form, some elements of a socialist realist architecture apparently crept into the design in the prominent front portico.

Finally, the National Agricultural Exhibition Center, located outside of the center of Beijing, was the most idiosyncratic of the three in its design.[29] The pagodalike roofs over main exhibition spaces were certainly traditionally Chinese in their inspiration, although the arched and domed structures elsewhere in the complex, as well as the rows of columns protruding like concrete fins, were modern. Around the extensive grounds of the complex could also be found large groups of socialist realist statues and futuristic light stanchions, adding further to the amalgam of architectural and sculptural styles. The spatial layout of the project combined axial, symmetrical neoclassical site planning with unfolding traditional patterns of organization also involving direction and symmetry—a further reminder of the confusion or "collaging" of traditional and modern that had been taking place in architecture from the Republican period on.

38   Beijing Railway Station, by Yang Tingbao, 1958–1959.
39   The National Agricultural Exhibition Center, Beijing, 1959.

Two of the ostensibly socialist realist projects were located opposite each other on two sides of the now renovated and enlarged Tiananmen Square, with the apparent mass of both buildings increased by the use of raised platforms at their base in the manner of the traditional *xumizuo*, described earlier. On the western side was the Great Hall of the People, designed primarily by Zhang Bo; it was enclosed along its main and end facades by a massive colonnade of three square columns rising up to a thick cornice that wrapped around the top of the entire building.[30] The huge front entrance, which protruded slightly beyond the remaining building line, included tall, well-proportioned columns and a strong cornice emblazoned with the seal of the People's Republic, designed by Liang Sicheng and a colleague at Qinghua University. In all, the complex was very large, at 336 meters by 174 meters; at the central building component it rose 40 meters high. Although it had the overall appearance of a single structure, the neoclassical layout allowed penetration of the building mass by light wells and courtyards. The central part of the complex was composed of the portico leading first to a grand entrance hall and

40　　The Great Hall of the People, Beijing, by Zhang Bo, 1959.

then to a large, three-level assembly hall with a seating capacity of 10,000. Another significant element of the overall building program was an elaborate banquet hall that could hold about 5,000 people. Traditional Chinese architectural elements were confined largely to decoration, including that along the eaves line and the vast fretwork of vertical and horizontal mullions of the glazed wall behind the columns of the front portico. The most-cited precedent for this complex was the League of Nations Building in Geneva. During its preliminary design phase, Zhou Enlai was deeply involved in the project, emphasizing, according to Zhang Bo, that the hall should be "safe, express greatness with reason," project "humanism," and be "inclusive," "embracing all the *jinghua* of old and new, Western and Chinese."[31]

The Museum of Chinese Revolution and History, located on the eastern side of the square and designed primarily by Zhang Kaiji (of earlier "Big Roof" notoriety), projected a similarly monumental presence.[32] Very tall, almost freestanding masonry and reinforced concrete columns along the front facade elongated the otherwise strong horizontal lines of the building

41   The Museum of Chinese Revolution and History, Beijing, by Zhang Kaiji, 1959.

complex. In plan, the layout blurred distinctions between neoclassical composition and traditional Chinese courtyard schemes, incorporating essences of both in a manner that Zhou Enlai probably would have approved. Also very large, the complex measured some 313 meters (along Tiananmen Square) by 149 meters.

The third building of the socialist realist group was the Military Museum of the Chinese Revolution, located away from Tiananmen Square on the west side of the city. There the plan arrangement was more thoroughly neoclassical in the Western tradition, with two courtyards again arranged symmetrically on either side of the taller central portion of the building complex, crowned by a spire that resembled simultaneously the tower of the Soviet Exhibition Hall and the top of a Buddhist stupa. The design intention, however, was probably more Western than Eastern in its orientation, given the star at the tower's top. Traditional Chinese decorative motifs were to be found on the building complex's interior, particularly in the main function rooms.

The Beijing Workers' Stadium was the most thoroughly modern of the buildings in the remaining group, largely devoid even of Chinese decoration except for the curving bridge structure, with traditionally influenced balustrades, that formed the main approach to the sports facility winding past large realist statues in various athletic poses.[33] The reinforced concrete structure of the stadium itself was an expression both of its function and of engineering exigencies. Two tiers of seating rose up from the open floor of the complex, curving in the form of a giant ellipse. But perhaps the most startling feature of the building was the Y-shaped overhang lightly poised above the entire complex. In all, the stadium was a celebration of China's newly acquired modern engineering prowess. Structure and function were also strongly expressed in Zhang Bo's Minzu Hotel, a large slablike eleven-story building with two wings extending back into the site.[34] Apart from the registration of floor slabs and columns, the external facades were punctuated by recessed window openings and protruding balconies at regular intervals. Traditional Chinese decoration was largely confined to the strong horizontal line of the balustrade running the entire length of the building above the main floor, the balcony enclosures themselves, and the cornice line at the top of the building. It also appeared around the main entrance, in a manner consistent with most of the other buildings in the anniversary celebration. The final "modern" building, the Overseas Chinese Mansion, also had Chinese decoration around its balconies, although the remainder of the building facade was a sober expression of window openings and an eight-story-high wall plane.[35] To follow the site boundaries, the plan of the building featured a chamfered corner near the center of the complex at the main entrance. Like all the other projects, the mansion was made to look as symmetrical as possible in its overall composition, with the building mass deployed to give a monumental appearance.

By 1962 misgivings were being expressed in China about modernist architecture in the West. While praising innovative construction methods, savings in material used, and engineering achievements, commentators criticized what they saw to be a formalist trend in current architectural thinking, which one writer put down to "capitalist companies' need for exaltation" that resulted in "bizarre forms and styles."[36] Coming under particular attack were Eero Saarinen's TWA terminal in New York, Hugh Stubbins's Berlin Conference Center, and Le Corbusier's Ronchamp chapel.[37] By contrast, Pier Luigi Nervi's slightly later exhibition hall, with its lightweight ferroconcrete shell roof, was admired as appropriate for displaying industrial and scientific products and praised for giving "the appearance of firmness and complexity."[38] At the core of the criticism seems to have been a mistrust of modern architecture in the service of the upper class, industry, and big business, which made it just another consumer product. As one critic put it, the early progressive position of modernism "in pursuit of a new and rational approach to suit the demands of production and life" had been abandoned, resulting in what he saw as a "tendency to abuse and misuse the latest technology and material, not to mention various extreme forms of ostentation and waste."[39]

Also at issue was the difficult problem of monumentality being confronted by the Chinese themselves, and what they saw as a failure on the part of modernist architects in the West to produce monuments of any value. According to Wu Huanjia, a noted historian of Western architecture in China, it was as if some essential purpose and soul had vanished from modern Western architecture, even though its technical expertise continued to develop and expand.[40] Once again this kind of analysis pitted "essence" against "use," as commentators looked for a deeper cultural meaning in contemporary architecture. In so doing, they concluded that architecture cannot exist artistically without a strong sense of progressive social ideology—which is, after all, its "essence." Clearly, it was this perceived essence of early modern architecture, Soviet influence notwithstanding, that first drew Chinese attention during the postrevolutionary era.

But the Chinese, unlike those in the West, could never entirely accept the idea of an architecture constituted by its own substance, function, and making.

Against this backdrop, architectural production in China during the early 1960s continued to look for a firmer cultural footing and an appropriate socialist style. Modernism continued to be employed in a relatively orthodox manner, as architects showed considerable interest in functional requirements and in corresponding engineering and construction innovations. The Beijing Workers' Gymnasium (1961), for instance, by Xiong Ming and Sun Bingyuan, had an audience rotunda some 94 meters in diameter that was the first in China to use a suspended cable structure.[41] The facility was reminiscent of Nervi's Olympic structure, with a similar program; its exterior facade was a straightforward expression of the gymnasium's columnar structure, intermittent stairways, and galleries at various levels. By contrast, Dai Nianci's National Gallery of Art (1962), another project in Beijing in which the state was highly involved, continued with the theme of the "Big Roof."[42] The tiled roofs ascended in layers above the entrance, topped by an upturned pyramidal form; they were emphatically traditional in overall presentation and detail, as was the latticework between the columns on the ground floor and around some of the windows. The horizontal symmetrical massing of the building, especially when approached from the front, also conveyed a palpable sense of traditional Chinese monumentality. At the same time, the curved external articulation of the main hall at the back of the complex and the planar walls, obviously built from contemporary materials, gave the building a modern quality.

Dai Nianci (1920–1991) was yet another distinguished Chinese architect of the second generation, who graduated from National Central University in Chongqing (one class ahead of Wu Liangyong, in 1942) and later studied and worked under Yang Tingbao.[43] He served as an adjunct professor at Qinghua University and succeeded Yang Tingbao as president of the Architectural Society of China. His earlier design of the west wing of the Beijing Hotel, in the 1950s, included a lobby with eight very ornate Chinese columns; and his later Queli Hotel, adjoining the Confucius Temple in Qufu in Shandong province, was also appropriately traditionalist in roof and other forms, while contemporary in its material palette and surface details.[44] Historicism was even more marked in the Jianzhen Memorial Hall at Yangzhou. Constructed in 1963, this was one of Liang Sicheng's few built architectural works; among other things, it demonstrated the con-

42   Shanghai in the manner of the Beijing Workers' Gymnasium, by Xiong Ming and Sun Bingyuan, 1961.

43   The National Gallery of Art, Beijing, by Dai Nianci, 1962.

sistent Chinese proclivity toward, and even preference for, traditional forms of expression when buildings were memorials or were close to historical sites.[45]

Criticism of current modern architecture in the West also coincided with the Socialist Education Movement (1962–1965). Serving as a preamble to the Cultural Revolution, it focused primarily on grassroots corruption in the countryside. A strong political shift to the left led to the "Four Cleanups" or "Purifications Campaign" that targeted wrongdoing in the increasingly decentralized management of communes, away from state collectives.[46] Specifically, the "Four Cleanups" investigated corruption in the keeping of collective accounts, the management of communal granaries, the use of public property, and activities at work locations. Many students, university officials, and others not directly concerned with these rural matters were ordered into the countryside to participate in the campaign. In the Cultural Revolution—the "Great Revolution in Proletarian Culture"—that followed, work teams were sent into the universities, polarizing national Red Guards into both defiance and defense of school administrations.[47]

Such vast disruption obviously affected architects and architecture. For example, posters attacking Liang Sicheng, then head of the architecture department at Qinghua, began appearing in 1966, unfairly accusing him of being a "reactionary academic authority" and (among other things) of collaborating with the former mayor of Beijing, Peng Zhen, against the Communist Party immediately after the revolution.[48] As elsewhere, conflict and denunciation escalated between 1966 and 1967, and terror reigned on the Qinghua campus as houses were ransacked and hapless victims suffered appalling physical abuse. In 1968 the People's Liberation Army was called on to disperse the Red Guards by "sending them down" (xiafang), mainly to rural areas. Many high-ranking Party members were purged as a result of the extreme factionalism that had broken out. The Cultural Revolution gradually wound down—particularly with the death of Lin Biao, the leader who had been named the official successor of Mao, after he allegedly participated in a coup attempt in 1971—but it ended only with the death of Mao Zedong and the arrest and trial of the "Gang of Four" in 1976.[49] In the meantime, many had lost their lives as a direct or indirect result of this terrible upheaval, including Liang Sicheng in 1972.

In this extreme ultraleftist political environment, little building of note was undertaken; even the term "architecture" was denounced as being too far removed from a direct reckoning and engagement with the real needs of the people for shelter, an attack that showed just how far theorizing in the direction of "production and life" had gone. Concepts like "functionalism" were also condemned, not simply as bourgeois but because some saw an architecture that was simply utilitarian as potentially lacking sufficient human dignity. In 1965 the Institute of Architectural Research abolished history and theory in the discipline; regional planning followed.[50] History and theory, in particular, were seen as being feudal, revivalist, and capitalist in orientation and thus incapable of reinvigorating the socialist revolution. Yet during this period of sharp contradictions, the libraries of major institutions like Qinghua University continued to subscribe to and circulate major Western architectural journals. Zheng Guoqing, the librarian at Qinghua, did much to keep the collection together and followed the administration's policy of discontinuing journal subscriptions only on economic rather than ideological grounds—except for stopping all the incoming Russian journals.[51]

Those few buildings of importance completed during this time were almost entirely intended to support external relations, such as they were, between China and the outside world and to put a good face on things. Thus Chinese domination of the World Table Tennis Championship in the 1960s spawned new sports halls and stadiums in several cities, and hotels were built to accommodate foreign trade exhibitions, particularly in the southern city of Guangzhou. The Capital Stadium in western Beijing, for example, built between 1966 and 1968 and designed principally by Zhang Depei, Xiong Ming, and Xu Zhenchang, contained a competition area large enough for twenty-four games of table tennis to be played at the same time, before some 18,000 people.[52] The same area could also be used for ice hockey and gymnastic competitions. A simple rectangle in plan, the building primarily expressed its architecture in the straightforward yet elegant column lines, with horizontally banded fenestration located behind, and in the interior sweep of the space-framed roof. Overall, the building had a monumental stature somewhat reminiscent of earlier projects, and like them it had a strong pedestal base. The Kuangquan Hotel (1964–1966) in Conghua, about two hours from Guangzhou, was far more organic, especially in its attempt to revive the Chinese tradition of combining landscape with architecture.[53] Also known as the Mineral Springs Resort, this complex was designed by Mo Bozhi, the chief architect of the Guangzhou Institute of Architectural Design. It featured the extension of a pool of water from a courtyard garden set between two wings of the hotel into the ground-floor lounge area. The interpenetration of internal and external space was further amplified by corridors and

44 The Capital Stadium, western Beijing, by Zhang Depei, Xiong Ming, and Xu Zhenchang, 1966–1968.

45 Nanjing Airport, by Yang Tingbao, 1971–1972.

46 East Wing of the Beijing Hotel, by Zhang Bo, 1972.
47 High-rise housing in the Jianguomenwai Diplomatic Compound, Beijing, by the Beijing Architectural Design Institute, ca. 1976.
48 Parallel-block housing at Melon Lane, Shanghai, ca. 1975.

stairways overhanging the landscaped space and by pathways encouraging movement between the inside and outside of the building.

By 1972 Deng Xiaoping (1904–1997), one of the early fathers of Chinese Communism who had been purged during the early days of the Cultural Revolution, had struggled back into power; as Party secretary, he began to impose political stability and make possible the country's economic revival. Against a ruinous background of mismanagement and neglect, he slowly yet effectively undertook a process of rebuilding and new construction, focusing particularly on the great need to improve infrastructure and provide housing. To implement these programs with the scanty resources available, a modern architecture appeared from the early to late 1970s of extreme simplicity and, at times, considerable elegance.

The Hangzhou Airport (1971), by the Zhejiang Provincial Institute of Architectural Design, for instance, was both modern and uncomplicated.[54] The Nanjing Airport, built a year later and designed by Yang Tingbao, was also very modern; its simple flat roof was supported at regular intervals by columns, which were clad in between with plain spandrel panels and straightforward glazing.[55] The control tower at one end of the building was elegantly proportioned and articulated architecturally in a modern idiom. Like Yang's railroad stations, which always seem to embody the essence of that building type regardless of other formal preoccupations, so too this airport terminal allows one to recall numerous others.

Zhang Bo's new East Wing of the Beijing Hotel, built in 1972 to host Americans in their new relationship with China, had many of the same qualities and strongly conformed to the modern hotel type.[56] Rising some twenty stories above the Avenue of Eternal Peace, the main street at the front of the building, the building also had several floors below grade. Consisting of a rectangular slab with wings at both ends, the entire building was articulated on the exterior by a regular rhythm of window openings and balconies. A prominent cornice line and roof structure completed the complex and also gave it a well-proportioned monumentality. Internal circulation was designed in an efficient and functional manner, with a central corridor providing access to rooms placed along its length on both sides.

This relatively simple modern architecture was to continue in the mid- and high-rise buildings of the Jianguomenwai Diplomatic Compound, constructed during the second half of the 1970s, as well as in the Three Gate Housing Complex along Qiansanmen Dajie, both in Beijing.[57]

Among the most notable buildings in the diplomatic compound were several well-proportioned and conspicuously modern apartment towers located along a main street and the well-detailed and also modern Beijing International Club, all by the Beijing Design and Research Institute. The construction of the Three Gate Housing Complex (1976) sparked a debate on the merits of residential towers versus smaller walk-up slab buildings; it was decided a little later largely in favor of the latter, for economic and technical reasons that included the need to adequately service elevators in towers. Generally well regarded, the first phase of the Three Gate Housing Complex was built on a 5-kilometer-long site, along much of the southern perimeter of what was once the old city. On about 22 hectares of land and to a maximum height of 45 meters, housing was provided for around 30,000 people.[58]

Given the previous ambivalence toward architectural modernism and given what was actually built through the early 1960s, it is perhaps surprising that these and other modernist buildings were constructed during the 1970s. There are several possible explanations for the style's endurance. First, modernism was never rejected by the Chinese, despite their criticism of many contemporary Western architectural practices. Indeed, as shown above, it remained a strong strand of architectural thinking and even became dominant in theoretical circles during the left-wing advocacy of "function, economy, and appearance where circumstances allow" and the essential reorientation of architecture to focus on "production and life."

Second, the Cultural Revolution and its immediate aftermath left the country impoverished; under such conditions, the value of economic use of building materials and efficient, functional layouts of buildings outweighed a few dissenting objections. Simple, modern buildings alone could meet China's needs for production and shelter. Thus, during the later 1970s rows upon rows of worker housing (*hanglieshi* or *danyuanlou*) were built in the form of five- to seven-story walk-up parallel apartment blocks, almost devoid of architectural character beyond a bare minimum of attention to the placement of window openings and doorways. Each block, on the model of its Soviet predecessors, was usually given a correct north-south orientation and located a distance of a little less than one and a half times its height from an identical, or almost identical, neighboring building.

Third, contemporary building programs and building types such as terminals, sports facilities, and large hotels were difficult to render, or seemed nonsensical, in anything but modern form. Fourth, as mentioned earlier, apart from infrastructure and housing, much of the ostensibly modern architecture during this later period was found in buildings associated with various kinds of foreign engagements, generally between China and the West. It was as if a modern architectural "face" was expected as the Chinese began to entertain a more open diplomatic policy and attempted to place themselves in the best light for their visitors.

Finally, the problem of symbolizing a new socialist order remained. The easier separation of expressive form from functional and material circumstances that was enjoyed, especially in prominent state-sponsored buildings, up to the early 1960s—a separation that made possible "popularization" by reference to the past while at the same time moving forward in the direction of contemporary social life—no longer held (though in many smaller-scale structures, such as some housing, traditional spatial rather than stylistic forms of organization still survived). Even the Memorial Hall of Chairman Mao in Tiananmen Square, completed in 1977, though classical in detail and overall conception, was comparatively modern in its clean lines and use of materials.[59] In stark contrast, Chiang Kai-shek's Memorial Hall of 1976 in Nationalist Taipei returned almost completely to a traditional Chinese appearance of building and site layout.[60]

Indeed, this comparison points tellingly both to the sociopolitical differences in nationalism and to the existence of moments in which realpolitik and architectural expression mesh, in spite of the slipperiness of such connections. In China, at least up to this point, such moments appear to have occurred when traditional motifs are either embraced or palpably abandoned at times of extreme political conditions. In search of solidarity, although laboring under different conceptions of history and the past, both the Nationalists in the 1930s and the Communists in the early 1950s adopted stylistic and outward expressions of traditional buildings. By the 1970s, when the Communists were at the beginning of their struggle to recover from the Cultural Revolution and the Nationalists in Taiwan were in a period of isolation, the Communists had ostensibly adopted their relatively extreme form of architectural modernism, in continuing pursuit of their socialist order, and the Nationalists had become even more grandiose in their traditional references, in pursuit of national legitimacy. Moreover, in hindsight, both architectural positions seem inevitable and even necessary: it is unlikely that other intermediary forms of expression would have served the same sociopolitical purposes so well under the cultural logics prevailing in both places at the time.

49 Chiang Kai-shek's Memorial Hall, Taipei, 1976.

"I AGREE! THE THREE ELEMENTS SHOULD STAY. After all, the Committee even subdivided the program that way," said Lu Hui, gesturing toward the summary sketch Wu Feng had made of their work so far. By now the table and floor around them were strewn with sheets of tracing paper, site plans, sections of aerial photos, and parts of the Library Committee's report. *"But why do they have to be aligned at odd angles?"* she asked.

"To activate the open space and to create an unfolding view of the complex as you move forward," responded Feng.

"The site is really too small for that," commented Zhang Shaoshu. *"Perhaps if the blocks were lined up more in parallel like so, and then we could think of it much like a courtyard scheme."* As he spoke, he laid a sheet over the drawing Feng had just completed.

"But what about the idea of an unfolding perception of the building as you move through it? That was your idea this morning—wasn't it?" Feng inquired.

"Yes, but it could still happen. . . . Think of the Imperial Library," Shaoshu replied quickly.

"Isn't that comparison a bit grandiose?" questioned Hui.

"Not really, it was quite a small complex," responded Shaoshu. *"Anyway, the cone of vision was clearly manipulated by the placement of pavilions and gateways, so that you could never really see the whole long courtyard at once."* He added, *"Furthermore, I don't see why those compositional principles wouldn't work for us today."*

"I thought we were all about xin shiji," said Feng with a certain touch of irony in his voice.

"The New Age! I thought that all ended in Tiananmen Square?" Hui broke in, not at all sure about the reference Feng was making.

"Tell me about it; I was there!" shot back Feng, with a certain pride in his voice.

"I didn't know that," said Hui, genuinely surprised.

"There's a lot of things you probably don't know. Besides, I don't mean it that specifically. I only meant the need to move past all the dichotomies between old and new we have been working with for so long," Feng went on, sounding to Hui more like Shaoshu than like himself.

"Another moment of foreign influence," Shaoshu chimed in, adding, *"and all those denunciations retracted."*

"Have you ever noticed that as soon as we have another round of foreign influence, the 'big roofs' come back?" commented Feng. *"Maybe it's some kind of defense mechanism."*

"What are you talking about?" demanded Shaoshu. He added tartly. "It was a lot more complicated than that, or were you asleep? A flowering of intellectual ideas does not just come down from the sky. Think of . . . think of the Weimar Republic. Yes, that's a good parallel."

"I'm sure it doesn't and I'd rather not," replied Feng wearily, trying to avoid the issue and get back to the project. Yet he could not help adding, "Although the question is: What to do with the flowering? And look what happened in Germany," again sounding a lot like Shaoshu but not wanting him to have the last word on the subject.

"If we go with the courtyard scheme, then the entrance and main circulation should be placed centrally," observed Hui, concentrating on the drawing in front of her.

"Thank you, Hui!" Feng said out loud, though to himself. "At least someone else wants to get on with it."

"Why do you say that?" asked Shaoshu, immediately pulled back into the fray. "Let me see what you've got up on the screen now."

THE "CULTURE FEVER"

THE "CULTURE FEVER" that gripped China between roughly 1979 and 1989 was a re-action to the revolutionary orthodoxy and official ideology of the contemporary state; at the same time, it was shaped by how individuals both absorbed and reacted to Western cultural the-ory, scholarship, and thinking. Sometimes referred to as the "Great Cultural Discussion," this cultural undertaking was very broad and self-reflective—probably the broadest since the May Fourth Movement, affecting many aspects of artistic and daily life. As an avant-garde move-ment Culture Fever was made possible and was formed by the sociocultural experience of Deng Xiaoping's China, beginning in 1978 with the "Four Modernizations" (*Sige xiandaihua*) of agricul-ture, industry, science, and technology and defense. The modernizations also involved a historic opening to the West in 1979, together with considerable economic reform—though that reform was still governed by socialist principles.[1] A common theme among the various strands of this broad cultural movement was a concern with opposing not Eastern and Western positions but tradition and modernization—or, more radically, an embrace of the idea of being both Chinese and modern, or neither Chinese nor modern. It thus put into question the universal and hege-monic notion of modernity, both examining China's status as an underdeveloped socialist nation and critically analyzing Western scholarship and technical expertise.

This "Cultural Discussion" had two almost immediate results: a significantly enlarged capacity of individuals to reposition their cultural selves outside the framework of official ideology, and a reassertion of traditional values—by now familiar, as it had recurred at every step of China's modernization. Many heard the Party's Central Committee discussions of December 1978, which advocated socialist modernization instead of class struggle and emphasized "emancipating the mind and seeking truth through facts," as a clarion call for open experimentation with cultural issues that either had lain dormant through the terror of the Cultural Revolution or were newly brought to popular attention through outside exchange. The movement was "feverish" because of rapid economic growth and the attendant social change, as well as the hopes raised by futuristic visions of what China might become, now that it was emerging from the sociopolitical and economic quagmire of the Cultural Revolution.

This fever was no doubt heightened by the collective sense of the magnitude of the gap, now more visible, between an isolated society and the rest of the modern world, and the corresponding length that China would have to go to catch up. By far the most explicit outpouring of these sentiments took place in literature, art, film, theater, and other media of high culture, although architecture (particularly architectural theory and criticism) was not as disengaged as it had arguably been during the May Fourth Movement. A "new wave," as it were, was sweeping through almost all forms of cultural discussion and production—belatedly, perhaps, in comparison with similar movements in the West, but nevertheless with candor and forcefulness. Another common theme was a growing concern for humanity itself under conditions of increasing modernity, often expressed as a need to avoid the trap of mechanical rationalism and the corresponding loss of a sense of dignity. In many significant ways, Gao Xingjian's book *Soul Mountain* (*Lingshan*) captured the contours and thrust of this wave.[2] Begun early in the 1980s and completed in exile in 1989, this voluminous work portrays a free repositioning of the self by intriguing multiplication of the narrator, as "I" alternates with "you," "she," and "he." As the narrative captures a trek in an isolated mountainous region, storytelling in encounters with villagers, and confrontations with the majestic splendors of nature, Gao's prose moves backward and forward through both his own and the country's history in a compelling search for higher meaning.

Within the Cultural Discussion several lines of thinking emerged; each was perhaps predictable, given prior cultural positions and the release that was taking place from earlier intellectual and speculative constraints.[3] Some focused on the here and now and on the near future as the only appropriate grounds on which contemporary culture could be formed. Picking up largely where the May Fourth Movement had left off, they broadly pledged themselves to apply positivistic scientific and logical thinking to social and cultural issues. Moreover, advocates of this position on cultural matters inevitably forged close links with members of the "reform bureaucracy" within the Chinese Communist Party, such as General Secretary Hu Yaobang and the then premier, Zhao Ziyang. Scientific management and political utilitarianism were natural allies. Gan Yang, a prominent voice among those with a near future orientation, was for wholesale Westernization, arguing that cultural debates were not abstract discussions but vital responses to modernity.[4] Another proponent—Jin Guantao, a chemist in the Chinese Academy of Sciences—edited and published a pamphlet titled "Toward the Future" that treated a diverse range of topics; in it, "contemporaneity" was presented as the only relevant ground for cultural production.[5] In this declaration, an echo of Mao Zedong's insistence that movement forward must be based on everyday objective facts could certainly be heard, though it lacked Mao's attention to past traditions and practices. Indeed, those who stressed contemporaneity without explicitly attending to the historical development of China's sociocultural space had difficulty articulating the crucial question of how Chinese modernity, because of its particular manner of emergence, could be an alternative to any other kind of modernity.

Others favored a second line of thinking, often followed in the past, as a concern for cultural identity led them initially to return to the past and to reexamine China's Confucian heritage and its prospects for adequately guiding contemporary cultural life. Many proponents of this position gathered around the Academy of Chinese Culture, which was presided over by Tang Yijie, a professor of Chinese philosophy at Beijing University; they were committed to the intriguing idea that the ongoing cultural enterprise was deeply rooted in a dynamic conception of tradition that could support different and even opposing positions about tradition and modernity.[6] For them, the cultural structure of tradition and that of modernity could be reconciled or even were identical. They also harbored the idea that if traditional elements exist and participate in the present, the result can be a salutary transcendence of the modern state through Confucian ideals such as the harmony between human and nature, as well as the practice of virtue. They therefore often conducted a critique of modernity in the name of the past.

Tang Yijie, for example, argued not for scientific methodology but for "modernization of humanity"; in that sense, he regarded the May Fourth "enlightenment project" as unfinished.[7] One way of going forward, according to him, was by paying special attention to the local ethnographic content, whose sum total helped define the national cultural tradition.

Another culturalist, Li Zehou, also advocated a strong place for Confucian ideals. Li, a philosopher and expert in the history of Chinese thought, as well as a significant influence on the younger generation of Chinese writers, took issue with Zhang Zhidong's nineteenth-century distinction between Chinese scholarship as "substance" and Western scholarship as "function"; his own formulation effectively reversed the terms, repositioning "the Western" as substance and "the Chinese" as function.[8] Li, however, here referred not to Western learning but to the socioeconomic process of modernization itself, and by invoking Chinese "function" he reaffirmed both the validity and practice of traditional values, morally and aesthetically. Rather than seeing Western technology as a force able to transform and hence modernize Chinese traditions and ways of life, he was arguing that Chinese traditions and values had the power to reform modern ways of life otherwise dominated by technology. His question was a relatively simple one. Can Chinese society remain consciously Chinese while fully adopting modern science, technology, and all the principles of social organization that go with it? As he put it, could China sufficiently "adopt or retain the moralism necessary to maintain its power and splendor of sacrificing the self for the other, private for public, . . . the customary handling of human relationships accumulated in Chinese culture, . . . and prevent China from slipping into cruel relationships involving money, extreme individualism, . . . mechanical rationalism, and so forth?"[9]

Those adhering to a third line of thinking, positioned roughly between the other two, evinced a "critical theoretical" concern with the reinterpretation of culture from a more subject-centered orientation—an orientation that would take into account a new understanding of the past, based more on contemporary approaches than on official ideology. They were sometimes dubbed "wholesale Westerners" or "hermeneuticists," labels acquired from their use and advocacy of "critical theory" and other Western cultural interpretive frameworks from the likes of Hans-Georg Gadamer, Martin Heidegger, and Paul Ricoeur.[10] Many adherents were either students or former students at Beijing University's Institute for Foreign Philosophy, who were all well-versed in various Western theoretical discourses, though for most of the institute's existence the intellectual environment was quite hostile to such theory. Indeed, it had been founded precisely because Mao Zedong had advised, in effect, "know your enemy." A critical quarterly, *Culture: China and the World,* was founded by the critical thinkers in Beijing around 1985; it helped shift the dominant binary in comparative thinking from East versus West to tradition versus modernity.

Members of this loosely affiliated group saw the infusion of strong foreign (i.e., modern) ideas as necessary to break the hold of official ideology as a cultural master narrative, essentially by helping to relativize its referents and sign system. Accordingly, this form of interpretation enabled the notion of the subject to be decentered, as had been done in the West, through a process of constant questioning and unraveling of accepted sociocultural positions regarding the present and the past, a process that Gadamer might have recommended. One proponent, Liu Xiaofeng, even suggested that the discussion of modernity and tradition be suspended in favor of questioning both in the unfolding of the present, and deplored the whole idea of comparative culture.[11] Again like Gadamer, he saw tradition not as something ready-made or invented but as part of contemporary cultural production, so that one simultaneously interprets it and participates in it.[12]

Inevitably, these three positions toward the past and near future also mixed and at least partially amalgamated, even as there was wholesale clamoring for what appeared to be new and popular elsewhere. It was an uncertain yet intoxicating time in China, as many in cultural circles were rather abruptly exposed to a broad array of new and foreign ideas and ways of conducting themselves intellectually and artistically—albeit with constraints, such as those imposed by the official "oppose spiritual pollution" campaign of 1983.

As noted, the Great Cultural Discussion spilled over into architecture, architectural education, and especially architectural criticism, as similar discussions had in the West, resulting in a comprehensive reevaluation of both the role of tradition and the promise of modernism. In this and other respects, debate returned to the central topic of the 1950s regarding expression, but now with a more extensive and better-informed critical perspective. Broader cultural discussions had equipped those in architecture, as elsewhere, with new logic and insight to carry on the same enduring tussle. Certainly the insularity of the former Soviet point of view had gone, and theorists and practitioners alike appeared willing to revise the "hard lines" of earlier positions.

After the onset of the Four Modernizations in 1978, Tong Jun published (in 1980) an impressive and well-documented survey titled *New Architecture and Styles*.[13] Subjects considered in the book, written in 1977, ranged from contributions by such people as Sir Joseph Paxton and John Ruskin in the nineteenth century, all the way up to present-day practitioners and theorists. Particularly noteworthy was the coverage of post–World War II developments in the West, including Team 10, the metabolists, brutalism, purism, and postmodernism, as well as an interesting chapter summarizing urban design and planning from Haussmann, Ebenezer Howard, Patrick Geddes, and Patrick Abercrombie forward. The tone of this publication differed from that of past studies, discussing the works both in much richer historical perspective and from a self-consciously contemporary viewpoint on architecture. In 1979, the history faculties at Qinghua, Tongji, Nanjing, and Tianjin Universities or Institutes of Technology also addressed the lack of readily accessible material in the field of twentieth-century and contemporary architecture, especially from the West, by coediting a reference book, *Foreign Architecture from Recent History;* it was eventually published in 1982.[14]

In addition, a reinvigorated Architectural Society of China in 1979 founded *The Architect (Jianzhushi),* a journal that was to become its primary organ for conducting discussions on a regular basis. In October 1978, the society also held a "reengagement conference" explicitly to discuss the modernization of architecture and the matter of architectural style. The speeches were generally short and timid—except for one. When it came his turn, Liu Hongdian was sharply critical of the prior period, recalling his experience while editing *Principles of Residential Architecture,* when the prevailing doctrine forced him to devote too little space to formal and aesthetic issues. He then noted, with a nod in the direction of a critical cultural concern for how matters might proceed, that this "narrowness of our mindset [had] yet to be remedied," expressing the hope that both the new and revitalized journals would promote more debate on theory and research.[15] One such journal was *World Architecture* (*Shijie jianzhu*), which began publication in 1980 under the auspices of Qinghua University. Another was *City Planning Review,* which under Wu Liang-yong's able editorship often focused on important cultural issues of the day in urban design.

Particularly with regard to architectural expression, reappraisal and stocktaking essentially operated on two levels. The first involved a vindication of past practices, including the "Big Roof," together with apologies for past repudiations. The second, engaged almost in the same breath, continued the debate over matters of expression first taken up during the postrevolutionary period of the early 1950s. Both conveyed a concern for how contemporary cultural production, like architecture, should be interpreted critically in light of past circumstances and of broad, subject-centered issues of identity.

For instance, in a 1978 article titled "Chinese Architecture in Recent History and Architectural Style," Wang Shiren placed the first generation of Chinese architects in a contemporary socialist context by referring to "the limitations of quasi-feudal and quasi-colonial social circumstances [which] prevented a full realization of their potential"; the result, he argued, was "a world view belonging essentially to the capitalist class."[16] In summarizing the present dilemma, Wang referred to contemporaneity without abandoning the past, still seen as useful: he asserted that "traditional architecture became obsolete without the content of a new way of life" and that "the newly imported Western architecture failed because it did not absorb the qualities of traditional architecture."[17] Taking something of a critical theoretical turn, Wang found the remedy in the "style developed in recent history"—for example, the vernacular of Shanghai's *lilong* housing, a hybrid, as described earlier, reflecting both Western and Chinese influences. This was particularly appealing to him because "it absorbed and transformed elements of traditional architecture like the balcony, the light well, and the back room, and reorganized them into a new uniform general framework, for the contemporary occasion."[18]

More sharply critical of the recent past, Chen Chongqing, writing in 1980, attempted to distance architecture further from politics without denying altogether that architecture can reflect political inclinations. He argued that politics and art should not be evaluated on the same grounds: the "political standard" and the "artistic standard" were fundamentally different. Chen thus concluded that "a work of art can be incorrect politically" even when it "may still have some artistic merit." This claim led to a remarkable rhetorical question: "How can we disagree that the 'Big Roof' was intended for the revival of our civilization?"[19] For him, the "Big Roof" was clearly and fundamentally a style, to be judged according to artistic standards; it therefore could not be stigmatized politically, as had happened in the recent past, as merely revivalist.

Wang Zhili was even more critical of the immediate past in his 1980 article "Two Lessons of History: Recollections from Two Phases of Architectural Work." According to him, the first phase, lasting from 1956 to 1964, "saw the prosperous development of architecture, through horizontal integration with related fields," while the second phase, coinciding with the Cultural Revolution (1966–1976), "saw destruction by dogma." He, like Wang, appears to take aim at the denial of the aesthetic dimensions of architecture, stating that "there has often been very damaging thinking in the past, namely avoiding the ideological aspect of architectural study."[20] Here and elsewhere, reservations about wholesale importation of foreign approaches to architectural design appeared, directed particularly at "cultural form," borrowed from the Soviet Union in the 1950s, and at "postmodernism," which began to enter from the United States around 1980. The positions of these writers also reflected some of the more general features of the Culture Fever: the assignment of a persistent if not entirely clear role to tradition in Chinese culture; a far more nuanced understanding of modernism, especially in historical writing (a stance they shared with critical theorists); and an interest in advanced technology not inconsistent with, although far more practical than, positions usually held by those concerned with the near future.

During the flurry of intellectual activity taking place in architectural circles in the 1980s, numerous topics came and went, as the Chinese tried to make up for lost time in an intense phase that contained, one observer later said, "almost too much for easy digestion."[21] Some discussed architectural semiotics—and the connotative, denotative, and otherwise languagelike characteristics of buildings as signs and symbols—much as did those immersed in hermeneutics, with little concern for an official ideological perspective, although here the issue of a correct language did emerge.[22] Those inclined to embrace traditional culture favored contextualism, which some dismissed as a craze that would soon pass but proponents lauded as a cultural view pertaining to far more than just the physical environment of a project site. And by 1986, architectural postmodernism and, with it, a pluralism of historicist and narrative forms of architectural expression were certainly beginning to be in play and under discussion.[23]

Yet debate never got much beyond a consideration of superficial influences, usually from external sources, and never really grappled with the crucial theoretical issues actively engaged by some in other cultural disciplines, such as literature and film. Many architects were too uncritical, as they, like so many others at the time, pursued novelty and the appearance of being up-to-date; moreover, neither the architectural education nor professional discourse in China, both isolated for so long, had prepared them to approach these architectural positions, which arose largely outside their country. Consequently, distinctions between "modernism" and "post-modernism" often were cast as merely stylistic, as those debating lacked a more fundamental understanding of the deeper differences at stake. In other instances, architectural post-modernism was roundly condemned—not without reason, from the earlier Chinese modernist-socialist perspective—as a convenient justification for what was otherwise seen as being retrogressive architectural thinking that ignored the contemporary world.[24] In any event, the widespread consciousness of culture that architecture shared with other fields was often felt in what one commentator saw as "the outcome of the clashes and intermingling of indigenous and outside influences which had permeated deeply into every corner of social life . . . and had been causing wholesale renovation in the cultural modes of society." He further declared, in the manner of early reformers, that this phenomenon was "leading to a common conviction that modernization could never be realized, in fact, without cultural renovation."[25]

As several analysts have noted, 1985 or thereabouts was a time when it became clear that there were crossed signals in the implementation of Deng Xiaoping's Four Modernizations, resulting in not a little confusion and even bewilderment as to what was an appropriate course of action.[26] In agriculture, for example, the subdivision of arable land into smaller parcels, which followed the dismantling of the communes and the creation of a contract system at the household level, made large farm machinery, capable of achieving economies of scale in northern provinces like Shaanxi, unusable. Needless to say, many who had profited from the collectivized and brigade forms of production deeply resented this change. Independent management of industry, in what were once state enterprises, also resulted in contradictions: while a system of "private" incentives reinvigorated production in some cases, the notion of a social compact between the state and its employees—"the iron rice bowl"—significantly eroded. Similarly, in defense and foreign policy, China often seemed to be sending contradictory signals regarding its stance toward both the Soviet Union and the United States, and some resented the paring down of the armed forces. In domestic matters, public policy seemed to run counter to private interest; for example, though the state insisted on the one-child family, the household incentive system, widely adopted in agriculture, placed a premium on family-based productive power. Intellectually, lines also began to be drawn between forms of expression that were considered to be "blossoming" and those regarded as "bourgeois liberalization," a return to the idea of "spiritual pollution."[27] Nevertheless, on precisely this subject Secretary General Hu Yaobang went so far as to declare that the Chinese "must never again espouse the radical leftist nonsense of preferring socialist weeds to capitalist seedlings."[28]

Little wonder that many had difficulty finding their bearings, even when dealing with fairly mundane aspects of life. Cynicism and hopeful promise were mixed, and a not unhumorous Chinese appreciation of the paradoxes involved often came to the fore. For example, the authors of the "Not-Not Manifesto" of 1986 described "Not-Not" as "not the negation of anything," but "only the expression of itself." In short, "Not-Not is aware that liberation existed in the indefinite."[29] Much more broadly, many became aware that a more open society was needed to work through these contradictions. In 1986, slogans and wall posters reading "No Democratization, No Modernization" and "Long Live Freedom" began to appear, together with mass street demonstrations. On December 20, 1986, some 30,000 students, joined by about the same number of townspeople, marched through People's Square and along the Bund in Shanghai. It was almost as if the manifestations of the May Fourth Movement had emerged once again.[30] Predictably, party hardliners became upset, and the fear of another massive round of student upheaval spread throughout the Central Committee. Accordingly, the students' behavior was roundly condemned, and their demonstration in early 1987 in Tiananmen Square was quashed and followed by a number of dismissals and purges; among those punished were popular figures like Fang Lizhi, a prominent university professor and scientist.[31]

In keeping with Deng Xiaoping's program of modernization and the economic opening of China to the outside world—not to mention China's lack of contemporary know-how and ready capital for construction—some of the first significant works of architecture of the 1980s came as joint ventures blatantly directed at external markets in an effort to court sources of further financial support. Among the most prominent of these enterprises were the Western-style hotels constructed in several major cities. The Fragrant Hill Hotel by I. M. Pei, for example, which opened in 1982, quickly drew considerable attention, both because of the stature of its architect and because of the clear attempt made there to situate the complex within an evolving modern Chinese culture.[32] Built on the dilapidated site of an eighteenth-century Qing dynasty garden known as the Garden of Quiet and Ease, the hotel was overtly modern and unmistakably Chinese at the same time. In overall concept it was built somewhat like a traditional enclosed garden villa, with two- and four-story buildings either joined directly or linked by single-story arcades to form about ten large and small courtyards, each landscaped in a time-honored Chinese manner. The setting of the entire complex on the side of a hill was further dramatized by an expansive rock garden that was both old and new: it included a large pond that often reflected the structures around it.

Given Pei's personal family background in Suzhou, the design approach was perhaps not surprising; he had ample examples of the garden-courtyard dwelling to draw on and could note

50   Fragrant Hill Hotel, outside Beijing, by I. M. Pei, 1982.

the prevalence of smooth white walls decorated with gray clay tile and brick moldings, the basic palette of the Fragrant Hill Hotel. Nevertheless, the design sparked intense discussion and in many ways had a liberating effect on Chinese architectural thinking. Indeed, in 1982, the Society of Chinese Architects hosted a conference about the project.[33] Though the design was criticized on several fronts—faults included its uneconomical construction and its reliance on overly sophisticated technology not yet appropriate for use in China—the results were often praised as being "elegant," "distinctive," and built to "good overall effect."[34] Once the hotel was built, Pei was sorely disappointed by the poor workmanship and maintenance; but he seems in his design to have appreciated and elaborated on several of the ideas of modernity inherent in traditional Chinese architecture, such as close relationships between interior and exterior, and a direct reckoning with rather than diffusion of different programmatic elements. Consequently the complex could readily be interpreted both as modern and traditionally based architecture—a duality that some critics saw as indicating Pei's ambivalence about the hotel's essential design.

Engagement with the landscape, although in a more contoured form (comparable to that of the Kuangquan Hotel of the 1960s), was also the centerpiece of the Jianguo Hotel in Beijing (1982) by Clement Chen and Associates from San Francisco.[35] In fact, this was the first Sino-American project in Deng's China. It was located on a narrow urban site in a rapidly developing section of the city. With a five-story wing of guest quarters on the north and a ten-story tower of accommodations on the west, it had the layout of a contemporary American motel. Toward the center of the complex, a garden and water environment was constructed, reminding some of landscapes found on much larger scale in parts of southern China; it created a thematic internal visual focus for the entire complex, not unlike overseas practice at the time.

Similarly, the White Swan Hotel in Guangzhou (ca. 1983) brought Western hotel planning and interior layout to the fore.[36] Designed by She Junnan and Mo Bozhi of the Guangzhou Institute of Architectural Design, the extensive 90,000-square-meter complex, located on the river edge of Shamian Island, included extensive restaurant, garden, and other semipublic facilities; car parking with direct access to the nearby roadway system; and the tower of the hotel proper. This tower was thirty-two stories, high by Chinese standards then. An attenuated hexagon in plan, the tower afforded views from each room of the majestic Pearl River. An ostensibly Chinese garden theme was also introduced in the external landscaping of the site to one side of the tower, as well as being insinuated in the otherwise American-style hotel atrium space inside the building complex itself. Since its opening, the White Swan Hotel has enjoyed considerable commercial success and has undoubtedly influenced other modern developments in China's fledgling but growing tourist industry. In pursuing tourism, China was cautiously opening itself up to a contemporary cultural and economic enterprise. For although tourism is nothing new, as a mass phenomenon it is largely a manifestation of the modern period, when individuals have had both the inclination and opportunity to engage in it.

The importation and full-fledged use of modern, internationally available building technology was a by-product of China's historical opening to the West, resulting most recently in numerous

51   The garden court of the Jianguo Hotel, Beijing, by Clement Chen and Associates, 1982.

52   The Great Wall Hotel, northeastern Beijing, by Beckett International, 1983.

glass- and metal-clad towers in such developments as Pudong in Shanghai, Dalian in northern China, and Guangzhou in the south. One of the first appearances of the glass curtain-wall system, commonplace at the time in the West, occurred at the thousand-room Great Wall Hotel (1983) in the northeastern outskirts of central Beijing.[37] Largely designed by Beckett International of Santa Monica, California, the complex was configured functionally into separate wings converging on a central circulation and service shaft, crowned by a restaurant. These wings, rising twenty-two stories, and the hotel function areas in between, about six stories high, were all clad in a seismically resistant system of silver reflective glazing. Also among the first curtain-wall structures was the Union Edifice (1985), an office building in Shanghai designed by Zhang Qianyuan, Yang Liancheng, and Wang Sixiao of the East China Architectural Design Institute.[38] At more than 100 meters in height, the building had a simple square floor plate supported by columns, with strong architectural articulation of the building's structure at the corners. Of modest size, the building included 28,000 square meters of floor space. Another technologically noteworthy early building was the Jinling Hotel in Nanjing (1980–1983) by the venerable Hong Kong–based firm of P & T (formerly Palmer and Turner).[39] Some thirty-seven stories high, the hotel's single tower rose from a verdant garden setting, again landscaped in a southern Chinese style.

The Jinling Hotel and similar buildings introduced into China a new round of high-rise construction made possible by advances in technology pertaining to elevators and other mechanical systems. These operating technologies were quickly transferred to other building types, including residential tower blocks; it appeared that both the debates and technologies of the 1970s were now obsolete. One example of residential housing employing the new methods was the Quyang New Village project of 1986, located on 80 hectares of land in northeastern Shanghai. Numerous twenty-four-story apartment towers were built alongside lower, six-story complexes and a full complement of nonresidential facilities, including a shopping center, an entertainment center, sports clubs, and libraries.[40] Designed by Cai Zheng and Wang Guanling, the overall planning of the village also owed a debt to Western subdevelopment practices and was far more varied in scope than the typical *danyuanlou* and residential districts of the late 1970s. Also consistent with the implementation of Deng's open-door policy generally, most of these early applications and experiments with contemporary building technology took place in a few major cities and in specially designated enterprise zones. Moreover, these zones, exhibiting a separateness reminiscent of that sought by the Self-Strengthening Movement, were developed beside existing urban areas. They thus were highly practical, providing the needed new quarters quickly and efficiently while avoiding—at least initially—massive displacements of populations and facilities.

In spite of the renewed intellectual contact and exchange with the outside world, in the design of major cultural institutions strong references to traditional Chinese architecture persisted, though usually in a qualified form. Theoretical discussions of culture and architecture, except perhaps those focusing narrowly on the present, had no effect on the design of many of China's new commercial buildings, whose designers felt overwhelming pressure to expediently follow internationally available technical and formal prescriptions. These structures were meant to be familiar and convenient for overseas trade, as well as to symbolize progress to the world at large. But for buildings aimed more at a domestic audience, the calls of theorists and others interested in moving the modern architectural project along to look critically at both the present and the indigenous past were being heeded, as reflected in at least some of what was being produced. Chief among these projects was the Beijing Library, completed in 1987 though first approved by Zhou Enlai in 1975; its construction was overseen directly by the State Construction Committee, a supraministerial organization of the State Council.[41]

Located on Baishiqiao Road in the northwestern suburbs of Beijing, the building site was opposite the well-known Purple Bamboo Park (*Zizhuyuan gongyuan*), roughly midway between Qinghua University and the city center. With a floor area of 140,000 square meters and a capacity to hold twenty million volumes, the library was conceived to be China's national depository of publications, and it is one of the largest libraries in the world. Design of the complex was entrusted to the Architectural Design Institute of the Ministry of Construction, along with the Northeastern Institute of Architectural Design and Research; the first design proposals were devised jointly by Yang Tingbao, Dai Nianci, Zhang Bo, Wu Liangyong, and Huang Yuanqiang, arguably the most distinguished practitioners available.[42] The organizing principle of the library was "high stacks [and] low reading rooms"; the majority of book stacks were grouped into a double-tower arrangement at the center of the complex, which extended seventeen stories above grade and three below.[43] The remaining three- to five-story buildings, containing reading

53   The Beijing Library, by Yang Tingbao, Dai Nianci, Zhang Bo, Wu Liangyong, and Huang Yuanqiang, 1989.

rooms, administrative offices, and cataloguing and other service areas, were grouped around the tower structure in a complicated though essentially symmetrical arrangement of building wings, attached pavilions, and courtyards. This organization enabled the very large program of accommodations to be spread out on the site and spatially deployed in a manner reasonably consistent with the comparatively low height of traditional architecture, despite the complex's otherwise monumental appearance. The entrance for visitors, located along the southern front of the complex facing Purple Bamboo Park, readily acknowledged the designers' two main considerations: to best place the entrance traditionally and to provide users with the most convenient and pleasant surroundings.

Cleaner in lines and less mannered than the earlier National Gallery of Dai Nianci, the Beijing Library nonetheless was replete with traditional architectural references, ranging from the *xumizuo*-like base approached by a monumental stair to the geometrically forthright gabled roofs and the large entry loggia, as well as the spatial layout of buildings and courtyards.[44] The balance between the otherwise modern facade and these formal elements was sufficiently restrained that the merger of the building's two pedigrees could be quite abstractly handled; enough of each remained that multiple interpretations could easily be supported. By contrast, in other cultural monuments the balance was sometimes weighted to one side or the other. Qi Kang's Memorial Museum of the Victims of the Nanjing Massacre, for instance, was formally modern and abstract in its architectural components; yet its symmetry and unfolding, through a spatial sequence of courtyards, stairs, and building pavilions, readily recalled the earlier Sun Yat-sen Mausoleum, as well as much earlier traditional referents like the western Qing Tombs.[45] Built in 1985, the museum lies just outside the Jiangdong Gate in Nanjing. It was one of several monuments designed by Qi; others included the Memorial of the Chinese Communists (1990). Qi Kang entered National Central University to study architecture in 1949 and then worked with Yang Tingbao for some thirty years; he is one of the last notable members of the second generation of Chinese architects.[46]

In the later 1980s, contextualism and a very real culturalist concern for the potential wholesale destruction of historic inner-city areas prompted several approaches to conservation and preservation.[47] Along Liulichang Street, in an old southern section of Beijing, several commercial blocks were refashioned as traditional two-story shophouses made of gray brick, with red-brick stringcourses and prominent, upturned gabled roofs. Planned primarily for tourists, this wholesale installation subsequently raised questions regarding the efficacy of literally recreating something from the past rather than conserving or preserving what was already in place.[48] Beginning at this time, similar traditional commercial streets were created in other tourist cities, such as Nanjing, Shanghai, and Xi'an, although usually as more strictly conservationist acts. Many traditional residential districts as well, again in frequently visited cities, such as Suzhou and Shanghai, began to be upgraded; thus Suzhou's garden villas and Shanghai's *lilong* houses were preserved.

There were also attempts to keep the traditional ambience of older urban areas, without literally preserving the existing structures. Indeed, as noted, in many cases such preservation was almost impossible because the structures were highly dilapidated or in outright ruin; their poor condition was often the result of severe overcrowding and the economic privations of the earlier Communist era. In Beijing's Ju'er Hutong (1989), by Wu Liangyong, a traditionally courtyardlike arrangement of housing was provided, though it rose, in a contemporary manner, to three stories and had several different dwelling units arranged around successive courtyards, instead of the traditional single house.[49] Dwelling units were modest in size, ranging from 50 to 80 square meters of livable space, and the entrance to each unit was provided from a courtyard. While clearly modern in its material finishes, composition, and unit layout, the gray-tiled gabled roofs, white walls, and proportions of both window openings and building masses again lent a strong traditional air to the housing complex. Throughout, Wu Liangyong appeared to have adhered closely to Li Zehou's theoretical culturalist formulation of tradition and modernism: he insisted on Western or at least modern "substance" in the planning, layout, and other accommodations of the housing, while using Chinese "function" or architectural means to temporize, ameliorate, and make familiar this otherwise contemporary housing complex. In practice, the validity of traditional values were reaffirmed at an aesthetic level, where such considerations were seen not as content so much as a manner of rendering architecture. In striking this balance, Wu was also registering the common understanding that vernacular traditions can be deployed readily in the service of contemporary circumstances so long as there are no dramatic transgressions in scale, density, and building type.[50]

54   Conservation of shophouses, Suzhou.

55 Housing in the Ju'er Hutong, Beijing, by Wu Liangyong, 1989.
56 Tongfangxiang Residential Quarter, Suzhou, by the Beijing Architectural Institute, 1996.

Other similar projects were to follow. For instance, the Tongfangxiang Residential Quarter in Suzhou (1996), by the Beijing Architectural Institute, covered a large square block (about 3.6 hectares in area) and replaced dilapidated and grossly overcrowded shelters. Throughout, the architectural quality of the project preserved many of the traditional urban values of old Suzhou—a city, as noted earlier, renowned for its gardens and canals—with a well-defined perimeter block subdivided internally by many small streets and lanes; they were lined with houses of different types, which accommodated enclosed gardens wherever possible. Again, the palette of building materials, the functional layout of the complex, and often the building massing were clearly modern, although the details—especially the tiled gable roofs, cornice lines, and door-ways—were traditional in appearance.

Institutionally, one of the driving forces in Tongfangxiang and in the Ju'er Hutong toward modern "substance" (to once again use Li Zehou's term) was the shift in 1984, during the Third Plenary Session of the Chinese Communist Party Central Committee deliberations, to a socialist planned commodity economy. Housing was no longer regarded as an item of welfare but as a commodity in China's fledgling property market, where use rights could be traded even though public ownership remained. This shift led almost immediately to the introduction of apartment units—a dwelling type by then a fixture in many other parts of the world—which replaced out-dated, shared nonspecialized accommodations. This widespread shift did more than change the physical form of the dwelling units themselves: for the increasing number of inhabitants who could afford to live in this new manner, it eventually began to promote a greater compartmen-talization of daily life, and the modern functional separation and special accommodation of vari-ous tasks and activities.

The pro-democracy movement once again seized national attention on April 17, 1989, when thousands of students from many Beijing-based universities joined in a rally in Tiananmen Square to mourn the passing of Hu Yaobang, the Communist Party general secretary who had showed some sympathy for liberal agitation, and to press for reforms in government and for greater participation in making decisions about university affairs. The next day they held a sit-in near the Great Hall of the People; and as the students continued to demonstrate, their rallies were joined by workers and other sympathetic Beijing residents. On May 17, as more than a million demonstrators gathered in and around Tiananmen Square, student representatives openly called on Deng Xiaoping and Li Peng, the premier, to resign. Though martial law was declared on May 20, the government took no decisive action until June 3 and 4, when army units loyal to Deng struck with devastating force. After effectively blocking all approaches to Tiananmen Square, troops gunned down unarmed students and other citizens both at the square and in other parts of the city.

This was, unfortunately, not the first such incident in Tiananmen Square, though none other was so bloodily indiscriminate or so well publicized in the rest of the horrified world. In the crackdown's aftermath thousands of students were arrested and interrogated. Still, the Party blamed the events on hooligans and counterrevolutionaries rather than on any broad-based support for a greater say in the affairs of the nation. As the historian Johnathan Spence notes, "by insisting to the last that economic reforms could be completely devoid from the immensely complex social and cultural effects that the reforms brought in their train, Deng, the party leaders, and the younger politicians in their clique threatened jointly to commit the government again to the nineteenth-century fallacy that China could join the modern world entirely on its own terms, sacrificing nothing of its prevailing ideological purity."[51] Jiang Zemin, the Party secretary of Shanghai who had managed to maintain order, was promoted by Deng to Party general secretary. Yet nothing could erase the public horror at the events of 1989 or counter the mounting evidence that dramatic economic growth would necessarily be accompanied by political and social change, as well as cultural openings to the outside world—even though one result of the crackdown, at least for a time, was widespread and often fearful self-censorship by many involved in the "Culture Fever."

But for architects, the proverbial genie was once again out of the bottle; they continued to experiment and develop their thinking in concert with outside influences as they had in the past, when China was more open to the world, particularly as economic circumstances continued to improve. A new round of internationally pioneered technologies and methods were introduced, especially (as before) in commercial construction, and new attempts were made to sinify aspects of architectural production—though now many earlier ascriptions of *ti* and *yong* were reversed, in favor of "modern content and Chinese form." In the process, the roles imagined for and played by contextual considerations and the indigenous landscape were amplified, even if the results were often rather superficial and uncertain because the architects failed to understand the deeper concepts involved in these changes. Finally, the tentative beginning of some measure of sophistication about expressive matters of both tradition and modernism could be discerned, at least in Chinese intellectual architectural circles, despite a relative lack of opportunities in a still poor country to apply such insights and despite professional misunderstandings and false starts. A decade or more earlier, the West had seen a similar sharp disjunction between theory and mainstream practice, which often led to profound differences in architectural discourse.

*"**AFTER ALL THAT TROUBLE,** greed seems to have taken over," Lu Hui observed seriously, as she and Zhang Shaoshu continued to drink their tea—Wu Feng stuck to his Coke even though it was far more expensive. "I suppose that's one way of forgetting," she went on pensively.*

"Yeah! And a lot of ugly stuff got built as a consequence," retorted Feng, as he didn't want to get into the events of '89. In fact, he still couldn't really talk about them. From his public persona one would think that he had already forgotten what had transpired, although nothing could be further from the truth. "Look what happened here at the Institute with everyone competing with each other for a new look—something different, something to get attention, something to get ahead. It's so crass!"

"What do you mean?" asked Zhang Shaoshu, "It's been a period of real experimentation and liberation, at least historically."

"Is that what you call it?" shot back Feng. "Look at what happened on the railway station. Look how many schemes they went through and look how different each one was. There was no integrity in the process," he ended emphatically.

"Speaking of that, look at what's happening in the schools," observed Shaoshu. "They are all taking things out of the magazines in such a mindless way, and the only things that seem to count are the pretty pictures, those overdone renderings that everyone gets excited about." His uncharacteristic complaints sounded to Hui more like something Feng would say.

"We all did a bit of that, it seems to me," continued Feng.

"Talking of rendering," interjected Hui, "what about lining up the main building program as three bars running across the site with links between them creating courtyards?"

"Not bad . . . very nice!" responded Feng, returning to the project at hand and pleasantly surprised by Hui's sudden insight. Maybe she wasn't so bad as a designer after all.

"Also, programmatically we should start at the entrance with administrative areas and then go to the reading room, with the stacks at the back," Hui continued, pleased by Feng's warm response, swiveling the screen of her PC in his direction.

"Why?" queried Shaoshu. "I don't understand."

"Because that way we can preserve the low height along the lane and have the pavilion rise in height as we go back," responded Feng quickly, already on the same wavelength as Hui.

"OK! I understand. Like in some imperial palace," observed Shaoshu.

"Well, you're the one who brought it up," Feng reminded him.

"Not a palace, the library, that's what I said, the library," Shaoshu pointed out with his usual pedantry.

"All right, before you two get into it again, it's getting late. Why don't we stop for now and continue in the morning?" interjected Hui.

"What's the rush?" asked Feng, wanting to continue, now that they were beginning to get somewhere with the project.

"Well, if you must know, I promised to meet some friends and go to the theater this evening," stated Hui rather emphatically, again looking at her watch, although not at all sure why she felt it necessary to give such a detailed explanation. She knew that Feng was interested in her, but she still felt undecided about him. "He can be so immature and all over the place, though interesting and talented at the same time. . . . It's probably my way of fending him off," she thought to herself quickly, as she reflected on what she had just said.

"I see," replied Feng, with a knowing look.

"All right, let's go on for a little while longer," interjected Shaoshu, also not entirely convinced that they should be stopping so soon, but understanding Hui's need not to stay too late.

A COMMODIFICATION AND INTERNATIONALIZATION OF ARCHITECTURE followed the renewed vigor with which economic development was pushed forward in China during the 1990s, heightening a trend that was beginning to become apparent during the previous decade. With annual growth in gross domestic product running in

double digits and the near ruinous inflation of the 1980s abated, though not entirely under control, average per capita income was rising at impressive rates. Although high rates of saving continued, the increased wealth among the Chinese translated fairly directly into increased buying power and higher levels of personal consumption, certainly in comparison to earlier generations. "Market fever" (*Shichang re*), as it was sometimes called, began to obliterate memories of the euphoric and tragic events of the 1980s for many Chinese; the substantial rise in production and consumption strengthened in many an underlying attitude of "let's get rich fast!"[1]

Undoubtedly, a further shift in state policy in the direction of a socialist market economy also had much to do with this prevailing mood. After his inspection tour of southern China in 1992, Deng Xiaoping spoke decisively on the relation between planning and market forces, which had long been a topic of ideological debate in China's economic reform, pronouncing them two parts of the same system, which would contain macroeconomic regulation and an ongoing market orientation. The economic boom, without a properly functioning market in place, also brought with it significant and unfortunate duplication of entrepreneurial economic activities, with the result that many communities competed unnecessarily with one another, all in search of newfound wealth.

Soon the ambiguous and often contradictory signals sent by officials in the 1980s gave way, in many places, to a headlong clamoring toward capitalism as a remedy for many of China's economic woes. Building boomed in many major cities, especially along the richer coastal regions, where most property markets were active; sometimes entirely new cities sprung up, like Shenzhen in the south, where there were once only backward villages and paddy fields. The boom, or at least its early prospects, brought more joint ventures between Chinese and overseas enterprises, particularly as many on the outside perceived in China enormous future markets to be tapped and profits to be made. These joint ventures, in turn, significantly changed and modernized Chinese ways of doing business, manufacturing things, constructing buildings, and generally managing their affairs. It was almost as if the "first" and "second" industrial revolutions, experienced much earlier in the West, descended on China simultaneously.[2] Privatization spread rapidly, and the competition between various work units for contracts developed an intensity never before seen in postrevolutionary China. State-established and state-run design institutes quickly shed their staid ways and entered into the fierce competition with each other, becoming like private firms in the West, complete with downsizing and mergers.

Standards of building practice began to shift dramatically, prompting the Ministry of Construction to promulgate new design standards and building codes as well as licensing procedures, often on American models. Architecture became an inextricable part of the new market system, enabling the product and image of one group to be distinguished from that of another. More significantly, perhaps, one city could base its claim to be more modern than another on the repertoire of its new buildings and apparent contemporary architectural prowess. Both the new economic freedom and openness to outside contact prompted clients to be bolder and even outrageous in their architectural demands. Perhaps not since the 1920s in Shanghai had architecture become such a sought-after commodity in China—and in retrospect that earlier period seems almost stately and mild in comparison to the 1990s.

The building boom was accompanied by an upsurge in forms of architectural expression, frequently varying considerably from project to project; this included much wider experimentation with formal devices having little precedent in China than had occurred during the 1980s. The prolific work of He Jingtang and his colleagues at the Design Institute of the South China Institute of Technology in Guangzhou was a clear case in point.[3] Office buildings, resorts, housing complexes, museums, and other institutions each seem to have been rendered so idiosyncratically that there were few, if any, indications that the body of work was designed by one group. Close examination always revealed an underlying rationale for a building's architectural expression, usually dependent on an obvious narrative about the place, or the program, to which a certain symbolism was attached. For example, in one institutional complex—the Memorial Hall of the Lingnan Party School (1993)—a notion of "turn of the century" was associated with the architectural work of Gaudí in Spain, and the building was rendered accordingly.[4] In another, the design of a memorial to the Sino-Japanese War of 1937 through 1945—the Museum of the September 18th Incident of 1931—was made to resemble the bent and presumably broken shaft of a samurai sword implanted in the ground.[5] The dramatic, abstract quality of the proposal almost managed to transcend the obvious symbolism involved. In both cases the design approach strongly denoted the occasion behind the building and not the material substance or other facts of the building itself, nor some continuing sense of architectural tradition.

57   A proposal for the Museum of the September 18th Incident of 1931, by He Jintang, ca. 1995.

He's architecture, like that of many others in the field, certainly had a didactic quality as strong as that found in earlier socialist realist projects, although its variety kept it from possessing the same narrative consistency. Perhaps his best work to date, in this regard, was the Museum of Nanyue King (1991), designed in collaboration with Mo Bozhi.[6]

The work of many other Chinese design institutes and their foreign collaborators, often tied symbolically to references both inside and outside of architecture, showed a similar variety of expression, sometimes closely emulating well-known contemporary buildings in other parts of the world. The Shanghai Securities Exchange Building in the Lujiazui area of Pudong, for instance, designed by WZMH of Canada in conjunction with the Shanghai Institute of Architectural Design and Research, is an unusual structure but strongly resembles the Grand Arch at La Défense built in Paris in the 1980s.[7] Rising twenty-seven stories above grade, the Securities Exchange Building is also large (91,564 square meters of floor area), and sited in a prominent location with an open area at the center of its main facade. Similarly, the Nextage Shopping Center Project by the same design institute, again for Pudong in Shanghai, incorporates stylistic references from a number of sources—including Aldo Rossi's civic building in Perugia, Italy, of 1989, in one of its towers.[8] The remainder of the proposal is a mixture of diverse elements, varying from a gently curved facade and arcade of tall arches to a modernistic group of stepped-back volumes at the center of the complex.

The new Shanghai Museum, sometimes known as the Heritage Museum, in People's Square (1995), another design by the Shanghai Municipal Institute of Architectural Design, under the direction of Xing Tonghe, also breaks with tradition by conforming to neither the time-honored use of the "Big Roof" nor the classical modernity of socialist realist projects.[9] Instead, the plain cubic volumes of the museum appear to follow a willfully sculptural rather than functional logic, and the cylindrical top portion of the museum—equally sculptural—is unprecedented in building. Alternatively, it can be seen in plan to follow the shape of ancient Chinese tripods, with a roof resembling a bronze mirror from the Han dynasty, though again this form has little to do with the building type as such. With a floor area of 37,000 square meters, the museum houses traditional Chinese artifacts, including furniture; perhaps its collection explains its rather literal image. Located almost opposite the Shanghai Municipal Government Building, the plaza in front of the museum is set within a park and enjoys substantial use by Shanghai's citizens. It also

58 The Shanghai Securities Exchange Building, Pudong, Shanghai,
by WZMH and the Shanghai Institute of Architectural Design and Research, ca. 1995.

59 The Shanghai or Heritage Museum, by Xing Tonghe, 1995.

conforms in some respects to Chinese tradition: together with the museum to the south and the later theater and construction museum alongside the municipal building to the north, it inscribes a T-shaped configuration resembling the character *zhong* (center), the original shape of Tiananmen Square in Beijing. This deliberate arrangement is further emphasized by statuary, a pair of *kilin*—mythical beasts—on the south side of the museum that mark a single urban space in the traditional manner.

Another Shanghai-based Chinese design institute—the East China Architectural Design Institute, founded in 1952, which now employs a few thousand people—has collaborated with numerous well-known foreign firms; it merged with the Shanghai Design Institute around 1997. It was responsible, in conjunction with Skidmore, Owings and Merrill from the United States as principal designers, for the Jin Mao Building project—at 420 meters high, one of the tallest structures of its kind in the world.[10] In fact, such unusual size, and the bragging rights that go with it, played a conspicuous role in the 1990s building boom. Indeed, as early as 1996, articles began appearing in the *Architectural Journal* taking issue with the scale and outlandishness of many new buildings.[11] The Jin Mao Building itself, however, has some similarities with the Kaifeng pagoda in Henan. Its overall form and the horizontal and vertical scalelike pattern on the *brise-soleil* curtain wall give the impression of a modern version of the decorated walls of the pagoda; moreover, the thirteen levels of distinct vertical rise correspond to the thirteen levels of the Kaifeng pagoda. The East China Institute also worked with John Portman on the Shanghai Center and with Obayashi, the giant Japanese construction firm, on the earlier Garden Hotel, as well as designing the Shanghai Broadcasting Building in the early 1990s.

One building type once again transforming the scale of the urban environment was the shopping center. It was also an integral part of the market fever that was sweeping at least the most affluent areas of the country. Like the earlier department stores in Shanghai along Nanjing Road, built during the 1920s and '30s, the new malls were large buildings, strategically located to take advantage of the commuting habits of prospective consumers and designed to have a strong presence on the street. The Sun Dong An shopping complex in Beijing (1997), by Wong Tung from Hong Kong, for instance, provided a new scale and commercial substance to the already bustling Wangfujing Dajie, one of Beijing's major shopping streets. Again like the earlier department stores, which brought open plans, well-coordinated vertical access, and other inno-

60 The Jin Mao Building, Pudong, Shanghai, by Skidmore, Owings and Merrill, in conjunction with the East China Architectural Design Institute, 1997–2000.

vations to building in China, the new malls introduced numerous merchandizing innovations, including spacious multifloor atria, glassed-in elevators, and food courts. Like the even larger trade marts that began looming on the suburban and urban landscape, they often incorporated other commercial uses such as offices and hotel accommodations, as was common in Japan and the United States.[12]

This commercial progress, especially in older urban areas, had the unhappy side effect of destroying the former city fabric and obliterating old patterns of life. Even smaller cities, flush with the initial success of township enterprises, frequently incorporated shopping malls into their new modernization plans. Zhangjiagang, for example, a prosperous, relatively small town in the Changjiang delta, northeast of Shanghai, recently completed construction of a new main street with multistory modern stores and a nearby shopping complex with residential and office components. Unfortunately, the slogan "build and they will come" has not proved true for some hapless communities, who clearly overreached during the early market boom and soon saw their once new and inviting commercial buildings lying vacant. All too often, low standards of construction have also meant that many buildings quickly fell into disrepair and needed to be replaced; this is a wasteful exercise that a poor though rapidly developing country like China can ill afford.

As a result of broad cultural contact coupled with Deng Xiaoping's economic opening, especially to the West, Chinese architects not only increasingly confronted outside references but also seemed to welcome a newfound demand for their services and a newfound freedom of expression. But at the same time, the lack of critical discussion in China about architecture led to buildings that often reflected little more than the pursuit of appearances or of what seemed to be the most fashionable image at hand. Moreover, this absence of an internal discourse was signaled not only by the lack of any real architectural consensus but also by the tendency of many practitioners, unable to cope adequately with the influx of new ideas, to accept new references uncritically. Indeed, given the hiatus in almost all theoretical discussions forced by the Cultural Revolution and the frenzied gorging on all that had been missed that followed, a vigorous critical viewpoint had little chance to develop. Furthermore, ensuing discussions suggested that neither tradition nor architectural modernism were widely understood; such confusion is hardly surprising, for modernism was received and subsequently deployed with

61 Interior of the Sun Dong An shopping complex, Beijing, by Wong Tung and Partners, 1997.
62 Main street, Zhangjiagang, 1997.

little critical analysis or articulation, and until recently few showed much interest in Chinese architectural history.

The approaches to traditional and modern architecture in the 1990s thus effectively blocked the opening up of avenues for exploring different versions of either. In short, as the demands of practice increased, almost no intellectual core remained to be drawn on to shape architectural ideas and to steadily guide architectural thinking on either side of the modern-traditional divide. In addition, the pursuit of architectural novelty as more or less an end in itself, a pursuit driven by the very new experience of competitive market forces, ran counter to a long tradition in which outmoded structures were often simply renovated with no attempt to change them. Moreover, in the rush to be different, many practitioners now refused to spend time on the steady process of discovery and to seek the innovations that come from long, autonomous work on architectural problems—if they ever had such habits; instead, they seized ready-made ideas springing up both inside and outside of architecture per se. Few, if any, followed the model of Yang Tingbao, who in midcentury had honed his architecture into what amounted to a reflective personal style: mindful of the cultural requirements flowing around him, he nevertheless focused on his own development as a modern architect and realized that neither traditional nor modernist forms of expression, about which he was more deeply informed than most, were ends in themselves. Consequently, design thinking often became unbalanced, conceived almost entirely according to the circumstantial aspects of a project and to the virtual exclusion of any internal disciplinary demands. Forced to take on so much, so soon, and with so little preparation, architects in China frequently created buildings uncouth, garish, and incoherent in their appearance and form, as well as downright ugly.

Fortunately, not all recent architectural production in China has been quite so free from any moorings. Large public infrastructure and transportation projects, for instance, often followed the compelling architectural logic found in the functional and engineering challenges presented by such large modern-day structures and facilities. The proposal for the new Shenzhen Airport Terminal (1995), by Wu Yue and his colleagues from the Building Design Institute of the Ministry of Construction, was a high-tech celebration of the possibilities of enclosure, span, and transparency; a highly functional arrangement of ramps led out from the main complex to the airplanes parked on the tarmac.[13] The curvilinear shape of the main terminal complex also allowed airport arrivals and departures to be handled in a readily accessible, clear, and understandable manner. Wu Yue's Futian (*Shixia*) Theater (1995–1998), again located in Shenzhen, shows a similar regard for modern architecture and the use of contemporary materials, structure, and forms of expression. Although relatively modest in size, the theater complex contains a large auditorium with a proscenium stage, flanked by a glass-enclosed backstage and administrative facilities. A raised, partly glass-covered open-air platform is reached via a monumental entry stairway, which doubles as a performance space in the style of the street theaters of old. In referring to a distinction between "old China" and "young China," Wu apparently felt at ease in Shenzhen's almost brand-new urban landscape to willfully deploy modern architecture without, as he put it, "feeling a need to confront the burden of tradition."[14]

Other members of the now-emerging fourth generation of Chinese architects, such as Ma Qingyun, Paul Chen, and Henry Wu, have also contributed to this trend, along with Cui Kai from the Beijing Ministry of Construction, Tang Hua from the same ministry's Shenzhen office, and Zhang Yonghe, a graduate of the University of California at Berkeley who works in the small, Beijing-based firm of Atelier Feichang Jianzhu.[15] Ma, a graduate of the University of Pennsylvania, made a proposal similar to Wu's for the Ningbo Cultural Center of 1996, working in conjunc-

63   Futian Theater, Shenzhen, by Wu Yue and the Ministry of Construction, 1995–1998.

175

tion with the Shenzhen University of Architectural Design. Also worthy of note is Zhu Wenyi from the Architectural Design Institute at Qinghua University, who was the winner of the Shanghai Residential Design competition of 1996 and, more recently, worked briefly with the French architect Paul Andreu.[16]

The massive new bridges across the Huangpu River in Shanghai, linking the newly developed areas of Pudong on the west with Puxi on the east, are other cases in point. The bold designs of reinforced concrete stanchions and cable structures are consistent with some of the best architecture of the contemporary era, including the construction that makes up the miraculous new Airport Core Program in nearby Hong Kong.[17] Unencumbered by the relatively unfamiliar pressures of the marketplace, or the felt need to tell some story or symbolize some event, these designs appeared to have profited in style and authenticity from engineering constraints that have pushed these structures to their formal, material, and functional limits. They also recalled earlier moments of Chinese architecture, like Yang Tingbao's earlier airport terminal, when parsimony and simplicity were elegantly and thoroughly brought to bear. At the same time, this renewed technical prowess was accompanied by a new awareness of the environment and of the need for China to conserve resources. Indeed, one of the platforms in the 1999 Beijing Conference of the Union Internationale des Architectes (UIA) was a call for an architecture designed in substantially greater harmony with its natural surroundings, although not at the cost of ignoring basic social purposes.[18] As one commentator had put it earlier in the decade, there was a very real need for "proceeding from realistic conditions in China and embodying the basic socialist principle of a maximum concern for human beings." For him, the proper approach included the "production and improvement of ecological conditions," along with the "creation and development of a pluralistic architectural culture, adapted to and capable of promoting new lifestyles."[19]

Meanwhile, architectural work continued in the "Big Roof" tradition. Freed from the criticism and repudiation that had flourished in the revisionist thinking of the 1980s, architects who wished could now return to exploring contemporary possibilities for a traditional Chinese design language. Chief among these architects in recent years has been Zhang Jinqiu (b. 1936), a leading member of the third generation of Chinese architects. Zhang earned a master's degree in architectural history and theory from Qinghua, where she studied with Liang Sicheng (she had been an undergraduate at Qinghua as well). She then started work as an intern at the

Northwestern Institute of Architectural Design in Xi'an; there she was steadily promoted, becoming chief architect in 1987 and accredited as a senior or master architect within the Chinese system in 1988.[20]

Zhang's noteworthy early work followed closely the orientation of her graduate studies in history, as she restored and made selective additions to structures in traditional settings in Xi'an. In 1978, she designed the Memorial to Abeno Nakamoro, an envoy and poet who did much for cultural exchange between China and Japan.[21] The monument itself was situated on a mound near a lake and designed in the style of the Tang dynasty, with an abstract modern base. The remainder of the project included adding corridors to link buildings and upgrading the existing Xingqing Park landscape, all in a traditional manner. The reconstruction of the Qinglong Temple and Memorial Court of Kukai, which followed in 1981, was developed along similar lines, though the temple project displayed considerably more authority and spatial sensibility.[22] The original temple, of Tang origin, was destroyed in the Song dynasty; Zhang's re-creation was based on excavated remains and wall paintings depicting the temple complex, and the garden design was reproduced through much the same process. With the Tri-Tang Projects of 1984, Zhang Jinqiu was able to give freer rein to her revivalist architectural sensibility while accommodating a contemporary building program.[23]

Situated in a southern suburb of Xi'an, the Tri-Tang Projects consist of the Xi'an Garden Hotel, developed to support rising tourism; the Tang Banquet Hall or Restaurant; and the Tang Culture and Arts Museum. All three buildings were located in a traditionally landscaped setting, again by Zhang, close to the Wild Goose Pagoda (*Dayanta*), a seven-story classical relic of considerable age and distinction. Although modern in its amenities, building materials, and functional layout, the hotel was also partly designed in a traditional style around courtyards containing ponds, bridges, outlooks, gazebos, and other accoutrements of traditional Chinese gardens. Architecturally, the three- and four-story linked pavilions of hotel rooms and suites were crowned with traditional gray-tiled gabled roofs; columnar pilasters ran along the upper walls, also in a traditional style. Li Zehou's idea of "modern content and Chinese form," as well as Yang Tingbao's earlier attitude, was clearly recognizable here, and the hotel complex was to have considerable influence on several other similar projects throughout China.

64   The Xi'an Garden Hotel, by Zhang Jinqiu, 1984.

With the Shaanxi Museum of History (1991), Zhang Jinqiu once again reasserted the monumental presence of Chinese revivalist architecture in a meaningful way, making a strong turn in the direction of the prominent "Big Roof" projects of the 1950s.[24] The museum itself, located near the center of Xi'an, was large (45,800 square meters) and could be entered on axis from a main street through a traditionally styled entrance gateway. The large paved courtyard behind the entrance led directly to the main gallery in front; temporary exhibitions were in a gallery on one side, special collections on the other. The front of the main gallery was imposing; reminiscent of the local Tang dynasty Forbidden City (*Daminggong*), it was situated on a broad plinth with stairs (*xumizuo*) and capped with a double-gabled upturned tiled roof. But the use of reinforced concrete columns, defining arcades around the courtyard, and a peristylar front to the main galleries was consistently and ostensibly modern in its abstraction. These devices were carried upward to the *dougong,* which acted as a clever transition between the modern columns and traditional roof as their implied bracketed forms under the eaves were enlarged and simplified. Here and elsewhere, the design of the project walked a fine line between unabashed revivalism and a sense of contemporaneity.

In the Bell Tower and Drum Tower Plaza project, which followed in 1996, Zhang blurred this distinction still further, using modernist planning principles to complement Chinese traditional landscape and related building techniques. In essence, the plaza project has become the main pedestrian-accessible open space in Xi'an, an extensive park above a below-grade shopping mall that links the traditional bell and drum towers both symbolically and physically.[25] Apart from anything else, this spatial arrangement thoughtfully subordinated the programmatic requirements for economic redevelopment of the site to the idea of what Zhang referred to as an outdoor "living room for visitors" to the city, including nearby inhabitants.[26] The plaza was flanked on one side by a four-story commercial building constructed in a traditional style and on the other by one of Xi'an's major cross streets. With an extensive area of the plaza the equivalent of several floors below street level, the shopping complex under the plaza was cleverly provided with what amounted to open street access. The very broad stairway leading down into the sunken plaza, running almost the entire length of one of its street sides, also enhanced the already monumental character of the nearby bell tower, as the size of its base seemed to increase when viewed from below. Vegetation was confined to a row of large trees on the perimeter and

65 Detail of the Shaanxi Museum of History, Xi'an, by Zhang Jinqiu, 1991.

66   The Bell Tower and Drum Tower Plaza, Xi'an, by Zhang Jinqiu, 1996.

a checkerboard pattern of grass and low shrubbery across most of the street-level portion of the plaza. Skylights above an atrium space near the main entrance of the shopping mall were raised in pyramidal forms reminiscent of the roof slopes of both the drum and bell towers, as well as I. M. Pei's celebrated pyramid at the Louvre in Paris. Of all Zhang Jinqiu's work, this project, in its blending of traditional Chinese and modernist references, most plainly suggested a direction that could be usefully followed in the future.

Since its completion in January 1996, Beijing's new Western Railway Station, another recent "Big Roof" project, has been the subject of intense controversy.[27] At first glimpse, it appears more out of context than Zhang Jinqiu's well-situated work and offers a more pointed contrast between modern and traditional architectural attitudes and elements. Designed by a member of the Beijing Institute of Architectural Design and Research, Zhu Jialu, who like Zhang graduated from Qinghua's department of architecture (and at about the same time), this new landmark—located in the southwest area of Beijing, about 6.5 kilometers from Tiananmen Square—boldly referred to China's architectural heritage by imposing a series of traditional Chinese pavilions on a monumentally scaled modern railway station.[28] In this and other respects, the project shared certain affinities with Yang Tingbao's Beijing Railway Station, one of the ten major projects of 1959, although the new project was larger in scale and incorporated more architectural elements. The main terminal of the Western Station was composed of three parts: a northern terminal building, a smaller southern terminal building, and an elevated concourse across the railway tracks between the two. As in Yang's earlier station, the concourse and the bulk of the other buildings were modern both in planning and in the expression of materials and building structure; the traditional iconographic elements were concentrated primarily near the center of the very extensive, 740-meter-long northern facade. Apart from the station functions, the project built to date contains offices, service areas, and some residential accommodations for workers. The rest of the original 62-hectare site remains to be completed; an additional million or so square meters of commercial and residential space is slated for construction on the southern side of the existing complex. Likewise, the plaza area with the roadway beneath it is still incomplete, with buildings planned on either side of a widened Nanyangfangdian Road, which will serve as a north-south axis and primary entry to the site. In addition to its considerable length, the height of the main northern terminal building was 102 meters, giving it considerable visual prominence within the overall city landscape.

Closer scrutiny of the Western Railway Station suggests a complex attempt to conform to State Council dicta asking for "cultural tradition, local characteristics, and a spirit of the time,"[29] as well as to the well-known liking of Chen Xitong, then Beijing's mayor, for traditional roofs on prominent buildings. In one interpretation, the five pavilions on the top of the northern terminal could be regarded as pavilions on a newly constructed ground plane, built much as had been the pavilions on Coal Hill, or the Pavilion of the Fragrance of Buddha (*Foxiangge*) on the hill at the New Summer Palace (*Yiheyuan*), on artificially made topographic features. Originally intended by Zhu to house a railroad museum, these linked enclosures quite faithfully reproduced features of the *ting* and *ge* pavilion types from the classical repertoire.

Furthermore, the large openings at the center of the complex suggested a traditional gateway; it could be argued that the *jianlou* gate type in particular had been rather ingeniously appropriated in order to syncretize the high-rise portion of the project. Historically, *jianlou* gates typically rose well above the buildings around them to afford archers a better defensive standpoint; so, too, the center portion of the northern terminal rises above its immediate context, although for a different purpose. The gateway metaphor also made some sense given the wall-like mass and length of the remainder of the facade, and the fact that thousands of citizens traveling from southern and western provinces enter the nation's capital literally as well as metaphorically through this huge portal rising above the central concourse. Taken together, the "pavilion," "gateway," and "wall" elements of the Western Station could also be seen as referring to a *guan*, a form of gateway structure not present in the West that consisted of an enveloped rectangular space (such as the concourse structure of the station) with two gateways in its axis (like the northern and southern station terminals).[30] Historically, the *guan* often acted as significant signposts—for instance, to mark the eastern and western ends of the Great Wall—and also to distinctively mark arrival at a specific place.

In addition, the two enormous pillars in front of the northern terminal building were each topped with a monumental clock, referring directly to a similar clock at the older Beijing Station to the east—and probably also to the *huabiao* pillar forms that once symbolized the guarding of important traditional monumental sites. By contrast, the faux *pailou,* or gate forms, that were al-

67 The Western Railway Station, Beijing, by Zhu Jialu, 1996.
68 Central gateway and entry to the Western Railway Station, Beijing, by Zhu Jialu, 1996.

most literally appliquéd across the central portion of the northern facade were far more gratuitous and less symbolically charged. Zhu wrote that when "we emphasized the cultural context, we also emphasized the spirit of the time. . . . The union between a gigantic steel structure and steel pavilion is itself modern. There is not a moment in history when the gate opening could afford such a span."[31] After an observer gets over the first visual shock, he or she finds in the Western Railway Station in Beijing many, though sometimes contradictory, metaphorical references; the justified criticism of the structure notwithstanding, it was something of a tour de force in "modern content and Chinese form." However, its architect, Zhu Jialu—unlike Zhang Jinqiu, who has remained generally committed to a particular revivalist approach—has also designed decidedly modern buildings, such as the recent City of Contemporary Commerce Complex in Beijing.[32]

The Western Railway Station in particular might make it tempting to write of the emergence of a "postmodern" architectural movement in China, which some have dated to the 1980s. Yet in contemporary discussions of Chinese architecture, like contemporary discussions of Chinese art, others have questioned whether postmodernism is a relevant conceptual category; some assert, for example, that China never really underwent a modernist phase of art. When Western postmodernism arrived in China around 1985 or 1986 the influential journal *Zhongguo meishu bao* (*China Art Journal*) called for a debate on it. Shao Dazhen was among those who saw postmodernism as a form of historical revival, and others applauded the pluralism and diversity it promised; but on the whole, art in China seems to have remained overwhelmingly simple, descriptive, and narrative in its format.[33] The same might also be said of architecture. To some, the escape from any moorings referred to earlier had all the visual hallmarks of a postmodern reaction to modern nonobjective aesthetic criteria. But it would be difficult to argue that such developments signify much more than a desire for a superficial level of variety, for they grew out of no preexisting firm, broad commitment to architectural modernism other than in its most reduced form, forced on designers largely by dire economic circumstances. In architecture as in art, the philosophical confrontation with modernism and postmodernism required a substantially different set of theoretical underpinnings and trajectories of development within the field itself. On this point, in fact, architectural experience during the past century in much of the West and in China differs markedly.

Another aspect of cultural commodification that has been taking place around the world is the pursuit of prestigious public works projects aimed at catapulting various cities and towns into international prominence. Encouraged by the example of Bilbao in Spain, with its Guggenheim Museum (1997) by Frank Gehry, many city officials have sought to draw attention to their own locales as special places. Often these efforts intend ambitiously to create not only readily recognizable architectural symbols but also broader environments of particular distinction. Of course, this phenomenon is not historically novel. Cathedrals of old were desirable in part because they burnished the image and heightened the prominence of the towns and cities in which they were built. However, as deliberate attempts have burgeoned to put places on the map and to enable them to compete successfully in an increasingly intense global market for tourism, conference patronage, and cultural sponsorship, the phenomenon has taken on a new significance in degree, if not in kind. Thus the deliberate creation of architectural symbols and what often amounts to the "theming" of urban environments have been pressed into the service of local commercial and political gain. In short, it is believed that distinctive architecture and urban design sell. Moreover, the public works concerned have been entrusted largely to a relatively small elite of internationally renowned architects, many of whom have achieved something akin to the star status previously reserved for those engaged in more popular cultural pursuits. In addition, much if not all of this same production displays an image of "hyper-" or "global" modernity, quite separate from how a given project might otherwise have been conceived of and couched in local circumstances and architectural traditions.

During the past dozen years or so, architecture and urban design in China have been actively commodified in this way. It might be argued that Hong Kong, which returned to the fold in 1997, has followed such a course for some time, with buildings such as I. M. Pei's Bank of China (1982–1990) and Norman Foster's Hong Kong and Shanghai Bank (1979–1986), although not with quite the same scope and authority as the current Airport Core Program already mentioned, the planned development of a high-tech development park, and the recent conference center by Skidmore, Owings and Merrill (1998).[34] In fact, the Airport Core Program, which has cost about $21 billion, is to date the largest public works upgrade on earth. First proposed in 1980, approved in 1989, and essentially completed in 1999, this improvement consisted of a huge new international airport, two world-class bridges—the Tsing Ma and the Kap Shui Mun—two tunnels un-

69   The Bank of China, Hong Kong, by I. M. Pei, 1982–1990.

der Hong Kong harbor, 34 kilometers of new highways and railroads, and a new downtown terminal facility, carefully linked into the existing rapid mass transit system.[35] The airport itself, designed by Norman Foster working as a part of the Mott Consortium, was built on Chek Lap Kok, an artificial island adjacent to Lantau Island, some 25 kilometers west of Hong Kong proper. Clearly, the aim was to replace the land-based and outmoded facility at Kai Tak in Kowloon and to handle the enormous passenger and cargo traffic necessary to maintain Hong Kong as a competitive international hub. With its graceful curving metal and glass-roofed structure lifted high above the main concourse, the airport is the epitome of high technology and design. At 1.2 kilometers in length it is very large indeed, enclosing some 430,000 square meters of floor area. Highly rational and spacious in layout, the building is one of a new breed of large regional-international airports that by now include Kansai in Japan, designed by Renzo Piano, and the Kuala Lumpur terminal in Malaysia, by Kisho Kurokawa.[36] In addition, the Tung Chung new town is being constructed nearby; its projected population is around 200,000 people, many of them airport employees. Although building this town was an immense undertaking, given the time constraints, it was also very much in the prior scheme of Hong Kong's satellite settlement patterns, dating back at least to the 1970s.[37]

In Shanghai both the Grand Theatre of 1998 and the nearby Museum of Planning, built slightly later, are symbols of progress and newly sought-after international recognition. The Grand Theatre, located next to the monumental Municipal Administration building in the park that forms People's Square, was designed in collaboration with the East China Architectural Design Institute by the French architect Jean-Marie Charpentier, who was also responsible for the Bastille Opera House in Paris (1994).[38] With its curving upturned roof, which purportedly will eventually house an open-air theater, this building appears to hover over a plinth of foyers and entry stairs in a symmetrical and well-composed manner. In spite of his ultramodern use of materials—sheer glass walls expose floor slabs, column lines, and interior stairways inside—Charpentier clearly makes references to traditional elements of Chinese public buildings, such as the *xumizuo* and a three-part vertical division of volumes into a base, a middle, and a top. In overall appearance, the sweeping curvilinear shape of the roof can be seen as another modern reinterpretation of the "Big Roof," though here in the concave form of the traditional southern style. Indeed, the conspicuous roof and the overall proportions of the front facade, as

70 The Grand Theatre, in Shanghai, by Jean-Marie Charpentier, in collaboration with the East China Architectural Design Institute, 1998.

71 The Shanghai Museum of Planning, by the Ministry of Construction, ca. 1998.

well as the forecourt, resemble the traditional theater in the nearby Yu Yuan garden.[39] The subject of an international competition held in 1994, the major auditorium seats 1,800 people; the complex houses two other smaller performance spaces and a museum of traditional Chinese musical instruments. The Shanghai Museum of Planning by the local design institute, located in People's Square on the other flank of the Municipal Administration building, similarly sports a fanned-out roof structure in metal and glass, terminating the distinctive columnar volumes that form the body of the building below. Also elegantly proportioned and detailed with a high-tech skin of glass and exposed steel, the building is very symmetrical in its layout and full of traditional decorative references; its four floors of exhibition space provide glimpses into Shanghai's past, present, and future.

By contrast, the expressive architectural language of Shanghai International Airport, which opened in late 1999, moves back in the direction of other similar recent facilities like Chek Lap Kok; it was designed by Paul Andreu, another French architect. Located on the seaward side of Pudong—Shanghai's major new development area—the terminal is entered, on axis, via a well-designed and landscaped highway installation, by Michel Desvisgne, from which the departure lounges and other embarkation halls are deployed symmetrically on both sides.[40] Courtyard gardens are interspersed between these structures at ground level, with references made to traditional Chinese gardens of the past through the choice of planting materials and the use of rock outcrops. The gently curving roofs have their distinctive supporting trusses whose vertical elements are most prominent, like pipes suspended from the upturned ceiling; they provide a spacious, almost skylike canopy to the complex. Throughout, considerable attention was paid to the constructive detailing of the materials, which are primarily glass and metal. Again, the overall effect is very contemporary and forward-looking, projecting an image of Shanghai and China as having well and truly arrived on the modern international scene.

In the latter respect, Paul Andreu's proposal for the National Grand Theater in Beijing, designed in collaboration with Qinghua University, is even more dramatic—and, according to official reports at the time, deliberately so. The winner of an international competition in 1999, the proposed complex resembles an otherworldly giant bubble made of titanium and glass.[41] Incorporating some 120,000 square meters of built-up area, the building is very large, slated to contain a 2,500-seat opera house, a 2,000-seat music hall, a 1,200-seat theater, and

72 The interior of the Shanghai International Airport, Pudong, Shanghai, by Paul Andreu, 1999.

smaller auditorium accommodations of 300 to 500 seats. Located next to the Great Hall of the People of 1959, the proposed complex is the biggest venture in the Tiananmen Square precinct since the construction of Mao's mausoleum in 1977, and it is clearly intended to leave the mark of the present political regime on the nation's administrative center. As one commentator has observed, it symbolically projects "openness and originality[:] . . . an avant-garde building by a European architect, as a sign of China's increasing wealth and modernity."[42] Occupying a site of about 10 hectares, with surrounding gardens and tree-lined paths and roadways, the complex, despite its obvious contemporary architectural references, is also quite traditional in the symmetry of its layout, its centered monumentality, and some of its details. The idea of surrounding the building by water, for instance, recalls much earlier traditional theaters, which were often placed in lakes; and the five bridges forming the entry to the complex were clearly modeled after the five bridges across the symbolic moat inside the nearby Forbidden City complex. That being said, the earlier distinctions between "essence" or "body" (*ti*) and "form" (*yong*) are not nearly so sharply drawn in all these recent projects.

In fact, Andreu's controversial scheme for the National Grand Theater was halted, though only temporarily, in mid-2000, owing to a protest from the Chinese Academy of Sciences that seems likely to again throw open the debate between traditionalism and modernism in Chinese architecture. As it had progressed through various phases of the architectural competition, Andreu's proposal had moved from a relatively squared-off building, with a proscenium-like stage setting at the main entrance and an equally squared-off cupola on top, to the final domed configuration. It thus became increasingly less traditional. By contrast, a competing scheme by Terry Farrell of the United Kingdom, along with Li Daozeng's proposal from Qinghua, had moved in almost the opposite direction; Farrell's scheme shifted from a transparent set of three enclosures to a design in which the tripartite division was less evident and a large curvilinear roof emerged across the top of the entire complex.[43] To understand the controversy, it is worth noting that Beijing has had far fewer foreign architects participating in its construction than, say, Shanghai.

The other urban architectural phenomena aimed at updating China's cities and giving them internationally a certain familiarity if not respectability are the active urban redevelopment programs. Chief among them are the creation of new business and administrative cen-

73 Proposal for the National Grand Theater, Beijing, by Paul Andreu, 1999–2000.

74   Model of the proposed development for the Lujiazui district of Pudong, Shanghai, ca. 1997.

ters, mostly within China's large cities—for example, the Lujiazui district of Pudong in Shanghai—and the construction of what seem likely to become extensive networks of pedestrian streets and plazas. The process of extending Shanghai's central business district across the Huangpu River into Pudong was begun in the early 1990s with an international competition that drew entries from such notable architects as Richard Rogers, from Britain; Dominique Perrault, from France; Toyo Ito, from Japan; and Massimiliano Fuksas, from Italy. The idea was hardly new: after the fall of the Qing dynasty none other than Sun Yat-sen had designs on Pudong, and the Guomindang government, like other planners, saw the area as naturally absorbing Shanghai's expansion to the east. However, only when the contemporary economic boom both made it possible to finance the extensive infrastructure projects described earlier and made real estate investments a stark necessity could Shanghai act. Instead of selecting one of the final entries in the competition, the city cobbled together a compromise design, with mixed results. In a plan based loosely on Richard Rogers's proposal, a complex of tall buildings was set around a large public park that was modeled, at least as we see it, on New York's Central Park. More recently, significant commercial stretches of the famous Nanjing Road stretching westward from central Shanghai have been pedestrianized, along the lines of designs provided by Charpentier in collaboration with Zheng Shiling and other local planners. Zheng until recently was the vice president of Tongji University and vice president of the Society of Chinese Architects; he is a prominent architect of the third generation and one of the authors of the 1986 plan for Shanghai.[44]

Beijing has recently added a similar pedestrian zone to one of its main shopping streets, Wangfujing Dajie, and has completed several other pedestrian parks and plazas, also located in the central district. Again, the models and references are clearly international, although it could also be argued that the tradition of the special, well-defined shopping street dates back well into China's Ming dynasty. Moreover, the form of urban redevelopment near or next to existing centers—favored in Shanghai's Pudong, Dalian's Dahei Hill, and Guangzhou's eastward extension—also squares well with traditions of the past, especially as seen in the treaty ports of the nineteenth century, while it lowers costs by developing largely unoccupied lands.

Since the tentative efforts of the 1980s, architectural production in China has accomplished at least four things. First, at least in the beginning, it exposed the weaknesses in the ex-

75 Pedestrian precinct along Nanjing Road, Shanghai,
by Jean-Marie Charpentier, Zheng Shiling, and others, ca. 1999.

isting educational and professional systems, which had led to ungrounded and uncritical architectural forms of expression and to plain awkwardness. Such a negative result is not all bad, as it often means (as it seems to here) that some recognition of the problem is at hand. Second, it led to the creation of some sophisticated contemporary architectural projects; even by international standards, these were the most distinguished Chinese works in a very long time. The theater projects, albeit in foreign hands, are cases in point, as well as some of the affordable housing. Third, it has recently allowed contemporary architectural expression to find a voice, guided in part by infrastructure projects and projects in so-called young China. As a result, some architects—particularly those in the youngest generation—have begun, like their counterparts elsewhere in the world, to tease apart aspects of modernism, especially with regard to constructive, material, and transparent qualities, in ways that effectively accommodate traditional architectural interests and requirements. Finally, on the other side of the coin, traditionalist architecture survived and flourished in many locales—but with room to accommodate some contemporary forms of expression, as exemplified in at least the details of some of Zhang Jinqiu's work in Xi'an.

ONCE OUTSIDE THE DESIGN INSTITUTE COURTYARD, *Lu Hui blinked, stopping to let her eyes adjust to the sudden darkness. It was well that she did, because with another step, as she turned right, she would have stumbled into a poorly marked construction ditch hastily cut into the pavement. "That wasn't here this morning," she observed to herself, with a start. "They are really tearing this place up. New construction is going on all over." Then, catching sight of her friends standing impatiently on the corner up ahead, she began zigzagging her way gingerly toward them, around piles of stone and what looked like pipes or pieces of scaffolding.*

At much the same time, Zhang Shaoshu finally turned off the overworked air conditioner and, with Wu Feng, headed for the door and then down the stairway, its peeling paint glimmering strangely in the fluorescent light. "I do hope we really get something better," remarked Shaoshu, gesturing at the space around him. "Yeah, that would be nice . . . something less basic, more modern," agreed Feng as he followed down the stairs, almost too closely on Shaoshu's heels.

Before drawing within greeting distance of her friends, Hui looked back suddenly and caught a glimpse of Shaoshu and Feng under the light as they exited the Institute, obviously, judging from their body language, deep in conversation. "They're at it again," she thought to herself, remembering the day's conversation with a smile. "Those two never quit!"

"Do you want to grab a bite?" asked Feng, although only half-heartedly. He and Shaoshu never really saw much of each other outside of work. "No, but thank you," responded Shaoshu courteously. "I've got to get home to my parents, they're expecting me . . . some family business." "OK—see you tomorrow," answered Feng. "Anyway, there is this act I want to catch at the club tonight," he went on with a wave as he walked away, knowing full well that this comment would only confirm Shaoshu's belief that he was casual and unserious.

Turning right and walking in the roadway to avoid all the construction debris, Feng reflected to himself on the day's discussion. "He isn't so bad! But I wish he would get more involved directly with what we are doing. He's not very hands-on."

Some minutes later, taking a slightly different route than usual toward his home in the First District hutongs, Shaoshu suddenly paused in front of the open gate of a large courtyard house under reconstruction. "At least this is one way of saving these things. . . . Sell them to rich people," he reflected. "Though I wonder whether it is worth it, in the end, with all those poor families that have to move."

About an hour later, the cleaning lady shuffled back into the deserted office and began to rearrange the stools and pick up all the pieces of paper that lay strewn on the floor. "Always the same mess," she mumbled to herself, with resignation. "I can't make out much of what they do here. . . . These smudgy pictures on pieces of paper and these computers that they never turn off, with all those swirling shapes. . . ." Genuinely perplexed, she began to sweep the floor and, in the process, knocked over a half-empty Coca-Cola bottle. "Young people these days! They're in a different world . . . not like mine!" she went on to herself, dimly remembering all the changes that had occurred.

MODERNIZATION IN CHINA, since the onset of the Opium War in 1840, has in general been a long and arduous process, full of ups and downs. Today, China is a moderately well-developed country by most measures, although still very poor in many places and saddled with outmoded economic and institutional practices, despite many recent changes. It has gone through three relatively distinct periods of modern development. The first, spanning 1840 to 1949, is characterized by fairly sustained foreign contact and occupation, as well as considerable internal turmoil and a clear diminution of the influence of feudal society. Modern industries were established, a break was made with a centuries-old dynastic form of rule, and modern cities began to emerge, often replete with foreign architectural accoutrements. For the most part, the beneficiaries of this progress were better-off members of society, as the differentiation between upper and lower social strata persisted and was even magnified; the middle class and its influence—so much a hallmark of modernization elsewhere—remained small and relatively ineffectual.

The second period, beginning with the foundation of the People's Republic of China in 1949 and lasting until 1978, was dominated by a revolutionary social ideology, as the country attempted to make a complete transition into a communist state. Most, if not all, of the socio-political and economic framework of the prior period was either eradicated or altered substantially, even though the search for a broader and, to many, a better socialist way of life involved a large bureaucratic organization whose operation often continued to follow well-trod lines. The economic and social consequences of this period were often grave and even disastrous, and for-eign influence was confined to the early stages—largely that of the Soviet Union, which had an ideological perspective similar to China's. But China charted its own course through the Great Leap Forward and the Cultural Revolution, strongly influenced by increasingly left-leaning political doctrines and making only micro readjustments in between.

The third period, in which China still finds itself, began in 1978; it was marked at first by sweeping economic and, to a lesser extent, social reforms, as well as an initially cautious opening up to the outside world, including its architectural influences. After numerous debates, policy adjustments, and experiments, a market economy has returned to China, including real estate development (albeit in an evolving socialist form) and a renewed interest in architectural production. Few if any countries have faced fluctuations quite so extensive during their process of modernization; as a result, modernization in China is still in its relative infancy, though it is developing quickly.

Against this background, modernization is certainly not taking place as a preordained pro-cess with a given set of characteristics. On the contrary, it is self-determining and has thus far differed in certain significant respects from what many regard as the "standard model."¹ Accord-ing to this model, industrialization, which is carried out to meet the needs and aspirations of a society, is accompanied by a diversification of occupations and a division of labor. Consequently, people give up their former livelihoods in agriculture and move to urban areas, the usual loca-tion of the new employment opportunities, where they can also generally enjoy better services and more personal amenities. As cities grow and industrial processes mature and become more complex, the need for managerial, logistical, and financial functions increases significantly, cre-ating more jobs and even greater occupational diversication, usually accompanied by more social and physical mobility. One result is that urban metropolitan areas expand further out into the countryside, and urban functions are provided in many more centers, surrounded by resi-dential communities of varying densities and social circumstances. Many individuals enjoy higher standards of living and improved prospects for a better life, and personal freedom under what is by then some form of liberal democracy becomes widespread. Thus the key components of this model are the causal relationships between industrialization and urbanization, between both these processes and occupational diversification and opportunities, and between all these factors and improved standards of living and greater personal choice.

In China, industrialization has not been followed by such a seemingly automatic shift of people away from the countryside; instead, integrated networks of township and village enterprises and other similar community initiatives soaked up the excess labor created by improvements in agricultural productivity at or near the original domiciles and centers of daily life. Consequently, levels of urbanization, even as industrialization advanced significantly and the service sector proliferated, have remained relatively low, and there have thus been relatively few opportunities for extensive production of urban architecture. At the end of the twentieth century, the overall proportion of the Chinese population living in urban areas stood at 35 percent, compared to about 78 percent for the United States, a similar percentage for Japan, and as much as 84 percent for Australia.[2] Another consequence is an emerging pattern of urban-rural population deployment with certain features that differ significantly in both kind and degree from those found in nations in the West judged to be developed or modernized. In one distinctive arrangement, relatively small communities combine both intensive agricultural and nonagricultural activities. The population continuum thus now moves from central cities through peri-urban development to the distinctive form of settlement just described and on into densely populated agricultural communities and finally dispersed forms of settlement, in what several geographers have described as an emerging "Asian city model" for the spatial distribution of functions.[3]

Furthermore, very large and dense Chinese cities, like Shanghai and Guangzhou, are still much smaller than comparable international cities.[4] To some extent their growth has been constrained by government policy, which seeks to balance regional economic opportunities inside China and to preserve valuable agricultural production within the fertile river basins that are also the sites of major urban development. Nevertheless, these lower-than-predicted levels of urbanization also reflect an effective self-organizing system of economic and other opportunities located outside of major metropolises. In short, the form and rate of urbanization occurring in China vary considerably from what the standard model of modernization seems to prescribe. All this may change in the future, with better infrastructure, increased horizontal mobility, and further urbanization, as well as the agglomeration of many industries in the interests of economies of scale; but it is also possible that the seamlessness and ubiquity of communication and transactions promised by the present information age may lend support to the more diversified and looser patterns of settlement now present in China.

Another exception to the standard model clearly occurs in the realm of social organization, for relatively obvious political reasons. To be sure, many Chinese have begun to enjoy some of the social benefits predicted by the standard model. Incomes and material well-being have risen dramatically, especially in the coastal regions of China. Employment and educational opportunities have likewise expanded, and a significantly greater diversity of living arrangements has become available. Nevertheless, nothing approaching a liberal-democratic way of life can be said to exist, and personal freedom in matters even as fundamental as where one lives remains largely controlled by the *hukou* system of official household registration; other abridgments of individual human rights are egregious. The middle class still remains relatively small and weak, though it seems to be gaining in both size and strength as the economic fortunes of the country improve and reform continues. Furthermore, market forces, a primary economic engine driving the development of enterprises, land, and buildings within the standard model, are nowhere fully in place.

All this may change in the future, though here again the outcome need not be inevitable. Significant decentralization of decision-making authority has occurred at many levels of municipal and provincial government in China. A variety of economic and social experiments have been undertaken—sometimes with mixed results—aimed at deliberately exploring different approaches to modernization, without jettisoning core social and political principles. Some semblance of civil society is also returning to Chinese life, at least in a more recognizable Western form. Yet the upshot of these trends could well be a form of social and political organization that achieves the progressive goals of modernization without a radical change in other values of community solidarity and well-being, and without allowing the pursuit of unvarnished individual freedom as an end in itself.

All this may seem far removed from a discussion of tradition and modernity in architecture, but these changing circumstances have clearly formed the backdrop to and have influenced the continuing master narrative underlying much architectural debate and shaping the opportunities for architectural production. More important for our purposes, it is a narrative containing strains at least conservative, if not traditionalist, as well as progressive, if not modernist. The specter of *ti* and *yong,* as well as the question of their final disposition in relation to one another, remains very much in play. And judging from the history of Chinese struggles with modernity and modernism in architecture, it seems very unlikely that any further substantial capitulation will occur without a corresponding broad theoretical realignment of how the balance between "essence" and "form" is to be maintained. Indeed, the consternation caused by the recent pell-mell thrust toward modernization in many parts of China suggests that this issue has become increasingly central within general as well as elite circles. For instance, recent building in the Changjiang delta, where there are prosperous village enterprises, indicates that when left to their own devices, many villagers habitually incorporate traditional motifs into their houses overtly and, one suspects, sometimes defiantly. Certainly officialdom today in places like Beijing remains concerned about the issue as they continue to search for a sense of modern yet indigenous identity.

The distinction between East and West is similarly less useful to the present discussion than it might have been during the early days of the treaty ports in China, or at the onset of the Self-Strengthening Movement around 1860. For one thing, the sheer contrast between the beliefs and practices of one sphere and the other is less marked than it once was, and it now manifests itself differently. Each sphere has become less homogeneous. Japan, for example, a thoroughly modernized country, is most certainly in the East; conversely, the differences in both the trajectory and outcome of modernization between, say, northern and southern Europe are now understood to be quite marked in many respects. The postcolonial "new world" of the Western Hemisphere also exhibits substantially different rates and degrees of modernization from one nation to the next, and even within those selfsame nations.

Consequently, today the geographic categories "Eastern" and "Western" have often been replaced by economic labels such as "developed," "less developed," and "underdeveloped," and countries are grouped variously in slightly more specific frameworks under "regional studies" for other cultural areas of inquiry. Moreover, the current interest in the processes of "globalization" and their effects in various regions of the globe reflects the sense that populations and places often seem very similar if not identical in certain regards—usually economic ones. Yet peoples actively maintain their differences in other respects, including in their sense of nationhood. Indeed, there are now more nations in the world, with the residents of many other areas clamoring for that right of self-determination, than there were when the United Nations was founded in 1945.

China can fit a confusing number of the above categories. It is simultaneously ostensibly "Eastern," not entirely "postcolonial" in any full sense, "lesser developed" rather actively participating in "globalization," and of great "regional" significance. Perhaps a better way to describe its position is to consider the effects of a rather sudden or sharp encounter with newness produced by both internal institutional changes and external influences, often clearly visible in China's architecture—an encounter leading to the emulation of other modern practices. From an internal perspective, encounters with newness have not led to the jettisoning of tradition and past practices, ample cultural and architectural evidence demonstrates. Moreover, the scale and structure of social and economic institutions, let alone their style of housing, have changed appreciably and comparatively rapidly, even if along well-established lines, and largely through exigencies generated from within China itself. Faced with external pressures, China has emulated others in substantial technological borrowing, again incorporating change relatively rapidly—with obvious architectural results, as well as a much broader sociocultural impact.

Specifically, periods of American, Russian, and now multinational influence have formed key episodes in China's modernization and in related architectural production during the past century. Furthermore, technological emulation—with all its attendant ideological characteristics, as John King Fairbank points out[5]—is usually nonlinear in its historical trajectory. Sometimes, as in the case of Japan since the Meiji Restoration, it involves straightforward copying followed by partial rejection and, last, a more thorough indigenization. In this pattern, the influence of the foreign source is first embraced, then disputed, and finally incorporated and transcended.[6] To date, China's response to influence has been somewhat more varied, with repeated episodes of acceptance and rejection and perhaps only the beginnings of assimilation. At the more specific level of individual designers, and in the unfolding of various indigenous generations of architects, emulation has played a role in various encounters with newness; here, too, the results have been mixed. Productions may continue to be derivative, even to bizarre extremes, or may be absorbed into an internationally consistent body of work, as has been the case in many commercial and some institutional projects. Others have resisted newness, even with full knowledge of the expediency of technology, choosing instead to pursue a more indigenous, often traditional, course, especially on government-sponsored projects. The architecture described above of He Jingtang, Zhang Bo, and Zhang Jinqiu, respectively, fits these three stances. To date, these varying encounters with newness have not resulted in either a common approach or a regional style. "Essence" and "form" are neither consistently aligned nor necessarily recognized as having equal significance, except perhaps in the usually conservative official stance toward architecture.

Explicitly or not, in all of these encounters authenticity is a significant consideration, even if its precise definition sometimes proves to be slippery. According to Lionel Trilling, an ardent student of the subject, authenticity is bound up with an idea of complete control, or mastery: something is authentic when it manifests its self-definition.[7] In historic preservation, for example, authenticity does not imply copying or, necessarily, painstaking reconstruction. And a religious ceremony or a sacred rite can be performed in a variety of ways without being inauthentic. Thus the Roman Catholic mass performed in the vernacular has no less authenticity than a traditional Latin celebration. In fact, one of the motivations for the widespread shift away from Latin was precisely to make the rite more meaningful and authentic to the participants by making it more familiar. Trilling also emphasizes the idea of the leitmotif, defined roughly as the theme associated with a particular person or, more important for Trilling, a self-defining set of cultural ideas.[8] Therefore, it is not just the brushstrokes of the early-seventeenth-century painter Caravaggio but the subject matter of his paintings and his characteristic treatment of light, shadow, and color—defining examples of chiaroscuro—as well as his use of commonplace, nonidealized models that rendered his paintings authentic. Moreover, it was also through this leitmotif that his work was recognized during his lifetime as being culturally authentic in such a poignant and socially challenging way. A personal leitmotif established his authenticity well beyond the frame of his canvases.

Thus architecture needs a cultural leitmotif to establish authenticity so that a work can be said to be honest and constitutive of an era. A modern analyst might initially be tempted to say that works of architecture with obvious traditional elements, like the Chinese "Big Roof," particularly if they are made out of contemporary rather than the original materials—in this case, concrete rather than wood—are inauthentic. However, once the roofs are seen as a leitmotif absolutely necessary according to the cultural politics in play at the time, they become critical to the design process, and therefore honest and authentic. They cannot be simply dismissed as a needless aberration on the way to rendering the modern condition somehow more "meaningfully" and "truthfully"—for instance, under the guise of contemporary architectural modernism. In hindsight, one might also wish to argue, given the critique of the "Big Roof" phenomenon in China itself, that these expressive devices were too literal to be a leitmotif and thus failed to meet the demands for authenticity made at the time. To satisfy Trilling's idea of the cultural leitmotif, the forms should have been further refined or merely implied. Such a claim might have some merit, though it clearly makes both "form" and "essence," as well as the relationship between them, somehow architectural abstractions unrelated to literal details of the sort invoked by Henry K. Murphy in his syncretic use of *dougong,* gorgeous colors, and *xumizuo,* or by Mao Zedong in his emphasis on aesthetics and popularization. Such abstraction may be a dangerous approach to take, relying too heavily on an idealized, historically independent understanding. What counts as being either literal or abstract can change from one moment to another. Of course, a rejection of abstraction does not mean that all "Big Roofs" were or remain authentic. But they should be judged on their inherent necessity, which was and remains a cultural decision to make.

Attention must be paid to the question of which leitmotifs are allowed to emerge, through the cultural politics of the day. In China considerable attention was paid and continues to be paid to the "Big Roof," together with the other obvious traditional architectural details it entrains, and not without reason: it has long powerfully symbolized a link to the past. Nevertheless, there could have been and are other architectural ways of making this link. In Paul Andreu's proposal for the National Grand Theater in Beijing, for instance, the necessary reference, or cultural leitmotif, took the form of the single pavilion in the lake and the bridges providing ceremonial entry. The concept thereby represented was as much spatial as figural; or, to put it another way, the spatiality of this aspect of the proposal constituted the figure and its potential literal understanding. The same can be said for other projects discussed here, ranging from Qi Kang's Memorial Museum to Wu Liangyong's Ju'er Hutong to the supercharged Western Railway Station in Beijing. But more often the formal-figural aspects of buildings, and not so much the space created around and within them, have been used to express a link with the past.

There are several possible reasons for reliance on form. First, traditional spatial arrangements frequently proved difficult to achieve with programs that are modern and constructed on a much larger scale. Second and perhaps more important, many found it difficult to see spatial arrangement, except of the most extreme type, as presenting a distinctive figural appearance; thus it could not adequately serve when clear and familiar traditional references were needed—for example, during the 1930s and the 1950s in China. Moreover, uneven knowledge of architectural history could often be seen at work among Chinese architects, who were generally familiar with the shape and appearance of traditional buildings but not with their essential spatial characteristics. Today this lopsided vision of tradition is being usefully challenged, as the examples mentioned above indicate, by architects who are replacing the prior dependence on the figure of the building with attention to spatiality.

In this discussion, it is difficult to conceive of identity other than as constructed. Moreover, such construction is fundamental to the concept of authenticity. Something is authentic if it gives rise to and thus encapsulates a shared sense of identity. This happens when a structure comes to thoroughly symbolize a cultural moment—as does the Eiffel Tower in Paris, though at the time of its construction it met with widespread disapproval.[9] A facsimile of the Eiffel Tower, built somewhere else, is thus inauthentic; conversely, the use of the symbol on advertisements quickly conveys a specific sense of identity—the product is "about" Paris. Curving roofs, along with images of the Great Wall, may have the same power in China. The question then to be addressed is how to use the symbols of a tradition in order to convey and sustain an appropriate sense of identity. Too many aspects of a tradition deployed too often would effectively diminish their power, especially when the symbolism obstructs other expressive impulses that have to do not with tradition but with a progressive, forward-looking vision. But too few or no references to tradition may, for an indigenous observer, render an expressive work placeless—or perhaps even worse, may make it appear to come from somewhere else.

Fortunately, a different answer emerges if the relationship between "identity" and the "subject" is reconceptualized so that the construction of identity is taken into account. That is, a statement like "I am Chinese, and therefore such-and-such must follow in order for this reality to be expressed" is replaced with something like "I am in a modernizing society that also happens to be Chinese, and therefore such-and-such must follow in order for this reality to be expressed." This reformulation doesn't entirely skirt the issue of identity in the instance of "Chineseness," but it avoids putting its symbolization first; that symbolization is thereby allowed to result from the cultural production of architectural space and form in a specific place and time. Moreover, the reformulation makes it possible to sort through matters of "essence" (*ti*) and "form" (*yong*) without a priori assumptions about expression and under varied circumstances, potentially leaving room for a more fully articulated sense of identity.

An examination of the modern period of Chinese architecture makes clear that on occasion, symbolism has been put first very forcefully. As noted earlier, during the rise of China's two versions of nationalism—in the 1920s and '30s with the Nationalists and in the 1950s with the Communists—architectural expressions of the past were actively promoted by those in power. Although nationalism per se was no longer the driving force, the same might also be said of the 1980s and particularly the 1990s, when China, equipped with more modern accoutrements, began to engage with the outside world actively and more completely. All three periods displayed a mix of confidence and anxiety about identity; and when architectural judgments were made, both sentiments often got in the way of the necessary efforts to sort through essence and form. At these times the architectural juxtaposition of something modern with something obviously traditional, reflecting such a monolithic construal of *ti* and *yong,* made the viewer wonder "Which is it?"—thereby raising questions of authenticity and hindering subtler understanding of both tradition and modernity. Because of its almost complete absence of reference to tradition, the 1960s, when a reduced form of architectural modernism was in play, might draw the same criticism.

The problem in all cases, of course, was the monolithic and simplistic manner in which the terms in the "traditionalist-modernist," or "essence and form," conceptual framework were understood and applied, often under official scrutiny; the obvious solution is to somehow tease these terms apart and then consider how they might be related more productively. Judging from the record, several avenues present themselves. The inclusion of architectural spatial devices by those considering tradition has already been discussed, as have tectonic treatments arising from the use of modern materials and constructive systems. The beginning of both can be found in the Beijing Library. Nevertheless, considerably more work along these lines could be done. For example, traditionally based and perhaps culturally ingrained qualifiers of modern ideas

209

about function might be exploited further. Also, the question of "Which is it?" could be reformulated as "How can it be both?"; some combinatorial approaches of this type have also been discussed, including the Fragrant Hill Hotel.

Setting speculation aside, at this juncture it is probably fair to say that a tacit agreement has been reached on the matter of modernity and tradition in Chinese architecture. Or, to put it in slightly less conspiratorial terms, a pattern appears to have developed of uses deemed appropriate for each form of expression, though in general much of the traditional language is now more abstract, and much of the modern language has become less pointedly charged, certainly in comparison to their manifestations in the 1950s and '60s. In some respects, the old binary distinctions between "essence or content" (*ti*) and "form or use" (*yong*) has thus begun to disappear. Nevertheless, at building scales and in institutional circumstances in which the Chinese architectural heritage has developed effectively during the modern era, it continues to be useful. Usually this has meant buildings such as museums and libraries, whose institutional purposes are linked directly to some form of cultural life, or to low-rise, moderate-density housing, where a vernacular tradition can still obtain. Moreover, from the perspective of constructed identity and authenticity the persistence of the distinction is probably appropriate, the preceding speculation notwithstanding.

One intriguing possible reason for the continued effectiveness of a contemporary development of tradition may be the modernist characteristics inherent in much traditional Chinese architecture. These include the use of particular buildings for special functions, the ready use of intermediate spaces such as courts and arcades, the tendency of structures to blend in with natural surroundings, a sense of transparency or layering between inside and outside, and the use of building surfaces that often tend to be flat and therefore abstract in their overall appearance. Another reason for its continued use is the cultural familiarity enjoyed by traditional forms, especially when they otherwise appear to fit in or serve the needs of particular clients and users. In China as elsewhere in the world, this dimension is particularly evident in some housing, as mentioned earlier, although it is compatible with many institutional functions as well. Furthermore, if modernism is regarded as a set of spatial concerns rather than as pertaining strictly to style, then architects such as Yang Tingbao and Wu Liangyong gain room for leeway, as suggested above, to achieve something akin to Li Zehou's "modern content and Chinese form."

By contrast, modernism as a form of architectural expression has been readily applied to a host of contemporary building programs that only recently have come to exist in China. Large office buildings, hotels, large sports facilities, railway stations, and airports are some obvious examples. Furthermore, the degree to which there was no prior experience with a building type even somewhat similar matched the degree to which modern "content" and modern "form"—in the long-standing Chinese sense of both terms—appear to have become inseparable. This condition was particularly apparent in stadiums and airports. In other contemporary buildings, such as office buildings, hotels, or even railroad stations, especially when seen as being composed of other architectural elements such as gateways and walls, the particular modernist inseparability of "content" from "form" has proven much harder to sustain under cultural pressures brought to bear in the name of tradition. As a practical matter, there seems to be no reason to expect that developing nations like China should have started afresh in devising an expressive language for the architectural products of their modernization, save, perhaps, for the purpose of national pride. Moreover, even if they had done so, there was no guarantee that the results would have been very different from those seen in many other contemporary cities around the globe. In a world of greater cultural self-consciousness and yet enormously heightened economic inter- action and global communication, modern architecture—a little like the English language— has now become the lingua franca: it is the mode of building necessary to accommodate the spatial exigencies of these communications in a direct, familiar, and practical manner.[10] Many aspects of modernization, therefore, demonstrate not necessarily the emulation of others but rather the comparatively limited number of ways of accomplishing something efficiently and authentically, in Trilling's terms; the almost inevitable result was that things, and in this case buildings, began to look much the same.

As far as *ti* and *yong,* or essence and form, were concerned, the meanings of the terms in Zhang Zhidong's nineteenth-century formulation often shifted and were even transposed. In fact, throughout the past century, a practice of resistance seems to have been at work, whereby tradition was pitted against the rising tide of modernization—or modernism, in the case of ar- chitecture—changing as it went along in order to meet new challenges and provide an adequate basis to ensure identity, though sometimes this was hard to discern. The "Chinese learning for essential principles and Western learning for practical purposes" of the Self-Strengthening

Movement gave way to the idea of providing an adequate Chinese foundation first, before using Western knowledge to preserve that core foundation. Then, elements of the May Fourth Movement advanced a more radical position: they called for a wholesale importation of Western knowledge and social institutions and took a more moderate stance of using Western interpretive and analytical methods within a broad Chinese cultural framework.

In architecture, the result was the reinterpretation of traditional Chinese forms, occasionally from a more historically or archaeologically correct point of view, by using modern methods and constructive practices. Later on, during the period immediately after the revolution, socialist content replaced traditional heritage, and cultural form and particularly monumentality replaced other Western practices; the status of architecture was quickly transformed, as its official focus became "function, economy, and appearance where circumstances allow." Today, following the "Culture Fever" of the 1980s, the terms seem to have been reversed (as they were for some during the 1930s); the emphasis, in architectural as well as in other cultural circles, is on modern content occasionally mitigated or rendered more compatible with prevailing taste through Chinese form. In essence, architecture concentrates on signifying modernist conditions, but only where appropriate.

Indeed, in this day and age there is no need a priori to explicitly pursue a national cultural orientation all of the time and at all costs, especially when a market economy—presumably, a market that rewards individual creative initiative—is replacing the unified strictures of officialdom. Surely such an orientation emerges inevitably from the complex interaction of habits of mind, background, and prevailing practices. In projects in which no obvious role could be found for tradition, modernism, or at least something contemporary, was pursued on all fronts, often haphazardly and unconvincingly because Chinese architects simply lacked an adequate foundation in these approaches. Thus the evolution of modernist architecture has reflected not so much a clear cultural vision as pressing considerations of tradition put forward in the name of nationalism and solidarity, even though the historical experience of modernity has clearly been transforming China, despite arriving late and sometimes progressing in fits and starts. Here, as is often the case in China, the juxtaposition between *ti* and *yong* is crucial. The key to a more comfortable relation between the two—architecturally speaking, at least—appears to lie in a deeper and more informed appreciation of their very foundations, especially with regard to tradition and modernism, as well as a more speculative and nuanced approach to both. At present, architectural education—and its important by-product, a more knowledgeable and critically informed profession and public—is only beginning to revive in China after being stifled for a half century by the country's massive sociopolitical changes. If carried out successfully, this improvement in education should have a salutary effect, helping to control much of the haphazard and garish architectural production whose design decisions seem to have become unmoored from any rationale. It would also aid the many Chinese institutions and enterprises that will undoubtedly enter into client relationships with overseas design firms. And, perhaps most important, it could move Chinese architecture into a position of international leadership. Certainly the higher levels of construction now taking place in China offer ample local opportunity for such developments.

It would be a mistake, however, to conclude that only the most up-to-date matters of contemporary construction and design should be emphasized. In many ways, the entire edifice of both traditional and modern architecture in China is badly in need of intellectual renovation, in many cases virtually from the ground up, without interference from on high. Fortunately, China's decreasing isolation will certainly help in this regard, combined with the examples of international projects close at hand. As recurrent debates and much practice made obvious, both traditional and modern architecture were poorly or superficially understood, with none but perhaps a few having a firm intellectual grasp of them. China was certainly not alone in this difficulty. Practitioners in many other places in the world have constantly struggled to adequately square client needs, professional responsibilities, and a broader critical and disciplinary basis for contemporary architecture. If Chinese architecture is to succeed in this longer-term creative project, the core elements of "essence" (*ti*) and "form" (*yong*) will have to finally come to rest, conceptually speaking—preferably, in forms different enough to enable a productive tension to continue and to ensure an essential role for history in the further production of architecture. Derrida was right to object to the much-heralded "death of history," if for no other reason than that history often curbs the excesses, faulty thinking, and sometimes insanity into which societies fall in their all-consuming contemporary pursuit of modernity.[11] Moreover, as we have argued here, the gap between "essence" and "form" must be filled by a specific history.

CHEN ZHI (CHEN BENJAMIN CHIH), B. 1902

A native of the scenic city of Hangzhou and scion of a family of literati and painters, Chen Zhi attended both Tsinghua College and, on a Boxer Scholarship, the University of Pennsylvania, graduating in 1928. An excellent student, he won first place in the Cope Architectural Competition at the University of Pennsylvania.

On returning to China, Chen joined Liang Sicheng to teach at Northeastern University. He later entered a partnership with fellow University of Pennsylvania graduate Zhao Shen in Shanghai; they were soon joined by Tong Jun, with whom they formed Allied Architects. This firm became noted for its modernist leanings, breaking its vow against overt traditionalist architecture only once, in the design of an addition to the headquarters of the Ministry of Railways in Nanjing. At the National Commercial Bank Building, Chen Zhi's use of expanses of glass for the facade, rather than the customary fortlike masonry with small windows, was a major breakthrough.

Between 1938 and 1944, Chen Zhi was professor at Hangchow (Zhijiang) University. After 1949, Chen was president and chief architect of the Shanghai Institute of Civil Architectural Design, leading such projects as the Lu Xun Mausoleum and the Jingshan Petrochemical Factory's residential district.

DAI NIANCI, 1920–1991

Dai Nianci graduated from National Central University in 1943. After graduation, Dai worked at Hsin Yieh Architects, which was led by Gin-djih Su (Xu Jinzhi) and Li Wei-paak (Li Huibo), and helped plan the National Museum in Nanjing under the guidance of its design consultant Liang Sicheng. Among Dai Nianci's many works are the National Gallery of Art in Beijing, the West Wing of the Beijing Hotel, and the Queli Guest House in Qufu. While Dai's works are often heavily formalist in appearance, conservative in materials, and traditional in scale and proportions, they are also invariably creative in spatial composition. His government appointments included being a special consultant to the Ministry of Construction and vice minister of the Ministry of

Urban Construction and Environmental Protection. Dai was also an adjunct faculty member at Qinghua (Tsinghua) University and president of the Architectural Society of China.

Zhang Zhugang et al., eds., *Dangdai zhongguo jianzhu dashi: Dai Nianci* (Modern events in modern Chinese architecture: Dai Nianci) (Beijing: Zhongguo jianzhu gongye chubanshe, 2000).

DONG DAYOU (DOON DAYU), 1899–1973

As advisor to and director of architecture of the Shanghai Central District Construction Commission, during the 1930s Dong Dayou was responsible for numerous projects in the new Central District of Shanghai (now located in the northwestern suburbs), many of which featured a unique adaptation of the traditional language. Dong received professional training at the University of Minnesota and pursued graduate studies in fine arts and archaeology at Columbia University. On returning to China in 1928, Dong first worked in the firm of Zhuang Jun and opened his own practice two years later. His buildings in Shanghai's Central District range from the more revivalist and courtly Shanghai Municipal Government Building to the understated eclecticism of the Shanghai City Stadium.

Dong Dayou's portfolio epitomizes the dilemma of the first-generation Chinese architects. A polemicist as well as a prolific architect, he contributed articles on architecture to *T'ien Hsia Monthly,* writing on the challenges facing traditional architecture and the progress made by his colleagues on expressive issues. Ironically, in 1935 he built his own residence in an extraordinarily modernist style.

Doon Dayu, "Architecture Chronicle," *T'ien Hsia Monthly,* November 1936, 358–362; Wu Jiang, *Shanghai bainian jianzhu shi: 1840–1949* (The history of Shanghai architecture) (Shanghai: Tongji University Press, 1997), 158–159; "Xin zhongguo zhumin jianzhushi: Dong Dayou (Famous architects of new China: Dong Dayou)," *Jianzhushi* (Architect), March 1982, 54–61.

ROBERT FAN (FAN WENZHAO), 1893–1979

Fan Wenzhao graduated from the University of Pennsylvania in 1922 and opened his own practice in China in 1927. He collaborated with Zhao Shen and Li Jinpei on the YMCA Building in Shanghai. The early work of Fan took a distinctively revivalist approach. His competition entry for the Sun Yat-sen Mausoleum won second place, and he designed such projects as the Ministry of Railways, the Officers' Club, and the Overseas Chinese Hostel, all sporting elaborate "Big Roofs." However, his design thinking changed sharply in 1933, when two young architects newly returned from the United States joined his practice. His later buildings, particularly the Yafa and Georgia Apartments and the Majestic Theater, were all modernist works reflecting this new thinking.

Wu Jiang, *Shanghai bainian jianzhu shi: 1840–1949* (The history of Shanghai architecture) (Shanghai: Tongji University Press, 1997), 152–155.

HUA LANHONG, B. 1912

Born in Beijing of a French mother, Hua Lanhong received his architectural training at the École des Beaux-Arts in Paris and first opened a practice in Marseilles before returning to Beijing in 1951. He was named chief architect of the Beijing Municipal Planning Commission, and in 1954 he designed the Beijing Children's Hospital. During the anti-rightist campaign of 1957, Hua was targeted for his allegedly elitist attitude and the questionable aesthetics of the Children's Hospital. In 1977, one year after the Cultural Revolution ended, Hua moved back to Paris. In 1990, he designed the Chinese Cultural Center in Paris.

Yang Yongsheng, *Jianzhu baijia yishi* (One hundred collected stories from architecture) (Beijing: Zhongguo jianzhu chubanshe, 2000).

KWAN, CHU, AND YANG

Founded in Tianjin in 1921 by S. S. Kwan, a graduate of MIT and Harvard, the firm was first joined by Pin Chu, a graduate of the University of Pennsylvania; T. P. Yang became the third partner in 1927. Later additions to the team included Quei-ling Yang, a noted engineer, and Zhang Bo. Kwan's connections in the elite circles of Republican China included Zhang Xueliang and T. V. Soong, securing the firm by far the largest share of commissions among Chinese architecture firms in the 1930s and 1940s.

With the founding of the new capital in Nanjing in 1927, Kwan, Chu, and Yang received numerous commissions for the new capital's massive building schemes; they were almost entirely designed by Yang Tingbao, who headed the studio. In 1937, the firm relocated to Chongqing and continued to receive government commissions for the wartime capital. After the war, the American firm of Skidmore, Owings and Merrill collaborated with Kwan, Chu, and Yang on Mobil Estates in Shanghai, unrealized because of the Communist victory. In 1949, S. S. Kwan followed the Guomindang to Taiwan, becoming the president of its architectural society, and Chu Pin left for Hong Kong. Both Yang Tingbao and Zhang Bo decided to stay on the mainland.

Zhang Bo, *Wode jianzhu chuangzuo daolu* (My journey in architecture) (Beijing: Zhongguo jianzhu gongye chubanshe, 1994).

LIANG SICHENG (LIANG SSU-CH'ENG), 1901–1972

With very few built projects, Liang Sicheng nevertheless left architecture in modern China a boundless legacy: it lies in his pioneering study of traditional architecture, his efforts to preserve Beijing's urban form and ancient monuments, and his creation of one of China's finest architecture schools.

Scion of one of the late Qing's greatest reformers, Liang Qichao, Liang Sicheng received a rigorous grounding in Chinese classics at home and Western professional training at the University of Pennsylvania. Liang followed the path of his older classmates at Tsinghua School, such as Yang Tingbao and Tong Jun, to the University of Pennsylvania's architecture school, where all studied under the famed Paul Cret. After graduating from the University of Pennsylvania, Liang went on to graduate studies in architectural history at Harvard. He returned to China in 1928, becoming head of the newly founded architecture department at Northeastern University in Shenyang (Mukden).

Liang's career in Chinese architecture began in 1925, when he started to read the newly rediscovered *Yingzao fashi* (*Building Standards*). In 1931, he was invited by Zhu Qiqian, who had unearthed the ancient text, to direct a research organization on traditional Chinese architecture. Liang directed the Society (later Institute) for Research on Chinese Architecture, partnered by his wife Lin Huiying and later joined by Liu Dunzhen. The team discovered some of the oldest timber structures in China, including Fuoguangsi in Shaanxi.

In a letter dated March 9, 1945, to Mei Yiqi, president of Tsinghua University, Liang urged Mei to consider creating an architecture department at the school. Liang wrote, "For a thousand years, living standards have been rising with the progress of civilization and the development of building technology. In recent years, European and American living has moved toward specialization, organization, and mechanization. In the near future, the dwelling will become a machine for living, and the city will become a organized working mechanism." In the same letter, Liang further suggested steering away from the Beaux-Arts curriculum offered at National Central University and looking to the reforms Walter Gropius had introduced at Harvard University.

The end of World War II brought new opportunities and laurels for Liang Sicheng, recognized for his research during the war years. Between 1947 and 1948, Liang taught at Yale University, represented China on the design committee for the new United Nations Headquarters in New York, and received an honorary doctorate from Princeton University. During his sabbatical in the United States, he was exposed to the latest currents in the West, especially the very vibrant developments in architecture and urbanism that had taken place since his student days at the University of Pennsylvania in the 1920s. Liang was elected a fellow of the Academia Sinica in 1948.

In 1949, Liang heartily endorsed the new regime and took vocal positions on such issues as Beijing's master plan, preservation of its wall, and its traditional style of architecture. He was at the center of the "Big Roof" debate throughout the 1950s and graciously accepted personal responsibility for a deeply rooted cultural and social movement. Today, Liang's name is often associated with the "Big Roof," but he never really advocated the style itself, instead devoting himself mainly to a scholarly pursuit of the history of Chinese architecture. Liang was far more concerned with historical verity, technical accuracy, and the continuation of Chinese tradition, in whatever form, than with the building of traditionalist architecture that mushroomed in China in the 1930s and 1950s.

Wilma Fairbank, *Liang and Lin: Partners in Exploring China's Architectural Past* (Philadelphia: University of Pennsylvania Press, 1994), and "Liang Ssu-ch'eng: A Profile" in *A Pictorial History of Chinese Architecture: A Study of the Development of Its Structural System and the Evolution of Its Types,* by Liang Ssu-ch'eng, edited by Wilma Fairbank (Cambridge, Mass.: MIT Press,

1984), xiii–xix; Lin Zhu, *Jianzhushi: Liang Sicheng* (Architect: Liang Sicheng) (Tianjin: Tianjin kexue jishu chubanshe, 1996).

LIN HUIYIN (PHYLLIS LIN WHEI-YIN), D. 1955

Lin Huiyin was one of the foremost female intellectuals of modern China. Lin received an exceptional education in secondary school in England, at the University of Pennsylvania as an undergraduate, and Yale University as a graduate student. By parental arrangement, she married Liang Sicheng, a classmate at the University of Pennsylvania, and entered a lifelong partnership with him. It is also worth noting that Lin Huiyin was the aunt of Maya Lin, well known to the American public as the designer of the Vietnam Veterans Memorial in Washington.

LIN KEMING, 1900–1999

Lin Keming studied architecture first in Lyons, France, and apprenticed with Tony Garnier before returning to China in 1926. He was a consultant to the Sun Yat-sen Memorial Hall project in Guangzhou, designed by Lu Yanzhi and executed by Li Jinpei. In 1932, Lin established the first school of architecture in southern China, the Guangdong Provincial Xiangqing University, which subsequently merged with the College of Engineering of Zhongshan University (later the South China Institute of Technology). After 1949, Lin assumed a series of positions in academia, design practice, and government. During his long professional career as an architect, he designed many of the monuments in Guangzhou, including the Guangzhou City Hall, much of the Zhongshan University campus, the *pailou* of the Mausoleum of the Seventh-two Martyrs at Huanghuagang, the Sino-Soviet Friendship Building, and Yangcheng (*Dongfang*) Hotel.

Wu Qingzhou, *Guangzhou jianzhu* (Guangzhou architecture) (Guangzhou: Guangdongsheng ditu chubanshe, 2000), 256–258.

LIN LEYI, 1916–1988

Lin Leyi received his architectural education from the Baptist Shanghai College (*Hujiang*) and the Georgia Institute of Technology. After returning to China in 1950, Lin became chief architect of the Architectural Design Institute of the Ministry of Construction. He was responsible for two major projects in the 1950s, the Beijing Telecommunications Building and the Capital Theater. Both are stately buildings at key locations in Beijing. One of Lin's most important legacies is *Architectural Design Resources,* first published in 1964; eventually more than 200,000 copies were printed, as the work became the industry standard in China.

Liang Yingtian, "Lin Leyi xiansheng de xueshu chengjiu: jinian zunjing de laoshi Lin Leyi xiansheng dansheng 80 zhounian" (The academic achievements of Mr. Lin Leyi: A Memorial of Teacher Mr. Lin Leyi upon his eightieth birthday), *Jianzhushi* (Architect), August 1996, 107–110.

LIU DUNZHEN (LIU TUN-CHEN), 1897–1968

Liu Dunzhen is considered one of the four pillars of modern Chinese architecture, with a reputation as an erudite scholar, a devoted teacher, and an able administrator. Liu was the partner of Liang Sicheng at the Institute for Research on Chinese Architecture and a colleague of Yang Tingbao and Tong Jun at National Central University.

Liu attended the architecture program at the Tokyo Institute of Technology, returning to China in 1922. After a brief period of practice in Shanghai, during which he opened the first all-Chinese architectural practice, Liu Dunzhen joined the faculty of Hunan University in Changsha. In the following year, Liu was invited to teach at Kiangsu Provincial Soochow School of Industry, founding the first architecture program in China. The Soochow School was merged into National Central University in Nanjing in 1928. Liu rejoined the faculty at National Central after his partnership with Liang Sicheng ended during World War II, and he continued to conduct research and publish on traditional Chinese architecture until his death during the Cultural Revolution. During his long career as a teacher, he oversaw the education of such figures as Zhang Bo, Zhang Kaiji, and Qi Kang, all of whom were to become important members of the second and third generations of Chinese architects. His publications include such key works as *Zhongguo zhuzhai gaishuo (Chinese Housing), Zhongguo jianzhu jianshi (A Concise History of Chinese Architecture)* and *Suzhou gudian yuanlin (Classical Gardens of Suzhou).*

Liu Xujie, "Chuangyezhe de jiaoying-ji jianzhu xuejia Liu Dunzhen de yisheng" (Footprints of an
explorer: The life of Liu Dunzhen, architect) in *Jianzhu Sijie: Liu Dunzhen, Tong Jun, Liang
Sicheng, Yang Tingbao*, edited by Yang Yongsheng and Ming Liansheng (Beijing: Zhongguo
jianzhu gongye chubanshe, 1998), 7–21.

Lu Qiansho (H. S. Luke), 1904–1992

Lu Qiansho was a graduate of the Architectural Association School of Architecture in London. In
Shanghai, he was director of architecture of the Bank of China. In that position, Lu was originally
commissioned to design the new headquarters of the Bank of China on Shanghai's Bund. However, T. V. Soong intervened and requested Palmer and Turner, which was reputed to be the best
foreign architectural practice in Shanghai. Thereafter, the design of the Bank of China Building
was a collaborative effort between the two firms. Because of the traditional Chinese elements
on the building and Lu's participation, the Bank of China Building is often referred to as the only
Chinese building on the Bund.

Zhang Qinnan, "Ji Chen Zhi dui ruogan jianzhu shishi zhi bianxi" (Recordings of Chen Zhi's iden-
tification of certain historical facts), *Jianzhushi* (Architect), June 1992, 5–7.

Lu Yanzhi (Lu Yen-chih), 1894–1929

Often called the most brilliant of the first generation of Chinese architects, Lu Yanzhi during his
short career designed two of the most significant works in the syncretic style: the Sun Yat-sen
Mausoleum in Nanjing and the Sun Yat-sen Memorial Hall in Guangzhou. Lu lived in Paris briefly
as a child, and graduated from the architecture program at Cornell. After graduation, he worked
for the office of Murphy and Dana, where he participated in the design of Ginling College in
Nanjing and the design of Yenching University. Eager to solidify the legitimacy of the Guomindang regime in Nanjing, the government organized a highly prestigious design competition for
the mausoleum of Sun Yat-sen, the first president of the Republic of China. Lu's scheme, consisting of a series of pavilions in an understated eclectic style tailored to the sloping Purple Hill,
won first prize and he was awarded the project. Soon after, Lu won a second competition for the
Sun Yat-sen Memorial Hall in Guangzhou. The Memorial Hall is a massive octagonal auditorium

that follows a more revivalist approach. Lu died of cancer before either building was finished. Both projects were carried forth by Lin Jinpei.

Who's Who in China, 3rd ed. (Shanghai: China Weekly Review, 1926), 113–114.

Mo Bozhi, b. 1914

A graduate of Zhongshan University, Mo Bozhi was former chief architect of the Guangzhou Planning Bureau and professor at the South China Institute of Technology. Mo's works include Mineral Springs Hotel in Conghua, Baiyun Hotel, White Swan Hotel, and, in collaboration with He Jintang, the Museum of the King of Southern Yue's Tomb. The Mineral Springs (Kuang Quan) Hotel is an exemplary work of the Lingnan School. Baiyun Hotel was the first high-rise modern building in China after the Cultural Revolution, heralding a new era of architecture and construction in China. Mo is a fellow of the Chinese Academy of Engineering.

Wu Qingzhou, *Guangzhou jianzhu* (Guangzhou architecture) (Guangzhou: Guangdongsheng ditu chubanshe, 2000), 272–276.

National Central University/Nanjing Institute of Technology/Southeastern (Dongnan) University

The architecture program at today's Southeastern (Dongnan) University was first founded in 1927, as part of the National Fourth Chungshan (Zhongshan) University; it was soon merged with the Kiangsu Provincial Soochow School of Industry. Between 1928 and 1949, the university was renamed National Central and was the key national institution of the Nanjing regime. During the Japanese occupation, the school was relocated to Shapingba in Chongqing; this difficult period is ironically remembered as a golden age for its unrivaled gathering of talent. In 1952, the architecture department became part of the Nanjing Institute of Technology, which was ultimately renamed Southeastern University in 1988.

One of the oldest architecture departments in China, the architecture program at Southeastern has produced a vast number of architects in key professional and teaching positions throughout China, including Wu Liangyong and Wang Tan of Tsinghua University, Dai Fudong of Tongji University, and Tang Pu of Chongqing University—all former deans or chairs at their respective institutions. Zhang Kaiji, Zhang Bo, and Dai Nianci are three of the most prolific and well-known of the many practicing architects the school has educated.

Southeastern's enduring quality was built, most of all, on an extraordinary faculty. Liu Dunzhen, Tong Chuin, and Yang Tingbao each taught there for up to four decades. Because of the department's longevity, its library also enjoys one of China's most extensive holdings in architecture.

Pan Guxi, ed., *Dongnan daxue jianzhuxi chengli qishi zhounian jinian zhuanji* (Memorial Symposium for the seventieth anniversaries of the Architectural Department of Southeastern University) (Beijing: Zhongguo jianzhu gongye chubanshe, 1997).

Qi Kang, b. 1931

Qi Kang attended Nanjing Institute of Technology under the tutelage of Yang Tingbao, and joined the faculty of the school after graduation. As Yang Tingbao's protégé, Qi Kang has also collected and edited almost all of Yang's existing writings and works. In addition, Qi trained dozens of graduate students and was elected fellow of the Chinese Academy of Sciences. As a professional architect, Qi established a distinctive and powerful style of memorial and monumental architecture. Among his works are the Memorial Museum of the Nanjing Massacre and Yuhuatai Memorial Hall.

Qinghua (Tsinghua) University

Tsinghua School was founded in 1911, in part with the American repayment of the Boxer Indemnity penalties, as a school to prepare Chinese youth to study in the United States. Chen Zhi, Liang Sicheng, Yang Tingbao, and Tong Chuin all attended it before going to the University of Pennsylvania. Although Tsinghua became a university in 1925, only in 1946 did it begin an architecture program. Founded by Liang Sicheng and Lin Huiying, the department quickly grew to rival its more established counterparts in Nanjing and Shanghai. Mo Zhongjiang, Wu Liangyong, Wong Guoyu, Zhou Poyi, Zhu Changzhong, and later Wang Tan formed a strong team of teachers led by Liang. Taking advantage of its location in Beijing, Tsinghua also invited practicing architects such as Dai Nianci, Lin Leyi, and Zhang Bo to join as adjunct faculty members.

Zhao Bingshi and Hu Shaoxue, eds., *Qinghua daxue jianzhu xueyuan (xi) chengli wushi zhounian jinian wenji: 1946–1996* (Tsinghua University Architecture School collection of articles celebrating the fiftieth anniversary) (Beijing: Zhongguo jianzhu gongye chubanshe, 1996).

TONG JUN (TUNG CHUIN), 1900–1983

Tong Jun was a master architect, teacher, and scholar. Although lesser known than his University of Pennsylvania classmates Liang Sicheng and Yang Tingbao, he was perhaps the most respected figure in modern Chinese architecture, remembered for his rigor and erudition. Son of a Manchu scholar, Tong was educated at Tsinghua College and the University of Pennsylvania, where he completed both the five-year curriculum of the bachelor of architecture degree and the one-year master of architecture program in three years, while garnering multiple honors and awards for his stellar scholarship. After graduation, Tong worked in the United States for two years; he returned to China in 1930.

After his return, Tong joined the faculty at Northeastern University at Shenyang and took charge as departmental chair for a very trying semester between Liang's departure for the Society for Research on Chinese Architecture in Beijing and the Japanese invasion of Manchuria. Reputed to be a demanding and rigorous teacher, Tong was devoted to his students. When Northeastern University was disbanded in 1933, Tong organized a group of architects in Shanghai, including Chen Zhi and Zhao Shen, to see them through the completion of their studies and secured them employment. Speaking for the architectural profession in China, Liang Sicheng commended Tong as "a glimpse of light in a broken nation."

After the Japanese invaded Manchuria in 1933, Tong joined Zhao Shen and Chen Zhi in Shanghai to establish the Allied Architects. The firm was responsible for such works as the Ministry of Foreign Affairs in Nanjing (1932–1933), the Nanjing Xiaguan Electricity Plant (1932–1933), and the Shanghai Metropole Theater (1933).

Tong Jun's legacy is in his vast body of scholarly works. In 1937, he published the pioneering *Chinese Gardens: Especially in Kiangsu and Chekiang and Jiangnan yuanli zhi* (*Annals of Gardens in China*), discussing the history of garden building, landscape painting, calligraphy, and philosophical thought in China and drawing comparisons with the Villa d'Este at Tivoli, the Alhambra in Granada, and the Ryoanji in Kyoto.

Though he was a scholar steeped in classical gardens, Tong advocated and practiced a disciplined style that was remarkably progressive. In an article published in *Tien Hsia Monthly* in October 1937, Tong wrote, "The Chinese roof, when made to crown an up-to-date structure, looks not unlike the burdensome and superfluous pigtail, and it is strange that while the latter is now a sign of ridicule, the Chinese roof should still be admired. . . . It would be at once an anachronism and a fallacy if the tiled roof is made to cover constructions of any size with modern interior arrangement."

Tong joined the faculty at National Central University in 1944 and remained there until his death in 1983. During his later years, even through the hostile decade of the Cultural Revolution, Tong maintained a habit of reading foreign journals and kept meticulous notes from his readings. The brief span between the end of the Cultural Revolution in 1976 and his death in 1983 saw decades' worth of Tong's work come to fruition. He published *Xingjianzhu yu liupai (New Architecture and Styles)*, *Jinbainian xifang jianzhu shi (Western Architecture History in the Last Hundred Years)*, *Rebenjingxiandai jianzhu (Japanese Architecture in Recent History)*, *Sulian jianzhu (Soviet Architecture)*, and *Dongnan yuanshu (Glimpses of Gardens in Eastern China)*. As the political climate shifted toward a liberal opening to the West, his books quickly filled the lacuna of Chinese works on up-to-date architectural currents in the West. This was a remarkable accomplishment for a seventy-seven-year-old man who had not stepped out of China since his student days at the University of Pennsylvania and whose work had been suppressed for more than a decade. It is all the more extraordinary that in the final chapter of his last book he would movingly lavish praise on the Centre Pompidou (Beaubourg), recently finished and itself a subject of controversy in the West.

Tung Chuin, "Architecture Chronicle," *Tien Hsia Monthly*, October 1937, 308–312; Yang Yong-sheng, "Chunpu er jiechu de Tong Jun" (The straightforwardness and excellence of Tong Jun) in *Jianzhu Sijie: Liu Dunzhen, Tong Jun, Liang Sicheng, Yang Tingbao*, edited by Yang Yong-sheng and Ming Liansheng (Beijing: Zhongguo jianzhu gongye chubanshe, 1998), 31–38.

TONGJI UNIVERSITY

Originally founded in 1907 as the Tongji German Medical School, Tongji University built its architecture program on those of Hangchow University and St. John's University, whose architecture departments merged into Tongji's in 1952. Hangchow University's architecture program, founded by Chen Zhi, was later joined by Tan Heng, Huang Huabing, and Wu Zhiao. St. John's University program was founded by Huang Zuoxin (Henry Wong). Huang was a graduate of the Architectural Association in London; he followed Walter Gropius, who was in London between 1934 and 1937, to Harvard, becoming Gropius's first Chinese disciple. Because of Huang and a number of younger colleagues who returned from the West in the 1930s and '40s, Tongji developed a Bauhaus leaning distinct from the Beaux-Arts tradition at Tsinghua and National Central/Nanjing.

Wu Jiang, *Shanghai bainian jianzhu shi: 1840–1949* (The history of Shanghai architecture) (Shanghai: Tongji University Press, 1997), 158–159.

WU LIANGYONG, B. 1922

Wu Liangyong has been a leading figure in the department of architecture at Qinghua University since its founding in 1946. Over the years, he has made numerous contributions to the study and practice of architecture and urbanism in China. Wu, who graduated from National Central University in 1944, joined Liang Sicheng in creating Tsinghua's architecture program. At the suggestion of Liang, Wu pursued graduate studies at the Cranbrook Academy of Art, graduating in 1948 and working briefly for the office of Eliel Saarinen before returning to China in 1950.

As professor and dean at Qinghua University, Wu founded the Institute of Architecture and Urban Studies. A fellow of the Chinese Academy of Science and of Chinese Academy of Engineering, he has served as vice chairman of the Union Internationale des Architectes (UIA). The United Nations recognized Wu's Ju'er Hutong project with the World Habitat Award. Wu is also the author of *Guangyi jianzhuxue* (*A General Theory of Architecture*) and *Rehabilitating the Old City of Beijing,* and he founded the *City Planning Review.*

Zhao Bingshi and Hu Shaoxue, eds., *Qinghua daxue jianzhu xueyuan (xi) chengli wushi zhounian jinian wenji: 1946–1996* (Tsinghua University Architecture School collection of articles celebrating the fiftieth anniversary) (Beijing: Zhongguo jianzhu gongye chubanshe, 1996).

Xia Changshi, 1903–1996

Xia Changshi was one of the pioneers of the Lingnan School. He studied architecture at the Technische Hochschule in Karlsruhe and obtained his doctorate in art history from Tübingen. After returning to China, he held faculty positions successively at the National Academy of Fine Arts in Beijing, Tongji University, National Central, Chongqing, and finally Zhongshan University in Guangzhou. A follower of the Bauhaus, Xia used his influence to resist overtly traditionalist trends in the early 1950s in Guangzhou. On a series of buildings he designed or participated in as a consultant, his advocacy of natural light, landscape elements, and lively composition was instrumental in defining the distinctive style of the Lingnan School.

Wu Qingzhou, *Guangzhou jianzhu* (Guangzhou architecture) (Guangzhou: Guangdongsheng ditu chubanshe, 2000), 265–267.

Yang Tingbao (Yang Ting-pao), 1901–1982

With works spanning from the railroad station at Shenyang (1927) to the new Beijing Library (1987), Yang Tingbao was China's leading architect in practice and teaching for more than fifty years. Among the positions he held were professor at National Central University/Nanjing Institute of Technology; partner at Kwan, Chu, and Yang; president of the Architectural Society of China; vice chairman of the Union Internationale des Architectes (UIA); and deputy governor of Jiangsu province.

A descendant of the Song painting and calligraphy master Mi Fu, Yang emerged as a prodigy at painting at a very early age. At Tsinghua School, he was a close friend of Wen Yiduo, who would later become China's finest modern poet. Yang attended the architecture program at the University of Pennsylvania and quickly emerged as one of Paul Cret's favorite students; he won a series of design competitions, including the Emerson and Sigma Xi prizes, and was offered a position at Cret's office after graduation.

Yang returned to China in 1927 and immediately joined S. S. Kwan and Chu Pin at Kwan, Chu, and Yang in Tianjin. The Shenyang Railway Station (1927), a rigorous Beaux-Arts masterpiece, was Yang's inaugural project in China.

The mastery of traditional Chinese architecture that Yang showed in his later syncretic buildings is owed to a commission from the Peiping Bureau of Public Works and Relics Management Commission to survey and restore the Temple of Heaven, the southeastern tower of Beijing's city wall, and the Imperial College. From the master craftsmen and artisans, Yang gained a thorough grounding in the intricacies of traditional architectural style and building techniques.

Yang's training in traditional building was well suited to the Nanjing government's building program even though his work demonstrated other interests as well. The 1930s marked the most prolific stretch of Yang's career, including the Nanjing Central Stadium (middle-ground merger), Music Pavilion at Chung Shan Park (Sun Yat-sen Mausoleum; middle-ground merger), Central Hospital (Beaux-Arts), Museum for (Guomindang) Party Relics (courtly), and Academia Sinica (courtly).

Between 1945 and 1949, reinstated links to the United States and increased resources made possible a new turn in Yang's architectural style. The Nanjing Xiaguan Railway Station (1946) and Sun Fo Residence (1948) displayed a newfound affection for and mastery of modernism. In 1948, Kwan, Chu, and Yang collaborated with Skidmore, Owings and Merrill on the design of the Mobil Estates in Shanghai. Yang led the design of the project, and the partnership with the United States' leading practice again reaffirmed Yang's position at the forefront of an international professional arena, both in the modernism of his work and in the program of mass housing.

In 1949, Yang Tingbao decided to remain on the mainland. In preparation for the Asia Pacific Regional Peace Conference in 1951, Yang was assigned the design of the Peace Hotel to house the delegates. Working with a modest budget and a very tight schedule, Yang created an exemplary work of modernist architecture, acclaimed for its modesty, sensibility, and elegance. During the modernism debate of the 1950s, Soviet advisors sharply criticized the building as the box *ne plus ultra*. It was no less than Premier Zhou Enlai himself who vindicated the building: "Isn't the building very sensibly designed? This hotel has solved our problem." His other works, after 1949, include the Wangfujing Department Store (Beijing, 1954), Beijing Railway Station (1959), Nanjing Airport Terminal (1971), and Beijing Library (1987).

Yang is almost unique among Chinese architects in his immense international reputation; he was elected vice chair of the UIA for two consecutive terms. Lin Jianye, one of his students, recalled a visit to Louis Kahn: on learning the nationality of the young man, the master asked him if he knew a Chinese genius named T. P. Yang.

Yang Tingbao, *Yang Tingbao jianzhu lunshu yu zuoping xuanji* (Selected architectural writings and works of Yang Tingbao), edited by Wang Jianguo (Beijing: Zhongguo jianzhu gongye chubanshe, 1997); Zhang Bo, *Wode jianzhu chuangzuo daolu* (My journey in architecture) (Beijing: Zhongguo jianzhu gongye chubanshe, 1994).

ZHANG BO, 1911–1999

Zhang Bo is among the most prolific of the second generation of major Chinese architects. Zhang was the son of the last viceroy of Guangdong and Guangxi and started his architecture education at Northeastern University, in a department led by Liang Sicheng and Tong Jun. Zhang transferred to National Central University shortly after the Japanese invasion of Manchuria. After graduating from National Central University in 1934, Zhang joined the firm of Kwan, Chu, and Yang; he eventually became a junior partner and headed the Hong Kong office before returning to the mainland in 1951. During his time in Tianjin, Zhang also led the architecture program at the Institut des Hautes Études Industrielles et Commercielles de Tientsin.

Among the many projects Zhang led are the Friendship Hotel, the People's Cultural Hall, the Great Hall of the People, the International Club, and the East Wing of the Beijing Hotel. Zhang attributed his masterly hand to the teachings of Liang Sicheng, Tong Jun, and Yang Tingbao. His autobiography, *Wode jianzhu chuangzuo daolu* (*My Journey in Architecture*), makes a substantial contribution to the study of architecture in China since the 1930s.

Zhang Bo, *Wode jianzhu chuangzuo daolu* (My journey in architecture) (Beijing: Zhongguo jianzhu gongye chubanshe, 1994).

ZHANG JINQIU, B. 1936

Zhang Jinqiu began her architectural studies in 1954 at Tsinghua University and enrolled in the graduate program in history and theory at the same school. Under the tulelage of Liang Sicheng, she completed a definitive dissertation on the back hill of Yiheyuan (the New Summer Palace). In 1966, Zhang began work at the Northwestern Institute of Architectural Design in Xi'an, eventually becoming chief architect of the Institute. As a professional architect and learned historian, she has a firm command of contemporary techniques and traditional aesthetics. Among her most acclaimed works are the Shaanxi Museum of History and Tri-Tang Project in Xi'an. Zhang is also an adjunct faculty member at Tsinghua University, a fellow of the Chinese Academy of Engineering, and one of China's few master architects; she continues to write extensively on architectural history and theory.

"Zhang Jinqiu," special issue of *Pro Architect* 12 (November 1998).

ZHANG KAIJI, B. 1912

Zhang Kaiji graduated from the National Central University and had a private practice in Shanghai and Nanjing in the 1940s. After 1949, he joined the Beijing Institute of Architectural Design and Research as chief architect. Among the numerous projects Zhang led are the Museum of Chinese Revolution and History and the Sanlihe Government Offices. As advisor to the Beijing government on architecture and planning and one of the most respected national figures in architecture, Zhang was a vocal critic of the proliferation in the 1990s of overtly traditional architecture in Beijing.

ZHAO SHEN (CHAO SHEN), 1898–1978

Zhao Shen's professional life is highlighted by his leadership positions at Allied Architects, where he was one of three partners, and at the East China Architectural Design Institute, where he was chief architect. A graduate of Tsinghua College and the University of Pennsylvania, Zhao collaborated with Tong Jun and Chen Zhi on such projects as the Ministry of Foreign Affairs in Nanjing and the Shanghai Metropole Theater.

ZHENG SHILING, B. 1933

A member of the third generation of Chinese architects, Zheng Shiling was educated in France, returning to Tongji University in Shanghai as a faculty member; there he rose to become dean and, more recently, vice president. Prominent in professional circles, Zheng became vice president of the Chinese Architecture Association and still serves as president of the Shanghai Architecture Association. Active in local practice, he was one of the authors of the 1986 plan for Shanghai and recently collaborated on the design and implementation of the Nanjing Road pedestrian area. He is also actively engaged in the preservation of historical architectural landmarks in Shanghai, including the remaining *lilong* housing.

Luigi Novelli, introduction to *Shanghai: Architettura e città: tra Cina e occidente = Architecture and the City, between China and the West* (Rome: Edizioni Librerie Dedalo, 1999); conversations with authors.

Appendix B Glossary of Terms

The following is a glossary of names and terms used in the text, relating English spelling with *pinyin,* standard Chinese, and alternative spellings, as well as the older Wade-Giles form of transliteration when appropriate. Please note that in the text, the form of the names used—for example, S. S. Kwan (Guan Songsheng)—reflects what the architects called themselves. The same holds for political figures like Sun Yat-sen.

Academia Sinica, Institute of Social Sciences	中央研究院社会科学研究所
Allied Architects	华盖建筑师事务所
Analects	论语
The Architect	建筑师
Architectural Design Resources	建筑设计资料集
Architectural Journal	建筑学报
Architectural Society of China	中国建筑学会
Asia Pacific Regional Peace Conference	亚太区域和平会议
Atkinson and Dallas	通和洋行
Avenue of Eternal Peace; Changanjie	长安街
Baiyun Hotel, Guangzhou	白云宾馆
Bank of China	中国银行
Bank of Communications	交通银行
Bei Shoutong (Jimei)	贝寿同 （季眉）
Beihai Government Offices, Beijing	北海政府机关大楼
Beijing Children's Hospital	北京友谊医院
Beijing Hotel; Hotel de Pekin; Peking Hotel	北京饭店
Beijing International Club	北京国际俱乐部
Beijing Library	北京图书馆
Beijing Metropolitan Planning Commission	北京市都市计划委员会
Beijing Railroad Station	北京火车站

Beijing Telecommunications Building	北京电报大楼
Beijing Western Railway Station	北京西站
Beijing Workers' Gymnasium	北京工人体育馆
Beijing Workers' Stadium	北京工人体育场
Bell Tower and Drum Tower Plaza, Xi'an	钟鼓楼广场
Big Roof	大屋顶
Bohai Bay	渤海湾
Book of Changes; Yijing; I-Ching	易经
Book of Great Harmony	大同书
Boxer Indemnity Fund	庚子赔款
Boxer Rebellion	义和团起义
Broadway Mansion, Shanghai	百老汇大厦（上海大厦）
The Builder	建筑月刊
Bund, Shanghai	外滩
Cai Fangyin	蔡方荫
Cai Yuanpei; Ts'ai Yuan-p'ei	蔡元培
Cao Xueqin	曹雪芹
Capital Stadium, Beijing	首都体育馆
Capital Theater, Beijing	首都剧场
Central Cultural College	中央民族学院
Chang Ede and Partners	启明建筑事务所
Changchun; Hsintsin; Xinjing; Shinkyo	长春
Chen Denmin	陈登鳌
Chen Duxiu	陈独秀
Chen Xitong	陈希同
Chen Zhanxiang	陈占祥
Chen Zhi; Chen Benjamin Chih	陈植（植生）
Chiang Kai-shek Memorial Hall, Taipei	中正纪念堂
Chinese Academy of Engineering	中国工程院

Chinese Academy of Sciences	中国科学院
The Chinese Architect	中国建筑
Chinese People's Political Consultative Conference	中国人民政治协商会议
Chongqing; Chungking	重庆
Chongqing Great Hall of the People	重庆人民大会堂
Chongqing University	重庆大学
City Planning Review	城市规划
Coal Hill, Beijing	景山
Confucius	孔子
Conghua	从化
Continental Bank	大陆银行
Cultural Revolution	文化大革命
Dai Fudong	戴复东
Dai Nianci	戴念慈
Dalian; Dairen	大连
Daminggong	大明宫
danyuanlou	单元楼
Daoli	道里
Deng Xiaoping	邓小平
Dewey, John	杜威
Di'anmen Government Dormitory, Beijing	地安门机关宿舍
Dong Dayou; Doon Dayu	董大酉
dougong	斗拱
Dream of Red Chamber	红楼梦
duo kuai hao sheng	多快好省
Embankment Building, Shanghai	河滨大楼
Exhortations to Study	劝学篇

Fairbank, John King   费正清

Fang Lizhi   方励之

Feng Guifen   冯桂芬

feng shui   风水

Five-Year Plan   五年计划

formalism   形式主义

Four Modernizations   四个现代化

Fragrant Hill Hotel, Beijing; Xiangshan Hotel   香山饭店

Friendship Hotel, Beijing   友谊宾馆

Fujiadian   傅家店

function, economy, and appearance
    where circumstances allow   适用，经济，可能条件下注意

functionalism   功能主义

Fuzhou   福州

Gan Yang   甘阳

Gang of Four   四人帮

Gao Xingjian   高行建

Garden Hotel, Shanghai   花园饭店

Ginling College   金陵女子学院

Glimpses of Gardens in Eastern China   东南园墅

Grand Theatre, Shanghai   大光明电影院

Graves (Frederick R.) Hall   格致楼

Great Hall of the People, Beijing   人民大会堂

Great Wall Hotel, Beijing   长城饭店

Greater Shanghai Reconstruction Commission   大上海建设委员会

guan   关

Guan Yiyo   关以有

Guangxu; Kuang-hsü   光绪

Guangzhou; Canton   广州

Hundred Days' Reform	戊戌变法
Hundred Flowers Campaign	百花齐放
hutong	胡同
Imperial Academy, Beijing	国子监
Institute des Hautes Études Industrielles et Commercielles de Tientsin	天津工商学院
Institute (Society) for Research on Chinese Architecture	中国营造学社
Japanese Architecture in Recent History	日本近现代建筑
Jardine Matheson Company	怡和洋行
La Jeunesse; New Youth	新青年
Jiang Zemin	江泽民
Jiangsu; Kiangsu	江苏
Jianguo Hotel, Beijing	建国饭店
Jianguomenwai Diplomatic Compound, Beijing	建国门外外交公寓
jianlou	箭楼
Jianzhen Memorial Hall, Yangzhou	鉴真纪念堂
Jin Guantao	金观涛
Jin Mao Building, Shanghai	金茂大厦
jinghua	精华
Jingshan Petrochemical Factory, Shanghai	金山石油化工厂
Jinling Hotel, Nanjing	金陵饭店
jinshi	进士
Jiujiang; Kiukiang	九江
Ju'er Hutong, Beijing	菊儿胡同
Kaifeng	开封
Kang Youwei	康有为

Kiangnan Arsenal	江南制造局
Kiangsu Provincial Soochow School of Industry	江苏省立苏州工业学校
Kuangquan Hotel, Conghua; Mineral Springs Hotel	矿泉宾馆
Kung, H. H.	孔祥熙
Kunming	昆明
Kwan, Song Sing; Guan Songsheng	关颂声
Kwan, Chu, and Yang	基泰工程司
Kwantung Army	关东军
Li Chung-kan; Li Zongkan	李宗侃
Li Dazhao	李大钊
Li Hongzhang	李鸿章
Li Jie; Li Chieh	李
Li Jinpei; Poy G. Lee	李锦沛
Li Wei-paak; Li Huibo	李惠伯
Li Zehou	李泽厚
li, i, lien, ch'ih	礼义廉耻
Liang Qichao	梁启超
Liang Shuming	梁漱溟
Liang Sicheng; Liang Ssu-ch'eng	梁思成
Liaodong Peninsula	辽东半岛
lilong/linong[1]	里弄[1]
Lin Biao	林彪
Lin Changmin	林长民
Lin Huiyin; Lin Whei-yin (Phyllis)	林徽音
Lin Keming	林克明
Lin Leyi	林乐义
Lin, Maya	林樱

1. The row house lanes found in Shanghai and Tianjin can be pronounced either as *lilong*, in the Shanghai dialect, or *linong*, in Mandarin.

Lin Yutang	林语堂
Lingnan University; Canton Christian College	岭南大学
Liu Dunzhen; Liu Tun-chen	刘敦桢（士能）
Liu Hongdian	刘鸿典
Liu Huixian	刘恢先
Liu Kaiqu	刘开渠
Liu Xiufeng	刘秀峰
Liulichang	琉璃厂
Lu Xun (Zhou Shuren); Lu Hsun	鲁迅（周树人）
Lü Yanzhi; Lü Yen-chih	吕彦直
Lujiazui	陆家嘴
Luke, H. S.; Lu Qianshou	陆谦受
Lüshun; Port Arthur	旅顺
Majestic Theater, Shanghai	美琪大戏院
Manchukuo	满洲国
Mann (Arthur) Hall	思孟堂
Mao Zedong; Mao Tse-tung	毛泽东
Market Fever	市场热
Mausoleum of the Seventy-two Martyrs at Huanghuagang, Guangzhou	黄花岗 72 烈士陵园
May Fourth Movement	五四运动
Meiji Restoration	明治维新
Memorial Court to Kukai, Xi'an	空海纪念碑院
Memorial Hall of Lingnan Painting School, Guangzhou	岭南画派纪念馆
Memorial Museum of Nanjing Massacre, Nanjing	侵华日军南京大屠杀遇难同胞纪念馆
Memorial to Abeno Nakamoro, Xi'an	阿倍仲麻侣纪念碑
Mencius	孟子
Mercantile Bank of India	有利银行
Metropole Hotel, Shanghai	都城饭店（新城饭店）

Nanshi	南市
National Agricultural Exhibition Center, Beijing	全国农业展览馆
National Assembly, Nanjing	国民大会堂
National Capital Construction Commission	首都建设委员会
National Central Museum, Nanjing	国立中央博物院
National Central University	国立中央大学
National Commercial Bank	浙江兴业银行
National Convention on Residential Standards	全国居住标准座谈会
National Gallery of Art, Beijing	中国美术馆
National Grand Theater, Beijing	国家大剧院
National Northeastern University; Tung-pei; Dongbei	国立东北大学
National Southeastern University	国立东南大学
National Southwest Associated University	国立西南联合大学
neoclassicism	古典主义
New Architecture and Styles	新建筑与流派
New Culture Movement	新文化运动
New Democracy Movement	新民主主义运动
New Life Movement; National Rejuvenation Movement	新生运动
New Summer Palace; Yiheyuan	颐和园
Nextage Shopping Center, Shanghai	新世纪商厦
Ningbo Cultural Center	宁波文化中心
Niu Ming	牛明
Officers' Club, Nanjing	励志社
Opium War	鸦片战争
Overseas Chinese Mansion, Beijing	华侨大厦
pailou	牌楼
Palace Hotel, Shanghai	汇中饭店
Palmer and Turner	公和洋行

Qingdao	青岛
Qinglong Temple, Xi'an	青龙寺
Queli Guest House, Qufu	阙里宾舍
Qufu	曲阜
Quyang New Village, Shanghai	曲阳新邨
revivalism	复古主义
St. Francis Xavier, Shanghai	董家渡天主堂
St. John's University	圣约翰大学
sanheyuan	三合院
Sanlihe Government Offices, Beijing	三里河政府机关大楼
Sassoon House, Shanghai (Peace Hotel)	沙逊大厦
Self-Strengthening Movement	自强运动
Shaanxi Museum of History, Xi'an	陕西历史博物馆
Shamian	沙面
Shandong; Shantung	山东
Shandong Rural Development Research Institute	山东乡村建设研究院
Shanghai	上海
Shanghai Broadcasting Building	上海广播大楼
Shanghai Center	上海商城
Shanghai City Library	上海市图书馆
Shanghai City Museum	上海市博物馆
Shanghai City Stadium	上海市体育场
Shanghai Club	上海总会
Shanghai Customs House	上海海关
Shanghai General Post Office	上海邮政总局
Shanghai Grand Theatre	上海大剧院
Shanghai Library	上海图书馆
Shanghai Municipal Government Building	上海市政府大楼

Study of Confucius as a Reformer	孔子改制考
Study of the Forged Xin Classics	新学伪经考
Su, Gin-djih; Xu Jinzhi	徐敬直
Sun Company, Shanghai	大新公司
Sun Dong An Market, Beijing	新东安
Sun Ke; Sun Fo	孙科
Sun Yat-sen; Sun Zhongshan	孙中山（孙逸仙）
Sun Yat-sen University; Zhongshan University; Chung Shan University	中山大学
A Survey of Garden South of the Changjiang River	江南园林志
Tang Banquet Hall, Xi'an	唐歌舞餐厅
Tang Culture and Arts Museum, Xi'an	唐艺术陈列馆
Tang Pu	唐璞
Temple of Heaven	天坛
Theory of New Democracy	新民主主义论
Three Gate Housing Complex, Beijing	前三门住宅
ti	体
Tiananmen; Gate of Heavenly Peace	天安门
Tianjin; Tientsin	天津
T'ien Hsia Monthly	天下月刊
Tokyo Institute of Technology	东京工业大学
Tong Jun; Tung Chuin	童寯
Tongfangxiang Residential Quarter, Suzhou	桐方乡
Tongji University	同济大学
Tongzhi Restoration	同治中兴
Tri-Tang Projects	三唐工程
True Story of Ah Q	阿Q正传
Tsur, Y. T.	周诒春

Xi'an	西安
Xi'an Garden Hotel	西安唐华宾馆
Xing Tonghe	邢同和
Xinmin congbao	新民丛报
Xiong Ming	熊明
xumizuo	须弥座
Yale-in-China	雅礼学堂
Yan Fu; Yen Fu	严复
Yang Quei-ling; Yang Kuanlin	杨宽麟
Yang Tingbao; T. P. Yang	杨挺宝 （仁辉）
Yangzhou	扬州
Yen (Young-kiung) Hall	思颜堂
Yenching University	燕京大学
Yiheyuan; New Summer Palace	颐和园
Yingzao fashi; Ying-tsao fa-shih; Building Standards	营造法式
YMCA Building, Shanghai	基督教青年会
yong; yung	用
youhuanyishi	忧患意识
Yu Qingjiang	余清江
Yu Yuan	豫园
Yuan Shikai	袁世凯
Yuhuatai Memorial Hall, Nanjing	雨花台纪念馆
zaopo	糟粕
Zeng Guofan	曾国藩
Zhang Bo	张镈
Zhang Depei	张德沛
Zhang Jiade	张嘉德
Zhang Jinqiu	张锦秋

Zhang Kaiji	张开济
Zhang Xueliang; Chang Hsüeh-liang	张学良
Zhang Zhidong	张之洞
Zhangjiagang	张家港
Zhao Shen; Chao Shen	赵深
Zhao Ziyang	赵紫阳
Zheng Shiling	郑时龄
Zheng Zhizhi	郑枝之
Zhenjiang	镇江
zhong	中
Zhongguo meishu bao	中国美术报
zhongxue weiti, xixue weiyong	中学为体，西学为用
Zhou Enlai	周恩来
Zhouli kaogongji; Record of Trades	周礼考工记
Zhu Bin; Chu Pin	朱彬
Zhu Changzhong	朱畅中
Zhu Jialu	朱家禄
Zhu Qiqian; Chu Ch'i-ch'ien	朱启
Zhu Wenyi	朱文一
Zhuang Jun; Tsin Chuan	庄俊
Zongli yamen; Office of Foreign Affairs	总理各国事务衙门

NOTES

TRADITIONALISM VERSUS MODERNISM IN CHINA

1. See Peter Ward Fay, *The Opium War, 1840–1842: Barbarians in the Celestial Empire in the Early Part of the Nineteenth Century and the War by Which They Forced Her Gates Ajar* (1975: reprint, Chapel Hill: University of North Carolina Press, 1997); John King Fairbank, *Trade and Diplomacy on the China Coast: The Opening of the Treaty Ports, 1842–1854* (Cambridge, Mass.: Harvard University Press, 1953).

2. William Theodore de Bary, *East Asian Civilizations: A Dialogue in Five Stages* (Cambridge, Mass.: Harvard University Press, 1988), 1–20.

3. See Clae Waltham, *I Ching: The Chinese Book of Changes* (New York: Ace Book, 1969), 204–206, on the hexagram of *li*.

4. De Bary, *East Asian Civilizations,* 9.

5. Ibid., 69–70.

6. For general accounts of the Second Opium War, see John King Fairbank, *China: A New History* (Cambridge, Mass.: Harvard University Press, Belknap Press, 1992), 198–205; Ray Huang, *China: A Macro History* (Armonk, N.Y.: M. E. Sharpe, 1997), 227–241; Immanuel C. Y. Hsu, *The Rise of Modern China,* 4th ed. (New York: Oxford University Press, 1990); Jonathan D. Spence, *The Search for Modern China* (New York: W. W. Norton, 1990), 147–164.

7. For general accounts of the Foreign Matters Movement, see Michael Dillon, ed., *China: A Historical and Cultural Dictionary* (Richmond: Curzon, 1998), 276; Fairbank, *China: A New History,* 217ff.; Huang, *China: A Macro History,* 238f.

8. Ssu-Yü Teng and John K. Fairbank, *China's Response to the West: A Documentary Survey, 1839–1923,* 2nd ed. (Cambridge, Mass.: Harvard University Press, 1979), 50f.; Seng Kuan, "Bivalency Constructed: The Big Roof Phenomenon in Contemporary Chinese Architecture" (B.A. honors thesis, Harvard College, 1998), 30–34.

9. Quoted in Huang, *China: A Macro History,* 238.
10. De Bary, *East Asian Civilizations,* 48.
11. William Theodore de Bary, Wing-tsit Chan, and Chester Tan, comps., *Sources of Chinese Tradition,* vol. 2 (1960; reprint, New York: Columbia University Press, 1964), 82.
12. De Bary, *East Asian Civilizations,* 47.
13. For general accounts of the Taipeng Rebellion, see Fairbank, *China: A New History,* 206f.; Jen Yu-wen, *The Taiping Revolutionary Movement* (New Haven: Yale University Press, 1973).
14. Feng Guifen, "On the Manufacture of Foreign Weapons," in de Bary, Wing, and Tan, comps., *Sources of Chinese Tradition,* 46.
15. Spence, *The Search for Modern China,* 197.
16. Feng Guifen, "On the Adoption of Western Learning," in de Bary, Wing, and Tan, comps., *Sources of Chinese Tradition,* 48; see also Teng and Fairbank, *China's Response to the West,* 52.
17. Dillon, *China: A Historical and Cultural Dictionary,* 99.
18. On Li generally, see Stanley Spector, *Li Hung-chang and the Huai Army: A Study in Nineteenth-Century Chinese Regionalism* (Seattle: University of Washington Press, 1964).
19. Dillon, *China: A Historical and Cultural Dictionary,* 196–197.
20. Fairbank, *China: A New History,* 217.
21. Ibid., 218–219.
22. Kang Youwei, "The Three Ages," in de Bary, Wing, and Tan, comps., *Sources of Chinese Tradition,* 70–71.
23. See Kung-ch'uan Hsiao, *A Modern China and a New World: K'ang Yu-Wei, Reformer and Utopian, 1858–1927* (Seattle: University of Washington Press, 1975). Guangxu, whose personal name was Zaitian, was the penultimate emperor of the Manchu Qing dynasty and the son of Prince Jun and the empress dowager Cixi's sister.
24. Huang, *China: A Macro History,* 244–247.
25. See also Liang Qichao, "A People Made New," in de Bary, Wing, and Tan, comps., *Sources of Chinese Tradition,* 93–97.
26. See Joseph R. Levenson, *Liang Ch'i-ch'ao and the Mind of Modern China* (Cambridge, Mass.: Harvard University Press, 1953); Philip Huang, *Liang Ch'i-ch'ao and Modern Chinese Liberalism* (Seattle: University of Washington Press, 1972).
27. Huang, *China: A Macro History,* 242f.
28. See Luke S. K. Kwong, *A Mosaic of the Hundred Days: Personalities, Politics, and Ideas of 1898* (Cambridge, Mass.: Council on East Asian Studies, Harvard University, 1984).
29. Zhang Zhidong, "Exhortation to Learn," in de Bary, Wing, and Tan, comps., *Sources of Chinese Tradition,* 81; see also Teng and Fairbank, *China's Response to the West,* 169.
30. Perry Link, *Evening Chats in Beijing: Probing China's Predicament* (New York: W. W. Norton, 1992), 249.
31. See Mary Clabaugh Wright, ed., *China in Revolution: The First Phase, 1900–1913* (New Haven: Yale University Press, 1968).
32. On Sun Yat-sen, see C. Martin Wilbur, *Sun Yat-sen, Frustrated Patriot* (New York: Columbia University Press, 1976).
33. Mary Clabaugh Wright, introduction to Wright, ed., *China in Revolution,* 3–11.
34. See Ernest Young, *The Presidency of Yuan Shih-kai: Liberation and Dictatorship in Early Republican China* (Ann Arbor: University of Michigan Press, 1977).

35. See Hsi-sheng Ch'i, *Warlord Politics in China, 1916–1928* (Stanford: Stanford University Press, 1976).

36. Sun Yat-sen, "The Three People's Principles," in de Bary, Wing, and Tan, comps., *Sources of Chinese Tradition,* 107.

37. Sun Yat-sen, "The Three Stages of Revolution," in de Bary, Wing, and Tan, comps., *Sources of Chinese Tradition,* 119.

38. See Tse-tsung Chou, *The May Fourth Movement: Intellectual Revolution in Modern China* (Cambridge, Mass.: Harvard University Press, 1960); Fairbank, *China: A New History,* 267; Vera Schwarcz, *The Chinese Enlightenment: Intellectuals and the Legacy of the May Fourth Movement of 1919* (Berkeley: University of California Press, 1986).

39. For a detailed account of the student demonstration, see Spence, *The Search for Modern China,* 310f.

40. Ibid., 311–312.

41. Ibid., 312.

42. Fairbank, *China: A New History,* 267–269.

43. Huang, *China: A Macro History,* 257–258; Spence, *The Search for Modern China,* 313–319.

44. Spence, *The Search for Modern China,* 314; on Cai more generally, see William J. Duiker, *Ts'ai Yuan-p'ei: Educator of Modern China* (University Park: Pennsylvania State University Press, 1977).

45. Chou, *The May Fourth Movement,* 53f.

46. On Chen's beliefs, see Lee Feigon, *Chen Duxiu: Founder of the Chinese Communist Party* (Princeton: Princeton University Press, 1983).

47. Spence, *The Search for Modern China,* 315.

48. Ibid., 315–317.

49. Huang, *China: A Macro History,* 259.

50. Spence, *The Search for Modern China,* 318.

51. Lu Xun, *Diary of a Madman and Other Stories,* translated by William Lyell (Honolulu: University of Hawaii Press, 1990).

52. See Leo Ou-fan Lee, *Voices from the Iron House: A Study of Lu Xun* (Bloomington: Indiana University Press, 1987).

53. Ibid., 379–381, and Huang, *China: A Macro History,* 257.

54. Xudong Zhang, *Chinese Modernism in the Era of Reforms: Cultural Fever, Avant-Garde Fiction, and the New Chinese Cinema* (Durham: Duke University Press, 1997), 43.

55. Spence, *The Search for Modern China,* 369; see also Liang Shuming, "Eastern and Western Civilizations and Their Philosophies," in de Bary, Wing, and Tan, comps., *Sources of Chinese Tradition,* 187–188.

56. Dillon, ed., *China: A Historical and Cultural Dictionary,* 233.

57. General Chiang Kai-shek, *Outline of the New Life Movement,* translated by Madame Chiang Kai-shek (Nanjing: New Life Movement Headquarters, China, 1934), 2.

58. William C. Kirby, *Germany and Republican China* (Stanford: Stanford University Press, 1984); Spence, *The Search for Modern China,* 415–416.

59. Chiang, *Outline of the New Life Movement,* 1.

60. Mao Zedong, "On New Democracy," in de Bary, Wing, and Tan, comps., *Sources of Chinese Tradition,* 181.

61. Mao Zedong, *Xinminzhuzhuyilun* (Theory of new democracy) (1940; reprint, Beijing: People's Press, 1975), 23.

FOREIGN INFLUENCES AND THE FIRST GENERATION OF CHINESE ARCHITECTS

1. See *The Summer Place* (Beijing: China Esperanto Press, 1993).
2. Nancy Shatzman Steinhardt, *Chinese Imperial City Planning* (Honolulu: University of Hawaii Press, 1990), 33.
3. Ibid., 34–35.
4. Andrew Boyd, *Chinese Architecture and Town Planning, 1500 B.C.–A.D. 1911* (Chicago: University of Chicago Press, 1962), 23–25; quotation, 24; see also Wu Jin, "The Historical Development of Chinese Urban Morphology," *Planning Perspectives* 8 (1993): 20–52.
5. See Yahong Shen, "The Ordering of the Chinese City" (Ph.D. diss., Harvard University, 1994).
6. Steinhardt, *Chinese Imperial City Planning*, 118.
7. S. C. Chiou and R. Krishnamurti, *The Fortunate Dimensions of Taiwanese Traditional Architecture* (London: Pion, 1995), 553–560.
8. Steinhardt, *Chinese Imperial City Planning*, 169f.
9. Liang Ssu-ch'eng, *A Pictorial History of Chinese Architecture: A Study of the Development of Its Structural System and the Evolution of Its Type,* edited by Wilma Fairbank (Cambridge, Mass.: MIT Press, 1984), 38–61.
10. Xu Ping, "The Gift and the Confucian Notion of Propriety, *Li*," in *Streetlife China,* edited by Michael Dutton (Cambridge: Cambridge University Press, 1998), 40–42.
11. Personal observation and measurement with Professor Zhang Jie of Qinghua University, 1998.
12. Wang Shaozhou, ed., *Zhongguo jindai jianzhu tulu* (Catalog of Chinese architecture from recent history) (Shanghai: Chinese Science and Technology Press, 1989), 15.
13. Jeffrey William Cody, "Henry K. Murphy: An American Architect in China, 1914–1935" (Ph.D. diss., Cornell University, 1989), 69.
14. F. L. Hawks Pott, *A Short History of Shanghai* (Shanghai: Kelly and Walsh, 1928), 81.
15. Wu Guangzu, "China," in *Sir Banister Fletcher's A History of Architecture,* 19th ed., edited by John Musgrave (London: Butterworths, 1987), 1457.
16. Wang Shiren et al., eds., *Zhongguo jindai jianzhu zonglan: beijing pian* (Catalog of Chinese architecture from recent history: Beijing) (Beijing: Zhongguo jianzhu gongye chubanshe, 1993), 52; Wu, "China," 1455.
17. Chen Congzhou and Zhang Ming, *Shanghai jindai jianzhu shigao* (Historical study of Shanghai architecture from recent history) (Shanghai: Sanlin Press, 1988), 107–109.
18. On Shanghai's history, see Linda Cooke Johnson, *Shanghai: From Market Town to Treaty Port, 1074–1858* (Stanford: Stanford University Press, 1995).
19. Pott, *A Short History of Shanghai*, 35–41.
20. Ibid., 63–64.
21. Ibid., 132.
22. Ibid., 133.

23. See Leo Ou-fan Lee, *Shanghai Modern: The Flowering of a New Urban Culture in China, 1930–1945* (Cambridge, Mass.: Harvard University Press, 1999).

24. On the middle class, see Marie-Claire Bergère, *The Golden Age of the Shanghai Bourgeoisie, 1911–1937*, translated by Janet Lloyd (Cambridge: Cambridge University Press, 1989).

25. Torsten Warner, *German Architecture in China: Architectural Transfer* (Berlin: Ernst und Sohn, 1994), 195–148.

26. Ibid., 196.

27. Ibid., 195.

28. Ibid., 210.

29. Ibid., 258.

30. Cody, "Henry K. Murphy," 77.

31. Ibid., 80.

32. Søren Clausen and Stig Thørgersen, *The Making of a Chinese City: History and Historiography of Harbin* (Armonk, N.Y.: M. E. Sharpe, 1995), 23–27.

33. David D. Buck, "Railway City and National Capital: Two Faces of the Modern Changchun," in *Remaking the Chinese City: Modernity and National Identity, 1900–1950*, edited by Joseph W. Esherick (Honolulu: University of Hawaii Press, 2000), 65–89.

34. Clausen and Thørgersen, *The Making a Chinese City*, 39–40.

35. Ibid., 108.

36. Ibid., 109.

37. Fujimori Terunobu and Wang Tan, eds., *A Comprehensive Study of East Asian Architecture and Urban Planning: 1840–1945* (Tokyo: Institute of Asian Architecture, University of Tokyo, 1996), 244.

38. Buck, "Railway City and National Capital," 73.

39. Ibid., 86.

40. Warner, *German Architecture in China*, 36–39.

41. Ibid., 40–41.

42. See Edward W. Said, *Orientalism* (New York: Pantheon Books, 1978).

43. Joseph W. Esherick, "Modernity and Nation in the Chinese City," in Esherick, ed., *Remaking the Chinese City*, 7.

44. Brett Sheehan, "Urban Identity and Urban Networks in Cosmopolitan Cities: Banks and Bankers in Tianjin, 1900–1937," in Esherick, ed., *Remaking the Chinese City*, 47.

45. On Beijing's public parks, see Madeleine Yue Dong, "Defining Beijing: Urban Reconstruction and National Identity, 1928–1936," in Esherick, ed., *Remaking the Chinese City*, 121–138.

46. Cody, "Henry K. Murphy," 100; *Zhongguo jianzhu* (Chinese architect) 1.1 (1933): 39–40.

47. See Zhu Lin, "Jianzhushi Liang Sicheng jianli" (Appendix I: curriculum vitae of the architect Liang Sicheng), in *Jianzhushi Liang Sicheng* (Architect Liang Sicheng) (Tianjin: Tianjin Science and Technology Press, 1996), 238–242; Wilma Fairbank, *Liang and Lin: Partners in Exploring China's Architectural Past* (Philadelphia: University of Pennsylvania Press, 1994), 10–12.

48. Fairbank, *Liang and Lin*, 42–43. In fact, Tong Jun and Liang were roommates at Penn.

49. *Zhongguo jianzhu* 1.1:31. See also Delin Lai, "Xiandai zhongguo jianzhushi yanjiu" (A study on the history of modern Chinese architecture) (Ph.D. diss., Qinghua University, 1992).

50. Cody, "Henry K. Murphy," 317.

51. Ibid., 330. For a fuller description of registration of architects, see Delin Lai, "The Formation of the Modern Building System in Shanghai," *Space Magazine* 1 (1993): 1–3.

52. Cody, "Henry K. Murphy," 331.

53. Wu, "China," 1450.

54. See, for instance, Charles Hodge Corbett, *Lingnan University: A Short History Based Primarily on the Records of the University's American Trustee* (New York: Trustees of Lingnan University, 1963); Zhao Bingshi and Hu Shaoxue, eds., *Commemorative Collection upon the Fiftieth Anniversary of Tsinghua University's School of Architecture* (Beijing: Chinese Architectural Press, 1996).

55. Wu, "China," 1450.

56. Cody, "Henry K. Murphy," 328.

57. *Zhongguo jianzhu* 1.1:38.

58. Ibid., 39. Generally, among the three Zhao was in charge of public relations, Chen supervised office procedures, and Tong was the designer. Tong also published widely at the time. See, for instance, Chuin Tung (Tong Jun), "Foreign Influence in Chinese Architecture," *Tien Hsia Monthly,* May 1938, 410–417.

59. Wu, "China," 1457.

60. Fu Chaoqing, *Zhongguo gudian shiyang xinjianzhu: 20 shiji zhongguo xinjianzhu guanshihua de lishi yanjiu* (New architecture of the traditional Chinese style: The historical study of twentieth-century courtly architecture) (Taipei: Nantian Press, 1993), 146–149.

61. See Michel Foucault, *The Order of Things: An Archaeology of the Human Sciences* (New York: Pantheon Books, 1971).

Four Architectural Attitudes toward Modernization

1. Barbara Miller Lane, *Architecture and Politics in Germany, 1918–1945* (Cambridge, Mass.: Harvard University Press, 1968).

2. See Peter G. Rowe, *Making a Middle Landscape* (Cambridge, Mass.: MIT Press, 1991), 67.

3. Jeffrey William Cody, "Henry K. Murphy: An American Architect in China, 1914–1935" (Ph.D. diss., Cornell University, 1989), 276f. See also Charles P. Musgrove, "Building a Dream: Constructing a National Capital in Nanjing, 1927–1937," in *Remaking the Chinese City: Modernity and National Identity,* edited by Joseph W. Esherick (Honolulu: University of Hawaii Press, 2000), 121–138.

4. Wu Guangzu, "China," in *Sir Banister Fletcher's A History of Architecture,* 19th ed., edited by John Musgrave (London: Butterworths, 1987), 1453.

5. Chen Congzhou and Zhang Ming, *Shanghai jindai jianzhu shigao* (Historical study of Shanghai architecture from recent history) (Shanghai: Sanlin Press, 1988), 144.

6. Wu, "China," 1451.

7. Ibid.

8. Ibid., 1452; Chen and Zhang, *Shanghai jindai jianzhu shigao,* 55.

9. Wu, "China," 1453.

10. Chen and Zhang, *Shanghai jindai jianzhu shigao,* 73.

11. Ibid., 183.

12. Luo Xiaowei, ed., *Shanghai jianzhu zhinan* (A guide to Shanghai architecture) (Shanghai: Shanghai People's Art Press, 1996), 224.

13. Ibid., 227.

14. See Lenore Hietkamp, "The Park Hotel, Shanghai, and Its Architect, Laszlo Hudec (1893–1958)" (M.A. thesis, University of Victoria, 1989); Chen and Zhang, *Shanghai jindai jianzhu shigao,* 182f.

15. Chen and Zhang, *Shanghai jindai jianzhu shigao,* 182f.; Wu, "China," 1457.

16. Luo, *Shanghai jianzhu zhinan,* 82.

17. Chen and Zhang, *Shanghai jindai jianzhu shigao,* 135.

18. Chuin Tung (Tong Jun), "Architecture Chronicle," *Tien Hsia Monthly,* October 1937, 312; Chen and Zhang, *Shanghai jindai jianzhu shigao,* 132.

19. Henry Killam Murphy, "An Architectural Renaissance in China: The Utilization in Modern Public Buildings of the Great Styles of the Past," *Asia,* June 1928, 468.

20. Ibid., 470–472; Henry Killam Murphy, "Architecture," in *China,* edited by H. F. MacNair (Berkeley: University of California Press, 1946), 363.

21. Murphy, "An Architectural Renaissance in China," 468.

22. Ibid., 473.

23. For an excellent and complete study of Murphy in China, see Cody, "Henry K. Murphy."

24. Ibid., 123.

25. Ibid., 163f.

26. Ibid., 128.

27. Charles A. Gunn, "Mission Policy in Mission Architecture," *Chinese Recorder* 55.10 (1924): 642–649; J. V. W. Bergamini, "Architectural Meditations," *Chinese Recorder* 55.10 (1924): 650–656.

28. Murphy, "An Architectural Renaissance in China," 508.

29. Murphy, "Architecture," 363.

30. Murphy, "An Architectural Renaissance in China," 508.

31. Yenching was founded as a missionary school by Americans and Peking University emerged from Metropolitan University, founded during the Qing dynasty. The two institutions merged in 1949 and the site became known as Beijing Daxue, the home now of Beida.

32. Cody, "Henry K. Murphy," 265. Similar sentiments are also to be found in Henry Killam Murphy, "The Adoption of Chinese Architecture," *Journal of Chinese American Engineers* 7.3 (1926): 2–8.

33. Cody, "Henry K. Murphy," 270f.; Office of the Commission on Capital Design, *Capital Plan: Nanjing* (Nanjing: Office of the Commission on Capital Design, 1929), 129f.

34. On the Peking Union Medical College generally, see Mary E. Ferguson, *China Medical Board and Peking Union Medical College: A Chronicle of Fruitful Collaboration, 1914–1951* (New York: China Medical Board of New York, 1970).

35. Ibid., 32.

36. Cody, "Henry K. Murphy," 124–141.

37. Fu Chaoqing, *Zhongguo gudian shiyang xinjianzhu: 20 shiji zhongguo xinjianzhu guanshihua de lishi yanjiu* (New architecture of the traditional Chinese style: The historical study of twentieth-century courtly architecture) (Taipei: Nantian Press, 1993), 126–154; Wu, "China," 1450.

38. Lai Delin, "Lu Yanzhi he Zhongshan Ling ji Zhongshan Tang," *Guangming Daily,* October 23 and 30, 1996.

39. Dong Dayou, "Guangzhou zongshan jiniantang" (Sun Yat-sen Memorial Hall, Guangzhou), *Zhongguo jianzhu* (Chinese Architect) 1.1 (1933): 2–6. Indeed, the auditorium was admired at the time as a good "adaptation" (i.e., imitation) of Chinese architecture. See Doon Dayu [Dong Dayou], "Architectural Chronicle," *Tien Hsia Monthly,* November 1936, 360.

40. Fu, *Zhongghuo gudian shiyang xinjianzhu,* 147–149.

41. Ibid., 147; Chen and Zhang, *Shanghai jindai jianzhu shigao,* 16–17.

42. Musgrove, "Building a Dream," 140.

43. Ibid., 140–141.

44. Ibid., 142.

45. Ibid., 145.

46. Sun Mou, Xia Quenshou, and Shen Zouwei, "Shoudu daolu xitong diaocha ruogan xiangfa" (Opinions on the investigation of the capital city road system plan), *Shoudu jianshu* (Capital City Architecture), November 1929, 42.

47. Louis Fung, *China Building Development: 1982/83* (Hong Kong: Trend Publishing, 1983), 12; more generally on Lin Keming, see Fu, *Zhongguo gudian shiyang xinjianzhu,* 7–48.

48. Lin Keming, "Achievements of Guangzhou Architecture in the Last Ten Years," *Architectural Journal,* August 1959, 6–9.

49. See Ai Dingzeng, "An Otherworldly Path: Forty Years of the Lingnan School," *Architectural Journal,* October 1989, 20–23; Ma Xiozhi, ed., *The Architectural Heritage of Modern China: Guangzhou* (Beijing: Chinese Architectural Press, 1992).

50. Ma, ed., *The Architectural Heritage of Modern China: Guangzhou,* 90–91.

51. Cody, "Henry K. Murphy," 294.

52. William H. Chaund, "Architectural Effort and Chinese Nationalism: Being a Radical Interpreter of Modern Architecture as a Potent Factor in Civilization," *Far Eastern Review* 15.8 (1919): 533–536.

53. Ibid., 536. See also Anderson Luther, "The Splendor of Chinese Architecture," *Asia* 17.4 (1917): 278–285, for a contemporaneous formulation of the same idea.

54. "Obituary of Comrade Yang Tingbao and *Curriculum Vitae,*" *Architectural Journal,* January 1983, 1.

55. On Yang, see Yang Tingbao, *Yang Tingbao jianzhu lunshu yu zuoping xuanji* (Selected architectural writings and works of Yang Tingbao), edited by Wang Jianguo (Beijing: Zhongguo jianzhu gongye chubanshe, 1997).

56. Ibid., 28–29.

57. Ibid., 38–39.

58. Ibid., 47–48.

59. Ibid., 84–85, 87–89.

60. Wu, "China," 1456; Luo, *Shanghai jianzhu zhinan,* 86.

61. Wu, "China," 1455.

62. Ibid., 1457.

63. Ibid., 1458; Luo, *Shanghai jianzhu zhinan,* 42.

64. Walter A. Taylor, "Chinese Architecture in Modern Buildings," *Chinese Recorder* 55.10 (1925): 661.

65. On *lilong* houses, see Zhang Shouyi and Tan Yang, "Early Development of Urban Housing from 1940 to 1949," in *Modern Urban Housing in China: 1840–2000,* edited by Lü Junhua, Peter G. Rowe, and Zhang Jie (Munich: Prestel, 2001), 31–48.

66. On *lilong* houses in Shanghai, see Luo Xiaowei and Wu Jiang, *Shanghai Longtang* (Shanghai: Shanghai People's Fine Art Publishing House, 1997).

67. For a thorough biographical portrait of Liang Sicheng, see Wilma Fairbank, *Liang and Lin: Partners in Exploring China's Architectural Past* (Philadelphia: University of Pennsylvania Press, 1994).

68. Ibid., 49–50.

69. After earning his degree from the University of Pennsylvania (M.Arch, 1927), Liang Sicheng went on to Harvard (September 1927–March 1928), principally drawing on the holdings in the Yenching Library for his research in Oriental architecture (ibid., 29).

70. Osvald Sirén, *Walls and Gates of Peking* (London: n.p., 1924); Ernst Boerschmann, *Picturesque China, Architecture and Landscape: A Journey through Twelve Provinces,* translated by Louis Hamilton (New York: Brentano's, 1923); as well as Ernst Boerschmann, *Chinesische Architektur,* 2 vols. (Berlin: E. Wasmuth, 1925).

71. Fairbank, *Liang and Lin,* 58.

72. Liang, quoted in Fu, *Zhongguo gudian shiyang xinjianzhu,* 125.

73. Liang Ssu-ch'eng, *A Pictorial History of Chinese Architecture: A Study of the Development of Its Structural Systems and the Evolution of Its Type,* edited by Wilma Fairbank (Cambridge, Mass.: MIT Press, 1984). See also Liang Sicheng, *Liang Sicheng zuo pin ji* (Collected works of Liang Sicheng), 4 vols. (Beijing: Chinese Architectural Works Publishing, 1982), vol. 1.

74. Wu, "China," 1454; Zhao Bingshi and Hu Shaoxue, eds., *Commemorative Collection upon the Fiftieth Anniversary of Tsinghua University's School of Architecture* (Beijing: Chinese Architectural Press, 1996), 9–11.

The "Big Roof" Controversy

1. Wilma Fairbank, *Liang and Lin: Partners in Exploring China's Architectural Past* (Philadelphia: University of Pennsylvania Press, 1994), 155.

2. Zhao Bingshi, "A Biography of Wu Liangyong," in *Commemorative Collection upon the Fiftieth Anniversary of Tsinghua University's School of Architecture,* edited by Zhao Bingshi and Hu Shaoxue (Beijing: Chinese Architectural Press, 1996), 164–169.

3. Commission of the Shanghai Metropolitan Plan, *Da Shanghai dushi jihua zongtu cao'an baogaoshu* (Proceedings of the Commission on the Shanghai Metropolitan Plan) (Shanghai: Commission of the Shanghai Metropolitan Plan, 1946); Yang Tingbao, *Yang Tingbao jianzhu lunshu yu zuoping xuanji* (Selected architectural writings and works of Yang Tingbao), edited by Wang Jianguo (Beijing: Zhongguo jianzhu gongye chubanshe, 1997), 73–76.

4. Wu Jiang, "Bauhaus Principles in the Architecture of Shanghai," in *Städte des 21. Jahrhunderts: Peking, Shanghai, Shenzen,* edited by Kai Vöckler and Dirk Luchow (Frankfurt: Campus Verlag, 2000), 519.

5. Ibid.

6. Ibid., 518.

7. On this period, see Suzanne Pepper, *Civil War in China: The Political Struggle, 1945–1949* (Berkeley: University of California Press, 1978). Stephen Levine, *Anvil of Victory: The Communist Revolution in Manchuria, 1945–48* (New York: Columbia University Press, 1987).

8. Jonathan D. Spence, *To Change China: Western Advisors in China, 1620–1960* (Boston: Little, Brown, 1969), 282–283.

9. Wu, "Bauhaus Principles in the Architecture of Shanghai," 517.

10. Ai Dingzeng, "An Otherworldly Path: Forty Years of the Lingnan School," *Architectural Journal,* October 1989, 22–23.

11. Gu Mengchao, "Zhang Bo and My Journey in Architecture," *Architectural Journal,* February 1994, 52–53; Zhang Bo, *Wode jianzhu chuangzuo daolu* (My journey in architecture) (Beijing: Zhongguo jianzhu gongye chubanshe, 1994). Zhang Bo's father, the last viceroy of Guangdong and Guangxi, was a close friend of Liang Qichao, Liang Sicheng's father.

12. Design Bureau of the Ministry of Construction, *Famous Architectural Design Institutes* (Hong Kong: A & U Publications, 1995). See also Chinese Architectural Association, *Famous Architectural Design Institutes of China, Exemplary Collected Works* (Beijing: Chinese Architectural Press, 1996).

13. See the Ministry of Construction Bureau of Design, *Beijing–Soviet Union Exhibition Hall* (Beijing: Industrial and City Architecture Design Institute, 1956).

14. Fairbank, *Liang and Lin,* 169–171.

15. Ibid., 170.

16. Zhang Jie and Wang Tao, "Development in the Socialist Planned Economy from 1949 to 1978," in *Modern Urban Housing in China: 1840–2000,* edited by Lü Junhua, Peter G. Rowe, and Zhang Jie (Munich: Prestel, 2001), 141.

17. Liang, quoted in ibid. A similar analogy had already been made in 1937 by Tong Jun—Liang's University of Pennsylvania roommate—who spoke in terms of "superfluous pigtails." See Chuin Tung [Tong Jun], "Architecture Chronicle," *Tien Hsia Monthly,* October 1937, 308.

18. Wu Guangzu, "China," in *Sir Banister Fletcher's A History of Architecture,* 19th ed., edited by John Musgrave (London: Butterworths, 1987), 1456, 1461.

19. Zhang Qinnan, "A Search of Forty Years," in *Forty Years of Chinese Architecture,* edited by Chen Baosheng (Shanghai: Tongji University Press, 1992), 18.

20. Ibid.

21. The First Five-Year Plan was not officially published until 1955.

22. Mao Tse-Tung [Mao Zedong], "On Art and Literature," in *Selected Works of Mao Tse-Tung,* vol. 4 (London: Chadwick, 1985), 70.

23. Ibid., 83.

24. Ibid., 84.

25. Mao Zedong, "On New Democracy," in *Sources of Chinese Tradition,* compiled by William Theodore de Bary, Wing-tsit Chan, and Chester Tan, vol. 2 (1960; reprint, New York, Columbia University Press, 1964), 181.

26. Zhou is quoted in Gong Deshun, Zou Denong, and Yide Dou, "The Phases of Modern Chinese Architectural History: 1949–1984," *Architectural Journal,* October 1985, 11.

27. Zhang Shouyi and Tan Ying, "An Important Period of the Early Development of Housing in Modern Cities," in Lü, Rowe, and Zhang, eds., *Modern Urban Housing in China,* 80.

28. The phrase is often attributed to Liu Xiufeng, who shortly thereafter became minister of construction. It is also formulated as "Utility, economy, and, if conditions allow, beauty." See Fairbank, *Liang and Lin,* 172.

29. The slogan of the late 1950s and the 1960s became "standardization, mechanization, and assembly-at-the-site."

30. Fu Chaoqing, *Zhongguo gudian shiyang xinjianzhu: 20 shiji zhongguo xinjianzhu guanshihua de lishi yanjiu* (New architecture of the traditional Chinese style: The historical study of twentieth-century courtly architecture) (Taipei: Nantian Press, 1993), 170.

31. Ibid., 171; *Architectural Journal*, February 1954, 15–16. Chen Dengao, in fact, consulted with Soviet advisors about adapting Chinese characteristics into buildings and with other leading Chinese architects such as Liang Sicheng, Zhao Shen, and Liu Dunzhen. See Chen Dengao, "Lessons from Designing High-Rise Buildings in Cultural Form," *Architectural Journal*, February 1954, 104–107.

32. Zhang Kaiji, "Sanlihe Government Offices," *Architectural Journal*, February 1954, 100–103.

33. For a general account, see Zhang and Wang, "Housing Development in the Socialist Planned Economy," 103–186.

34. Zhang and Tan, "An Important Period of the Early Development of Housing in Modern Cities," 85.

35. Illustrated in *Architectural Journal*, February 1955, 24.

36. Li Yongguang, "Some Problems and Discussion Covering the Current Standard Design of Housing," *Architectural Journal*, February 1956, 5–10.

37. Niu Ming, "How Has Mr. Liang Sicheng Twisted the Architecture and Cultural Form," *Architectural Journal*, February 1955, 8.

38. Wang Ying, "An Examination of Formalist and Revivalist Architectural Thinking: A Critique of Mr. Liang Sicheng and Me," *Architectural Journal*, February 1955, 12.

39. Liu Huixian, "The Poison of Formalism and Revivalism," *Architectural Journal*, February 1955, 15–19.

40. Zhang Qinnan, "A Search of Forty Years," 18.

Struggles with Modernism

1. "We Need Modern Architecture," *Architectural Journal*, January 1956, 1f.

2. Wu Guangzu, "China," in *Sir Banister Fletcher's A History of Architecture*, 19th ed., edited by John Musgrave (London: Butterworths, 1987), 1460.

3. Yang Tingbao, *Yang Tingbao jianzhu lunshu yu zuoping xuanji* (Selected architectural writings and works of Yang Tingbao), edited by Wang Jianguo (Beijing: Zhongguo jianzhu gongye chubanshe, 1997), 94–95. In fact, Yang traveled frequently to the United States during 1948, while working in partnership with Skidmore, Owings and Merrill on the Mobile Estates project in Shanghai; he became very interested in Walter Gropius's work. See Zhang Bo, *Wode jianzhu chuangzuo daolu* (My journey in architecture) (Beijing: Zhongguo jianzhu gongye chubanshe, 1994), 35f.

4. "We Need Modern Architecture," 6.

5. See Roderick MacFarquhar, ed., *The Hundred Flowers Campaign and the Chinese Intellectuals* (New York: Praeger, 1960).

6. "Editorial: Deepening the Anti-rightist Struggle in Architecture," *Architectural Journal*, September 1957, 1f. Hua was not just a foreign-trained architect (educated in France); he was half French and married to a French woman.

7. Dai Nianci, "From Hua Lanhong's Architectural Theory and Children's Hospital to Thoughts in Modernism," *Architectural Journal*, October 1957, 65–69.

8. Architectural History Unit, Nanjing Institute of Technology, Department of Architecture, "Replacing White Flags with Red Flags from the Research and Teaching of Architecture History," *Architectural Journal*, October 1958, 40–42.

9. Ibid., 40.

10. Ibid., 41.

11. Ibid., 42.

12. Song Jian, *Zhongghua renmin gongheguo jingjishi: cong 1949 nian dao 90 niandai chu* (The economic history of the People's Republic of China from 1949 to the early 1990s) (Beijing: People's University of China Publishing House, 1992), 227f.

13. Ministry of Construction, "Resolutions of the Architecture History Conference," *Architectural Journal*, November 1958, 6f.

14. Liang Sicheng and Liu Dunzhen, "Replacing White Flags with Red Flags: The Renunciation of Bourgeois Scholarly Thinking at the National Architecture History Conference," *Architectural Journal*, November 1958, 6.

15. Ibid., 6, 7.

16. Ibid., 8.

17. Zhang Qinnan, "A Search of Forty Years," in *Forty Years of Chinese Architecture*, edited by Chen Baosheng (Shanghai: Tongji University Press, 1992), 18. See also Liu Xiufeng, "Creating the New Architectural Style of Socialist Choice," *Architectural Journal*, September 1959, 3–12.

18. Liang Sicheng, "From 'Function, Economy, and Appearance Where Circumstances Allow' to Tradition and Innovation," *Architectural Journal*, June 1959, 2–3.

19. Ibid., 2, 4.

20. Zhao Bingshi and Hu Shaoxue, eds., *Commemorative Collection upon the Fiftieth Anniversary of Tsinghua University's School of Architecture* (Beijing: Chinese Architectural Press, 1996), 72–74.

21. Wu, "China," 1460, 1464.

22. *Architectural Journal*, January 1957, 27–38.

23. See *Architectural Journal*, September–October 1959, on entire double issue devoted to the Ten Great Buildings.

24. Liang, "From 'Function, Economy, and Appearance' to Tradition in Innovation," 3.

25. Liu, "Creating the New Architectural Style of Socialist China," 8.

26. *Architectural Journal*, September–October 1959, 52–60.

27. Fu Chaoqing, *Zhongguo gudian shiyang xinjianzhu: 20 shiji zhongguo xinjianzhu guanshihua de lishi yanjiu* (New architecture of the traditional Chinese style: The historical study of twentieth-century courtly architecture) (Taipei: Nantian Press, 1993), 191–192.

28. *Architectural Journal*, September–October 1959, 47–51.

29. Ibid., 44–46.

30. Ibid., 23–30.

31. Zhang Bo, *Wode jianshu chuangzuo daolu*, 60.

32. *Architectural Journal*, September–October 1959, 33–39.

33. Ibid., 61–68.

34. Ibid., 69–73.

35. Ibid., 74–76.

36. Gu Qiyuan, "Certain Problems with Modernist Architecture in Capitalist Countries," *Architectural Journal,* November 1962, 18.

37. Ibid., 18–20. The journal's editors did note, however, that "Comrade Gu Qiyuan's article represented [only] one opinion" (1).

38. Wu Huanjia, "On Ten Buildings from the West," *Architectural Journal,* June 1964, 30.

39. Gu, "Certain Problems with Modernist Architecture," 18.

40. Wu Huanjia, "On Ten Buildings from the West," 29–33.

41. Chen, ed., *Forty Years of Chinese Architecture,* 40.

42. Fu, *Zhongguo gudian shiyang xinjianzhu,* 198.

43. "Obituary of Dai Nianci, President of the Architectural Society of China," *Architectural Journal,* January 1992, 63; Wu Liangyong, "Comrade Dai Nianci's Premature Departure," *Architectural Journal,* March 1992, 2.

44. Chen, ed., *Forty Years of Chinese Architecture,* 109.

45. Zhao and Hu, *Commemorative Collection upon the Fiftieth Anniversary of Tsinghua University's School of Architecture,* 9–11.

46. Anita Chan, *Children of Mao: Personality Development and Political Activism in the Red Guard Generation* (Seattle: University of Washington Press, 1985), 12; Michael Dillon, ed., *China: A Historical and Cultural Dictionary* (Richmond: Curzon, 1998), 66.

47. On this period, see David Zweig, *Agrarian Radicalism in China, 1968–1981* (Cambridge, Mass.: Harvard University Press, 1989); Jonathan D. Spence, *The Search for Modern China* (New York: W. W. Norton, 1990), 602–617.

48. Wilma Fairbank, *Liang and Lin: Partners in Exploring China's Architectural Past* (Philadelphia: University of Pennsylvania Press, 1994), 176.

49. See Dillon, *China: A Historical and Cultural Dictionary,* 195, on Lin Biao, the People's Liberation Army commander in chief and minister of defense from 1959 until his death. The Gang of Four (*Siren Bang*) were Jiang Qing (Mao's widow), Zhang Chunqiao, Yao Wenyuan, and Wang Hongwen, all members of the radical faction based in Shanghai.

50. Wang Zhili, "Two Lessons of History: Recollections from Two Phases of Architectural Work," *Architectural Journal,* June 1980, 1–2.

51. Zhang Guizhi, interview with authors, Qinghua, March 30, 1999; he worked, at the time, with Zheng Guoqing.

52. Chen, ed., *Forty Years of Chinese Architecture,* 40.

53. Wu Guangzu, "China," 1460, 1465.

54. Ibid., 1460.

55. Yang, *Yang Tingbao jianzhu lunshu yu zuopin xuanji,* 105.

56. "The New Wing of the Beijing Hotel," *Architectural Journal,* May 1974, 18–27, 80; Zhang Bo, *Wode jianshu chuangzuo daolu,* 51. Zhang himself saw the building in traditional terms and not as strictly an adaptation of the International Style.

57. "The Three Gate Housing Complex," *Architectural Journal,* May 1976, 16–22.

58. Ibid., 16–17.

59. Wu Guangzu, "China," 1460, 1463.

60. Fu, *Zhongguo gudian shiyang xinjianzhu,* 51.

THE "CULTURE FEVER"

1. See Richard Baum, *China's Four Modernizations: The New Technological Revolution* (Boulder, Colo.: Westview Press, 1980).
2. Gao Xingjian, *Soul Mountain,* translated by Mabel Lee (New York: HarperCollins, 2000).
3. For another account, see Xudong Zhang, *Chinese Modernism in the Era of Reforms: Cultural Fever, Avant-Garde Fiction, and the New Chinese Cinema* (Durham, N.C.: Duke University Press, 1997), 37–68.
4. Ibid., 37; more generally, see Gan Yang, ed., *Cultural Consciousness of Contemporary China* (Hong Kong: Southern, 1990).
5. Jin is cited in Zhang, *Chinese Modernism in the Era of Reforms,* 39. Jin was also quoted in a documentary series (ca. 1987) titled "Elegy of the River," which was very controversial, airing only once before being banned.
6. Zhang, *Chinese Modernism in the Era of Reforms,* 46. This conception of tradition is also linked with the idea of a "Third Era of Confucianism" and works like Lu Weiming, *Prospects and Questions of the Third Era of Confucianism* (Taipei: National Taiwan University, 1989).
7. Zhang, *Chinese Modernism in the Era of Reforms,* 46–47.
8. Li Zehou, *Essays on Modern Chinese Intellectual History* (Beijing: Beida Press, 1988).
9. Li, quoted in Zhang, *Chinese Modernism in the Era of Reforms,* 52.
10. Ibid., 55. See also Richard L. Bernstein, *Beyond Objectivism and Relativism: Science, Hermeneutics, and Praxis* (Philadelphia: University of Pennsylvania Press, 1983).
11. Liu Xiaofeng, *Zhengjiu yu congrong* (Redemption and easiness) (Shanghai: Chu-Ban-She, 1988).
12. See Hans-Georg Gadamer, *Truth and Method* [translation edited by Garrett Barden and John Cummin] (New York: Crossroads, 1975).
13. Tong Jun, *New Architecture and Styles* (Beijing: Chinese Architectural Press, 1980).
14. Liu Xianjue, Shen Yulin, Wu Huanjia, Luo Xiaowei, et al., *Jiudai xifang janzhu* (Foreign architecture from recent history) (Beijing: Taxiang zhongguo jianzhushi, 1982).
15. Liu Hongdian, "Speech," *Architectural Journal,* January 1979, 29–30. See also Liu Hongdian, ed., *Zhuzhai jianzhu gangling* (Principles of residential architecture) (Beijing: Taxiang zhongguo jianzhushi, 1974).
16. Wang Shiren, "Chinese Architecture in Recent History and Architectural Style," *Architectural Journal,* April 1978, 28.
17. Ibid., 29.
18. Ibid., 32–33.
19. Chen Chongqing, "Revindicating Big Roofs," *Architectural Journal,* April 1988, 23.
20. Wang Zhili, "Two Lessons of History: Recollections from Two Phases of Architectural Work," *Architectural Journal,* June 1980, 2.
21. Liu Kaiji, "On Architectural Semiotics," *World Architecture,* May 1984, 10.
22. Liu Kaiji, "Language Signs and Architecture," *Architectural Journal,* August 1984, 13–15; "The Aesthetics of Semiotics and the Art of Architecture," *Architectural Journal,* October 1985, 15f.
23. "Postmodern Pluralism" and "Postmodernism and Contemporary Chinese Architecture," *Architectural Journal,* November 1986, 8, 11.

24. Zou Denong, "The Lessons of Twice Importing Architectural Theory: From Cultural Form to Postmodernism," *Architectural Journal*, November 1989, 47–50.

25. Zhang Qinnan, "A Search of Forty Years," in *Forty Years of Chinese Architecture*, edited by Chen Baosheng (Shanghai: Tongji University Press, 1992), 21.

26. See, for example, Jonathan Spence, *The Search for Modern China* (New York: W. W. Norton, 1990), 712f.

27. Ibid., 713–716.

28. Hu is quoted in ibid., 716.

29. Quoted in ibid., 719.

30. Ibid., 724.

31. Ibid., 723.

32. Wu Guangzu, "China," in *Sir Banister Fletcher's A History of Architecture*, 19th ed., edited by John Musgrave (London: Butterworths, 1987), 1465, 1467.

33. Gu Mengchao, ed., "Conference on Beijing's Fragrant Hill Hotel," *Architectural Journal*, March 1983, 57–64.

34. Liu Kaiji in ibid., 58.

35. Wu, "China," 1466–1467.

36. Chen Baosheng, ed., *Forty Years of Chinese Architecture*, 95.

37. Wu, "China," 1466–1467; Louis Fung, *China Building Development, 1982–83* (Hong Kong: Trend Publishing, 1983), 73.

38. Chen Baosheng, ed., *Forty Years of Chinese Architecture*, 270.

39. Wu, "China," 1467.

40. Chen Baosheng, ed., *Forty Years of Chinese Architecture*, 240–241.

41. Ministry of Construction and the Northeastern Institute of Architectural Design, "Design of the Beijing Library," *Architectural Journal*, January 1988, 26–32.

42. The team was headed by Yang with Zhang as deputy. In the mornings the three juniors—Dai, Wu, and Wang—debated and sketched; in the afternoons, summaries were presented to Yang by Zhang. Zhang Bo, *Wode jianzhu chuangzuo daolu* (My journey in architecture) (Beijing: Zhongguo jianzhu gongye chubanshe, 1994), 23.

43. Ibid.

44. Fu Chaoqing, *Zhongguo gudian shiyang xinjianzhu: 20 shiji zhongguo xinjianzhu guanshihua de lishi yanjiu* (New architecture of the traditional Chinese style: The historical study of twentieth-century courtly architecture) (Taipei: Nantian Press, 1993), 198.

45. Chen Baosheng, ed., *Forty Years of Chinese Architecture*, 76.

46. See Qi Kang, *Condensation in Memorial Thought* (Beijing: Chinese Architectural Press, 1996).

47. Puyi Zhou, "The Contextualist Craze among Chinese Architects," *Architectural Journal*, February 1989, 7–12; Zhang Qinnan, "In Defense of Contextualism," *Architectural Journal*, June 1989, 10–11.

48. Conversation with Zhang Jie of Qinghua University, March 31, 1999.

49. Wu Liangyong, *Beijing Ju'er Hutong New Courtyard Housing Project* (Beijing: Institute of Architectural and Urban Studies, Qinghua University, 1993).

50. Wu Liangyong, *Rehabilitating the Old City of Beijing: A Project on the Ju'er Hutong Neighborhood* (Vancouver: University of British Columbia Press, 1999).

51. Spence, *The Search for Modern China,* 745–746.

A COMMODIFICATION AND INTERNATIONALIZATION OF ARCHITECTURE

1. Xudong Zhang, *Chinese Modernism in the Era of Reform: Cultural Fever, Avant-Garde Fiction, and the New Chinese Cinema* (Durham, N.C.: Duke University Press, 1997), 18f.

2. See William H. Overholt, *The Rise of China: How Economic Reform Is Creating a New Superpower* (New York: W. W. Norton, 1993).

3. For an overview of the Institute's work, see Architecture Design and Research Institute of the South China University of Technology, *Portfolio* (Guangzhou: Architecture Design and Research Institute of the South China University of Technology, 1999).

4. Ibid., 13–14.

5. Ibid., 16–17.

6. Ibid., 3–6.

7. Design Bureau of the Ministry of Construction, *Famous Architectural Design Institutes* (Hong Kong: A & U Publications, 1995), 72.

8. Ibid., 70.

9. Ibid., 71.

10. Ibid., 72.

11. *Architectural Journal,* February (1996).

12. The varied models for the Chinese stores apparently came primarily from Japan and secondarily from the United States. Peculiarly European concerns seem to dominate the French Carrefour chain, the German Metro, and the Japanese Yaohan.

13. Wang Mingxian and Xu Fang, *Chuantong he xiandai jianzhu* (Traditional and contemporary architecture) (Beijing: Chinese Architecture Press, 1996), 26.

14. Yue Wu, "The Futian Theater Complex in Shenzhen," presentation made at the Asia GSD Asia Pacific Design Conference, Harvard Graduate School of Design, Cambridge, Mass., March 8, 2000.

15. On Zhang, see Greg Hall, "Uncertain Politics Don't Stop Foreign-Trained Architects from Returning Home," *Architectural Record,* July 1996 PR5 [Pacific Rim Report] 5.

16. On Zhu, see Lu Haiping, *Sheji zuopin he lunwenji* (Selected projects and dissertations of the Shanghai International Residential Design Competition) (Shanghai: China Architecture and Building Press, 1996), 6–13.

17. See John J. Kosowatz and Andy Ryan, "Building a New Gateway to China," *Scientific American,* December 1997, 102–111.

18. On environmental concerns, see Wu Liangyong, *The Future of Architecture: Reflections at the Turn of the Century* (Beijing: Chinese Architectural Press, 1999).

19. Zhang Qinnan, "A Search of Forty Years," in *Forty Years of Chinese Architecture,* edited by Chen Baosheng (Shanghai: Tongji University Press, 1992), 22.

20. "Zhang Jinqiu," special issue of *Pro Architect* 12 (November 1998): 215.

21. Ibid., 36–43.

22. Ibid., 44–56.

23. Ibid., 56–87.

24. Ibid., 88–109.

25. Ibid., 144–159. See also China Northwest Building Design Research Institute, *Selected Works of Architectural Design* (Xi'an: China Northwest Building Design Research Institute, 1999), 8–9.

26. Conversation with Zhang Jinqiu, March 28, 1999.

27. Wang and Xu, *Chuantong he xiandai jianzhu,* 42–43.

28. Zhu Jialu, "Gateway to Beijing: The Design Concept of Beijing's Western Station," *Creative Architecture* 4 (1997): 10–22.

29. State Council, "Guowuyuan dui Beijing zhongti guihua pifu" (Permission for Beijing's urban master plan from State Council," state memorandum (Beijing, 1993), 144.

30. See Seng Kuan, "Bivalency Constructed: The Big Roof Phenomenon in Contemporary Chinese Architecture" (B.A. honors thesis, Harvard College, 1998), 91f.

31. Zhu, "Gateway to Beijing," 21.

32. Wang and Xu, *Chuantong he xiandai jianzhu,* 46.

33. Ellen Johnston Liang, "Is There Post-Modern Art in People's Republic of China?" in *Modernity in Asian Art,* edited by John Clark (Sydney: Wild Peony, 1993), 213.

34. Vittorio Magnago Lampugnani, ed., *Hong Kong Architecture: The Aesthetics of Density* (Munich: Prestel, 1993); also the authors' personal observation.

35. Kosowartz and Ryan, "Building a New Gateway to China."

36. "Theme," *Architectural Review* 104 (1998): 50–71.

37. M. Castells, L. Goh, and R. Y.-W. Kwok, *The Shek Kip Mei Syndrome: Economic Development and Public Housing in Hong Kong and Singapore* (London: Pion, 1990).

38. Luigi Novelli, *Shanghai: Architettura e città: tra Cina e occidente = Architecture and the City, between China and the West* (Rome: Edizioni Librerie Dedalo, 1999), 34–39.

39. Ibid., 30.

40. Alan Riding, "An Architect's Great Leap Forward," *New York Times,* December 19, 1999, 50–52; and Paul Andreu, "Recent Work in Asia," presentation at Asia GSD Asian Pacific Design Conference, Harvard University, Cambridge, Mass., March 8, 2000.

41. Hannah Beech, "The Tale of Two Cities," *Time,* May 8, 2000, B12–B15.

42. Mark O'Neill, "Jiang Theatre a Bubble Set to Burst," *Sunday Morning Post* (Hong Kong), September 5, 1999, 9.

43. Editing Committee of the International Architectural Competition of the Grand National Theater, *A Collection of Design Schemes* (Beijing: Construction and Industry Press of China, 2000), 53–101.

44. See Zheng Shiling, ed., *The Renewal and Redevelopment of Shanghai* (Shanghai: Tongji University Press, 1996).

MODERNIZATION IN CHINA

1. See Peter G. Rowe, *L'Asia e il moderno* (Ancona: Transeuropa, 1999).

2. Charles Goddard, *China Market Atlas, 1997 Edition* (Hong Kong: Economist Intelligence Unit, 1997), 123–128, and subsequent *Nation Reports* produced by the Economist Intelligence Unit.

3. See Norton Ginsburg, Bruce Koppel, and T. G. McGee, eds., *The Extended Metropolis: Settlement Transition in Asia* (Honolulu: University of Hawaii Press, 1991).

4. Based on an analysis of the Zipf distribution and other relative measures of size and scale of centers and subcenters, Graduate School of Design, Harvard University, 1999.

5. John King Fairbank, *China: A New History* (Cambridge, Mass.: Harvard University Press, Belknap Press, 1992), 217.

6. Samuel P. Huntington, *The Clash of Civilizations and the Remaking of World Order* (New York: Simon and Schuster, 1996), 75.

7. See Lionel Trilling, *Sincerity and Authenticity* (1972; reprint, Harcourt Brace Jovanovich, 1974).

8. Ibid., 99–100. We are also indebted to Eduard Sekler for his reinterpretation of Trilling's concept, during the Asia GSD Asian Pacific Design Conference, March 2000.

9. Charles Rearick, *Pleasures of the Belle Époque: Entertainment and Festivity in Turn-of-the-Century France* (New Haven: Yale University Press, 1985), 119.

10. Rowe, *L'Asia e il moderno*, 62.

11. See Jacques Derrida, *Positions,* translated by Alan Bass (Chicago: University of Chicago Press, 1981), and *Specters of Marx: The State of the Debt, the Work of Mourning, and the New International,* translated by Peggy Kampf (New York: Routledge, 1994).

ILLUSTRATION CREDITS

All illustrations are by the authors, except for the following.

Cover. Calligraphy by Wu Yue.

Figure 1. Redrawn from a facsimile of the *Map of the Peking Urban Area,* prepared by the Beijing Ancient Architecture Research Institute and the Beijing Real-Estate Management Research Center (Beijing: Yanshan Press, 1996).

Figures 5, 10. From Chen Congzhou and Zhang Ming, *Shanghai jindai jianzhu shigao* (Historical study of Shanghai architecture from the recent past) (Shanghai: Sanlian Press, 1988), 109, 17. Published with permission.

Figure 6. From an original photograph owned by the authors, date and photographer unknown.

Figure 9. Redrawn from Wang Shiren et al., eds., *Zhongguo jindai jianzhu zonglan: Beijing pian* (Catalog of Chinese architecture from recent history: Beijing) (Beijing: Zhongguo jianzhu gongye chubanshe, 1993), 52.

Figure 17. Published with permission of the United Board of Christian Colleges in China, New York.

Figure 19. Published with permission of the China Medical Board of New York.

Figure 21. From Zheng Shiling, *Shanghai jinbai jianzhu jianzhushi* (Shanghai: Shanghai Jiaoyu Chubanshe, 1999), 241.

Figure 22. Redrawn from *Shoudu jianshe* (Chinese Architect), November 1928, 7–8.

Figures 24, 25, 35, 45. From Yang Tingbao, *Yang Tingbao jianzhu lunshu yu zuoping xuanji* (Selected architectural writings and works of Yang Tingbao), edited by Wang Jinguo (Beijing: Zhongguo jianzhu gongye chubanshe, 1997), 105, 107, 94, 105. Published with permission.

Figure 32. From Fu Chaoqing, *Zhongguo gudian shiyang xinjianzhu: 20 shiji zhongguo xinjianzhu guanshihua de lishi yanjiu* (New architecture of the traditional Chinese style: The historical study of twentieth-century courtly architecture) (Taipei: Nantian Press, 1993), 171.

Figure 57. Published with permission of the Design Institute of the South China Institute of Technology, Guangzhou.

Figure 72. Photograph by Mr. Zhou Li/Point Photography Studio. Published with permission of Paul Andreu and H. Langlais-A. Buonomo.

Figure 73. Photograph by H. Langlais-A. Buonomo. Published with permission of Paul Andreu.

INDEX